Just Enough Data Science and Machine Learning

T0265304

Just Enough Data Science and Machine Learning

Essential Tools and Techniques

Mark Levene
Martyn Harris

♦ Addison-Wesley

Library of Congress Control Number: 2024947279

ISBN-13: 978-0-13-834074-2
ISBN-10: 0-13-834074-9

1 2024

Contents

List of Figures

Preface

The topic. Data science is an interdisciplinary field that has evolved from a synergy between computer science and statistics. While data science focuses on the analysis and interpretation of data, machine learning is its algorithmic part enabling the discovery of patterns from a statistical model formed from the data.

In recent years, the field of data science and its subfield machine learning have emerged as indispensable tools for extracting valuable insights and making predictions from potentially vast amounts of data. As these disciplines continue to shape our world, it becomes increasingly important, not only to a wide range of information technology (IT) professionals and researchers, but also to enthusiasts who wish to grasp their fundamental principles and techniques.

Motivation. Our aim in this book is that it will serve as an introductory guide to data science and machine learning. In our journey to explore the fundamentals of these fields, we focus on their applied side, giving practical examples of the concepts and methods. However, we do not shy away from presenting the fundamental theory of these subjects.

Thus our motivation for writing this book stems from a desire to provide a middle ground within the vast spectrum of literature on these topics. Our aim was to strike a balance between theoretical rigour and practical utility, offering readers an applied perspective enriched with algorithmic insights and essential statistical foundations.

Coded examples. Recognising the evolving nature of programming languages and the potential deprecation of code examples, within the book itself we have chosen to present the core concepts without listing the actual code, in order to ensure the longevity and relevance of the content for years to come. Nonetheless, all of the illustrative examples in the book are drawn from real-world data sets. The code that was used to produce data summaries and plots presented in each of the examples is hosted on a dedicated web site enabling readers to reproduce them, and ensuring a hands-on learning experience while future-proofing the material against evolving programming languages.

The audience. This book is tailored for anyone seeking a comprehensive, yet accessible, introduction to data science and machine learning. Whether you are a student venturing into these fields for the first time an IT professional or researcher looking to broaden your skill set, or an enthusiast eager to explore the potential of data-driven decision making, this book is designed to cater to your needs.

Prerequisites. We present an overview of data science with minimal mathematical prerequisites, ensuring that readers can grasp the fundamentals without the need for grasping complex equations. A basic understanding of mathematics and statistics will suffice to embark on this journey. We hope you will enjoy the book as much as we have enjoyed writing it.

Acknowledgments

We extend special thanks to our editor at Pearson, Kim Spenceley, who patiently guided us through the publication process. We would also like to thank the reviewers of the draft version of the book for their constructive comments.

Dedications

Mark Levene dedicates this book to his wife Sara and their three children Tamara, Joseph, and Oren. Martyn Harris dedicates this book to his wife Ilaria, their three children Zeno, Carolina, and Susanna, and to the memory of Angela and Nigel Harris.

Mark Levene and Martyn Harris

London, 2024

About the Authors

Mark Levene is emeritus professor of Computer Science at Birkbeck University of London. His main area of expertise encompasses Data Science and Machine Learning, including Applied Machine Learning, Trustworthy and Safe AI.

Martyn Harris is a lecturer and Programme Director at Birkbeck University of London. His areas of expertise include Data Science, Applied Machine Learning, and Natural Language Processing.

1

What Is Data Science?

I do not fear computers. I fear the lack of them.

Isaac Asimov, Science fiction writer

Any sufficiently advanced technology is indistinguishable from magic.

Arthur C. Clarke, Science fiction writer

Data science is inherently an interdisciplinary activity that has evolved from a synergy between computer science and statistics.

To do data science, we need data! So we have a data set; it could be a structured database of employee records with all their details, an unstructured collection of textual documents (say emails), a large collection of images of animals, a time series of financial data from the stock market, epidemiological data giving the number of infected individuals per day for a given region over a period of time, or geographical data pertaining to businesses in central London.

Having data is not enough; we need to have a problem we would like to solve or some questions we wish to answer using the data. For example, in an employee data set, we may wish to know the employee characteristics that determine their salary band or, in an epidemiological data set, we may wish to determine how fast a virus is spreading in the population. Now, in a broad sense, once the data is available and we have a well-defined problem to work on, several steps determine the tasks a data scientist should perform to tackle the problem at hand and find out what the data is telling us.

It is always sensible to start with an exploratory data analysis phase, which is carried out with the aid of visualisation tools. Exploring data will help us form some hypotheses about the data, which in turn allows us to build a statistical model of the data. Inevitably, we will use an algorithmic method, based on our model, whose output will assist us in verifying or refuting the hypotheses we have formed.

In a nutshell, this is what data science is about. The algorithmic method essentially enables the discovery of patterns in the data, which may be large in size and/or complex, according to the statistical model we have formed. This is often referred to as *machine learning*; however, the general process of pattern or knowledge discovery is known as *data mining*. In our exposition of data science, we prefer to use the term *machine learning* as the subfield of computer science responsible for the algorithmic part of data science.

Therefore, in a very broad sense, data science comprises the methods and algorithms used to analyse the data and present the findings from the ensuing analysis.

Taking this a step further, who are the stakeholders in this discipline and activity called data science? Computer scientists, such as the authors, are responsible for designing and implementing the algorithms in such a way that they scale to very large and potentially complex data sets. Then statisticians are responsible for model building, which is an essential part of data science. However, one could argue that the data scientist combines skills from these two disciplines of computer science and statistics, leaning toward one side or another depending on their background. Still, we have a third group of stakeholders who bring the data and the problems to the table: they may be social scientists, economists, epidemiologists, or any other professionals from any other discipline that would like to use data science to aid them in answering questions they have about the data they possess.

For successful data science to take place, more often than not, an interdisciplinary team needs to be working on the problem at hand. There is also a breed of data scientists who, from the start, build their expertise in this field rather than in the field of computer science or statistics. Moreover, others, such as the authors, started off in computer science or statistics and have moved their expertise to the middle ground of data science.

Ultimately, the question of what exactly is the relationship between data science, statistics, and computer science/machine learning will remain an ongoing debate. It is important from our perspective to appreciate that data science demands the application of expertise from both these disciplines to solve real-world problems emanating from data. Furthermore, our goal in this book is to provide a relatively brief technical introduction to this exciting field that can be understood by practitioners and researchers alike, coming from diverse backgrounds.

In Chapter 2 we introduce the basic statistical notions needed to become a data scientist. In Chapter 3 we introduce the fundamental data types that data scientists need to understand when going about their daily job. Chapter 4 is a machine learning crash course for budding data scientists. In Chapter 5 we examine several topics of the authors' choice in data science that will enhance data scientists' knowledge and give them insight into typical applications they may come across during their work. Finally, in Chapter 6 we summarise the material we have covered in this introduction.

2

Basic Statistics

In this chapter we will limit ourselves to introducing some basic concepts that are needed for introducing the subject in a manner that is as self-contained as possible.

2.1 Introductory Statistical Notions

A random or *stochastic* process is a function that evolves over time and assigns a value to the result of a random experiment, at each time point. Examples of random processes are (i) flipping a coin, (ii) rolling a die, (iii) measuring the temperature at a given place, and (iv) measuring the wind velocity at a given place. A *random variable* maps the outcome of such a random process to the value it generates at a given time point.

The first two random variables are discrete since they can take on only a finite number of possible values (or more technically, a countable number, which may actually be infinite). This gives rise to *discrete random variables*, which map outcomes of random processes to discrete values; random variables are denoted by uppercase letters such as X, Y, and Z, and their values are denoted by the corresponding lowercase letters x, y, and z. For example, in (i), the random variable X would map the random process of flipping a coin to its two possible outcomes: heads, represented numerically as $x = 0$, or tails, represented numerically as $x = 1$.

On the other hand, the third and fourth random variables are continuous and thus can take on an infinite number of values. This gives rise to *continuous random variables*, which map outcomes of random processes to continuous values. For example, in (iii), the random variable Y would map the random process of measuring the temperature in a building to its possible values y in degrees Celsius.

An *event* is the set of outcomes for which a random variable X takes on the value x, and its probability is a non-negative value, denoted as $P(X = x)$; at times we will use $P(x)$ as a shorthand for $P(X = x)$ whenever X is understood from context. Moreover, $P(X)$ is the sum of the probabilities of all outcomes that comprise the event X. So, for example, if we roll two dice, the event that the sum of the dice is 3 comprises two outcomes: either the first die is 1 and the second is 2, or the first die is 2 and the second is 1. The probability of this event, assuming the dice are fair, is $1/18$.

Two events $p_1 = P(X = x_1)$ and $p_2 = P(X = x_2)$ are *independent* if the outcome of p_1 does not have any effect on the outcome of p_2. A simple example is that of flipping the same coin two times in a row. Knowledge of the result of the first coin toss does not have any influence on the future result of the second toss. In the case of independence, the *joint probability* of the two events is equal to their product, that is,

$$P(X = x_1 \cap X = x_2) = P(X = x_1)P(X = x_2),$$

where the intersection symbol $\cap$ is read as *and*; the above joint probability can also be written as $P(X = x_1, X = x_2)$, with a comma replacing $\cap$.

For random variables X and Y having joint probability $P(X = x, Y = y)$, we can recover the *marginal probability* $P(X = x)$, respectively, $P(Y = y)$, by summing over all the values $Y = y$, respectively, $X = x$, that is,

$$P(x) = \sum_y P(x, y) \quad \text{and} \quad P(y) = \sum_x P(x, y),$$

using our shorthand notation, where Σ denotes summation.

Two events A and B are, in general, not independent, when one is conditional on another in some way. For example, when you are picking two cards out of a deck of cards, the probability of the second card being a king (event A) depends on what the first card was (event B). Another example, from weather forecasting, is the probability that it will rain today (A) given that it rained yesterday (event B). Their joint probability is captured by *Bayes'* theorem, which reads

$$P(A \cap B) = P(B)P(A|B),$$

where $P(A|B)$ is the *conditional probability* of event A occurring given that event B has already occurred. When $P(A|B) = P(A)$, then events A and B are independent.

A *probability mass function* (PMF) p_X is a function (known as a probability distribution) that returns the probability $P(X = x)$ of a discrete random variable X taking on the value x, that is, $p_X(x) = P(X = x)$. Similarly, a *probability density function* (PDF) f_Y is a probability distribution that returns the probability of a continuous random variable Y. As opposed to a PMF, which is a discrete probability distribution, a PDF is a continuous probability distribution that specifies the probability of a continuous random variable Y being in a range of values (or an interval), that is, $P(a \leq Y \leq b)$ for values a and b, since for a PDF the probability of any particular value is zero due to the continuous nature of its random variables. The probability $P(a \leq Y \leq b)$ is computed as the integral from a to b of f_Y.

A PMF satisfies the constraint that the sum of p_X over all values of X is equal to 1 and, correspondingly, a PDF satisfies the constraint that the integral of f_Y over all values of Y is equal to 1.

The *cumulative distribution function* (CDF) F_Z of a random variable Z is a function that returns the probability that Z is less than or equal to a value z, that is, $F_Z(z) = P(Z \leq z)$.

Correspondingly, the *survival function* (also known as the *complementary* CDF) F_Z returns the probability that Z is greater than z, that is, $S_Z(z) = P(Z > z) = 1 - P(Z \leq z) = 1 - F_Z(z)$.

Example 2.1. A histogram is a visual representation of count data for a random variable, grouped in a similar manner to a bar chart. The histogram for the heights of a sample of women recorded in a telephone survey in the United States in 1990 (see Table 2.1) is shown on the top left of Figure 2.1. The corresponding fitted PDF is shown on the top right of Figure 2.1. The histogram can be viewed as an approximation to the normal distribution (introduced below), and the PDF is generated from the parameters resulting from maximum likelihood fitting of the normal distribution to the data set. (*Maximum likelihood* is a well-established method for estimating the parameters of a distribution that is assumed to fit the data.) A further plot of the *empirical cumulative distribution function* (ECDF, introduced at the end of Section 2.1), is shown on the bottom left of Figure 2.1, and a plot of the CDF is shown on the bottom right of Figure 2.1.

Three parameters—*location*, *scale*, and *shape*—are commonly used to describe the characteristics of a distribution. The location parameter determines how far a distribution is shifted on the horizontal axis to the left or to the right from its standard value, which is often zero. On the other hand, the scale parameter determines the spread of the distribution on the horizontal axis and has the effect of stretching/compressing the distribution the larger/smaller its magnitude gets. As an alternative to the scale parameter, we may use the *rate* parameter, also called the *inverse scale* parameter, which is the reciprocal of the scale parameter. A third type of parameter, the *shape* parameter, is distinct from the location and scale parameters and determines a family of distributions distinguished by their general shape. We note that the location and scale parameters may correspond, respectively, to the mean (see Section 2.2) and standard deviation (see Section 2.3) of a distribution, as they do for the normal distribution introduced later. Moreover, the shape parameter can, for example, help describe the skewness or kurtosis (see Section 2.3) of a distribution.

Table 2.1   A sample of the data for height (in centimeters) and weight (in kilograms) of American women, recorded in a telephone survey in 1990.

Height	Weight
149.63	46.31
165.68	64.10
160.96	59.44
163.78	58.14
156.95	58.87

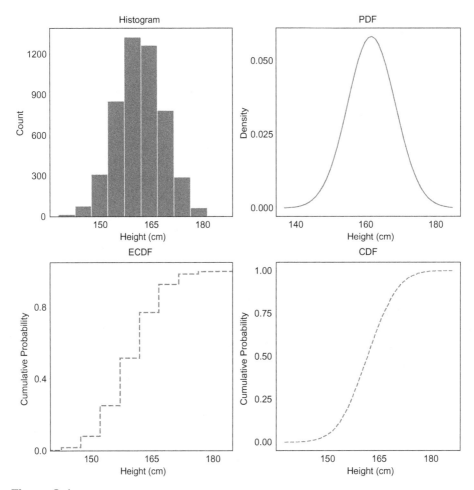

Figure 2.1   Histogram (top left) and corresponding PDF (top right), ECDF (bottom left) and CDF (bottom right).

A distribution that is characterised by parameters, like those just described, are called *parametric*. On the other had, a *nonparametric* distribution makes very few, if any, assumptions regarding the parameters that may be used to model the data. For example, a nonparametric distribution can be generated using *kernel density estimation* (kde), which creates a smooth curve of the data, known as a kernel distribution.

Example 2.2. The data set in this example is based on the recorded flipper length (in millimetres) of 342 penguins captured and measured on the Palmer Archipelago (Antarctica); see Table 2.2. The data captures three different species of penguin, along with data on their location (island), bill length and depth, and flipper length in millimetres. The distribution of the data is fit using a kde function with a suitable smoothing parameter value is shown in Figure 2.2 overlaid in red on top of the histogram.

Table 2.2 Sample of the Palmer Archipelago (Antarctica) data set; the lengths are in millimeters.

Species	Island	Bill length	Bill depth	Flipper length
Adelie	Torgersen	39.1	18.7	181.0
Adelie	Torgersen	39.5	17.4	186.0
Adelie	Torgersen	40.3	18.0	195.0
Adelie	Torgersen	36.7	19.3	193.0
Adelie	Torgersen	39.3	20.6	190.0

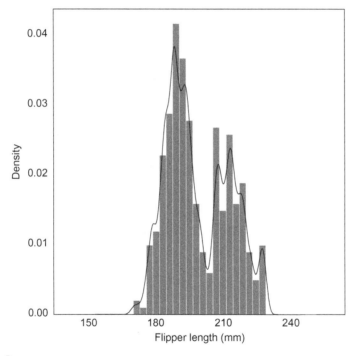

Figure 2.2   The histogram for the flipper length of penguins from the Palmer Archipelago (Antarctica) data set and the corresponding kde plot (overlaid in red).

We now briefly introduce the most widely used distributions (noting that there are many other useful distributions), where the random variable X is assumed to be either discrete (when referring to a PMF) or continuous (when referring to a PDF).

The *Bernoulli* distribution is a discrete distribution with probability of success p and two possible outcomes $k = 1$ (success) and $k = 0$ (failure). Its PMF p_X takes on the form

$$p_X(k|p) = \begin{cases} p & \text{if } k = 1, \\ 1 - p & \text{if } k = 0. \end{cases}$$

Table 2.3   The total number (#) of votes (in millions) received by Biden and Trump in the 2020 US presidential elections.

Candidate	#Votes
Joe Biden	81.28
Donald Trump	74.22

If a random variable X has a Bernoulli distribution with parameter p, we write $X \sim \mathrm{Bern}(p)$. To summarise, a Bernoulli random variable can be thought of as a random experiment with two possible outcomes: success with probability p and failure with probability $1 - p$.

Example 2.3. Consider the election results for the main candidates for the US presidency in 2020, where Joe Biden received 81,281,888 votes and Donald Trump received 74,223,251 votes; see Table 2.3. A Bernoulli distribution is fitted to the data set through maximum likelihood, resulting in the model parameter $p = 0.52$ representing Biden's winning proportion. That is, $X \sim \mathrm{Bern}(0.52)$, where X is a random variable indicating whether a vote will be counted for Biden rather than Trump. The histogram (left) and the corresponding PMF (right), for the proportion of candidate votes for each candidate, are shown in Figure 2.3. It is worth noting that the PMF is a scaled version of the histogram.

The *binomial* distribution is a discrete distribution with n trials and probability of success p. Its PMF p_X takes on the form

$$p_X(k|n,p) = \binom{n}{k} p^k (1-p)^{n-k},$$

for $k = 0, 1, 2, \ldots, n$, where

$$\binom{n}{k} = \frac{n!}{k!(n-k)!},$$

is called the *binomial coefficient* and $m!$ denotes the factorial of an integer m. If a random variable X has a binomial distribution with parameters n and p, we write $X \sim \mathrm{Bin}(n,p)$; note that $\mathrm{Bern}(p) = \mathrm{Bin}(1,p)$. To summarise, a binomial random variable can be thought of as a sequence of n independent random experiments, where each individual experiment is a $\mathrm{Bern}(p)$ trial.

Example 2.4. Consider data generated from 100 repeated experiments, where each experiment consists of $n = 100$ tosses (i.e., 100 trials) of an unbiased coin (i.e., $p = 0.5$), a sample of which is provided in Table 2.4. A binomial distribution, assuming $n = 100$, is fitted to the data set through maximum likelihood, resulting in the model parameter

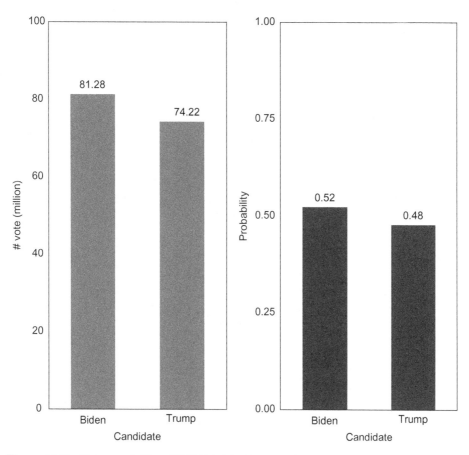

Figure 2.3 Histogram (left) and PMF (right) for the proportion of candidate votes; a Bernoulli distribution with $p = 0.52$ is fitted to the data, that is, $X \sim \text{Bern}(0.52)$.

Table 2.4 Sample results of the first five experiments for a binomial distribution with $p = 0.5$ and $n = 100$.

Experiment	#Heads
1	42
2	51
3	52
4	49
5	48

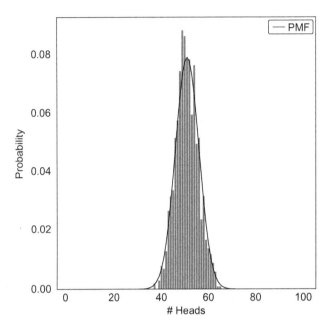

Figure 2.4 Histogram and PMF (overlaid in red) for the proportion of heads; a binomial distribution with $p = 0.5$ and $n = 100$ is fitted to the data, that is, $X \sim \mathrm{Bin}(100, 0.5)$.

$p = 0.5$ representing the number of heads in 100 trials. That is, $X \sim \mathrm{Bin}(100, 0.5)$, where X is a random variable indicating the number of heads obtained during the 100 trials. The histogram and the corresponding PMF (overlaid in red) for the proportion of resulting heads are shown in Figure 2.4.

The *Poisson* distribution is a discrete distribution with rate parameter $\lambda > 0$. Its PMF takes on the form

$$p_X(k|\lambda) = \frac{\exp(-\lambda)\lambda^k}{k!},$$

for $k = 0, 1, 2, \ldots$

If a random variable X has a Poisson distribution with rate parameter λ, we write $X \sim \mathrm{Pois}(\lambda)$. The mean and variance of a Poisson distribution are both equal to λ. It is worth noting that the Poisson distribution is used to model the number of random events occurring in a unit interval of time or space. The Poisson distribution is the limit of the binomial distribution with np tending to λ, as n gets larger and p gets smaller.

Example 2.5. Consider the count of births per hour in a single 24-hour period at a hospital in Brisbane, Australia; see Table 2.5. The data appeared originally in the Brisbane-based newspaper *The Sunday Mail* on December 21, 1997. A Poisson distribution is fitted to the data set through maximum likelihood, resulting in the model parameter

Table 2.5 Sample data of the number of births recorded each hour on a single ward and day.

Hour	#Births
00:00	1
01:00	3
02:00	1
04:00	4
07:00	2

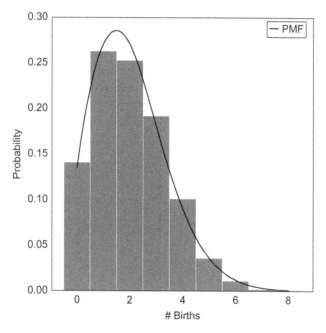

Figure 2.5 Histogram and PMF (overlaid in red) for the number of births within a period of an hour; a Poisson distribution with $\lambda = 2.01$ is fitted to the data, that is, $X \sim \text{Pois}(2.01)$.

$\lambda = 2.01$ representing the mean number of births, and its variance, within an interval of an hour. That is, $X \sim \text{Pois}(2.01)$, where X is a random variable indicating the number of births within a period of an hour. The histogram and the PMF (overlaid in red) for the probability of the number of births occurring within an hour are shown in Figure 2.5.

The *normal* or *Gaussian* distribution is a continuous distribution with mean μ being its location parameter and standard deviation σ (i.e., σ^2 is its variance) being its scale parameter. Its PDF f_X takes on the form

$$f_X(x|\mu,\sigma) = \frac{1}{\sigma\sqrt{2\pi}}\exp\left(-\frac{(x-\mu)^2}{2\sigma^2}\right),$$

where exp is the exponential function. If a random variable X has a normal distribution with parameters μ and σ^2, we write $X \sim N(\mu,\sigma)$. The standard normal distribution has a mean of zero and a standard deviation of 1; that is, it is $N(0,1)$.

The normal distribution, also known as the bell curve due to its shape, is the most familiar distribution to most of us. It is commonly used in many applications in the social and natural sciences. One reason for this is the *central limit theorem*, which intuitively states that if we take a sample of a large number of independent random values all coming from the same distribution (not necessarily normal), having a finite mean and variance, then the distribution of the average of these random variables will be approximately normal, and the approximation will be more precise as the sample gets larger.

Example 2.6. Consider the heights of women recorded in a telephone survey in the United States in 1990; see Table 2.1. A normal distribution is fitted to the data set through maximum likelihood, resulting in the model parameters $\mu = 161.820$ and $\sigma = 6.848$. That is, $X \sim N(161.820, 6.848)$, where X is a random variable indicating the height of a woman in the 1990 telephone survey. The histogram and the PMF (overlaid in red) for the probability of a woman having a certain height are shown in Figure 2.6.

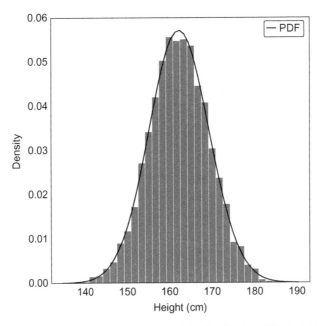

Figure 2.6   Histogram and PDF (overlaid in red) of the distribution of the heights of women; a normal distribution with parameters $\mu = 63.709$ and $\sigma = 2.696$ is fitted to the data, $X \sim N(63.709, 2.696)$.

The *exponential* distribution is a continuous distribution with rate parameter $\lambda > 0$. Its PDF f_X takes on the form

$$f_X(x|\lambda) = \lambda \exp(-\lambda x).$$

If a random variable X has an exponential distribution with parameter λ, we write $X \sim \text{Exp}(\lambda)$. To summarise, an exponential random variable can be thought of as modelling the waiting time between independent events, which occur continuously at a constant average rate.

Example 2.7. Consider two data sets, one recording the survival time in days after a heart transplant from a 1967–1974 study of 304 individuals (see Table 2.6), and the second recording the inter-arrival time of approximately 550,000 posts published on HackerNews between 2006 and late 2017 (see Table 2.7). Exponential distribution is fitted to both data sets through maximum likelihood, resulting in the model parameters $\lambda = 223.28$ for the first data set representing the survival rate in days after a heart transplant, and $\lambda = 0.99$ for the second data set representing the rate in seconds before a new post arrives. That is, $X \sim \text{Exp}(223.28)$, where X is a random variable indicating the survival time in days after

Table 2.6 Sample of data for heart transplant survival rates of individuals, measured in days alongside the age of the individual.

Survival	Age
15.0	54.3
3.0	40.4
624.0	51.0
46.0	42.5
127.0	48.0

Table 2.7 Sample of post data received on HackerNews, with postage timestamp and inter-arrival time in seconds.

Score	Author	Timestamp	Inter-arrival time
1	cthackers	1387536536	106.0
1	lecowski	1387536593	57.0
1	brianchu	1387536759	166.0
3	rb2e	1387536769	10.0
0	finerolla	1387537034	265.0

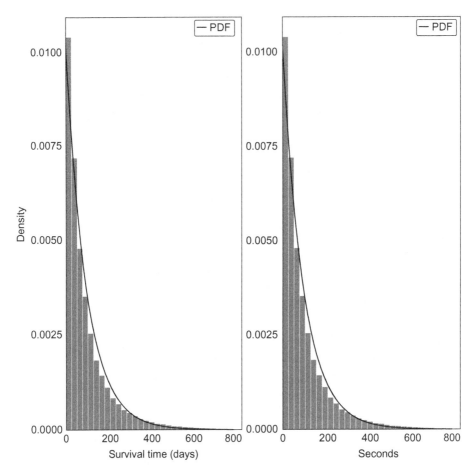

Figure 2.7 Histograms and PDFs (overlaid in red) of heart surgery survival rates (left), and HackerNews posts (right); an exponential distribution with $\lambda = 223.28$ is fitted to the heart data, that is, $X \sim \text{Exp}(222.28)$, while an exponential distribution with $\lambda = 0.99$ is fitted to the HackerNews data, that is, $X \sim \text{Exp}(0.99)$.

a heart transplant, and $X \sim \text{Exp}(0.99)$, where X is a random variable indicating the inter-arrival time in seconds of HackerNews posts. The histograms and the PDFs (overlaid in red) for the probability of survival after a heart attack (left) and for the arrival of a HackerNews post (right) are shown in Figure 2.7.

Lastly, we introduce the *Pareto* or *power law* distribution (see Subsection 5.2.3 in Chapter 5), which is a continuous distribution with scale parameter $x_{min} > 0$ and shape parameter $\alpha > 0$. Its PDF f_X takes on the form

$$f_X(x) = \alpha \left(x_{min} \right)^\alpha x^{-(\alpha+1)},$$

for an exponent α and some positive constant $C = \alpha \left(x_{min} \right)^\alpha$ acting as a normalisation constant (since the integral of f_X over all values x of X must be equal to 1), with the constraint that the data value x satisfies $x > 0$, recalling that $x^{-\alpha} = 1/x^\alpha$.

If a random variable X has a Pareto distribution with parameters x_{min} and α, we write $X \sim \text{Pareto}(x_{min}, \alpha)$. The Pareto distribution, discussed in more detail in Section 5.2.3, captures situations that cannot be modelled by the central limit theorem, due to the finiteness assumption of the mean and variance, such as the distribution of wealth in society.

Example 2.8. Consider two data sets, one recording the salaries of football players from FIFA 2019 (see Table 2.8), and the second recording the counts of words in the Brown corpus (see Table 2.9). A Pareto distribution is fitted to both data sets through maximum likelihood, resulting in the scale and shape parameters $x_m = 2.46$ and $\alpha = 0.13$,

Table 2.8 Sample of FIFA 2019 data showing the salary information in Euros for each player with the top 20 removed.

Name	Age	Nationality	Salary
L. Messi	31	Argentina	565,000
Cristiano Ronaldo	33	Portugal	405,000
Neymar Jr	26	Brazil	290,000
De Gea	27	Spain	260,000
K. De Bruyne	27	Belgium	355,000

Table 2.9 Sample of data representing the total count of each word in the Brown corpus.

Word	Count
the	69971
and	28853
is	10109
he	9548
be	6377
not	4610
but	4381
they	3620
one	3292
her	3036

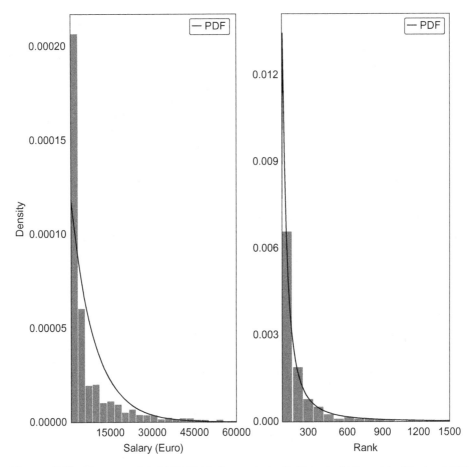

Figure 2.8   Histogram plot of FIFA 2019 player salaries (left), and a further plot of the top 1,500 words and their frequency counts in the Brown corpus (right); a Pareto distribution with parameters $x_m = 2.46$ and $\alpha = 0.13$ is fitted to the football salary data, that is, $X \sim$ Pareto(2.46, 0.13), while a Pareto distribution with $x_m = 72.192$ and $\alpha = 1.0435$ is fitted to the word count data, that is, $X \sim$ Pareto(72.192, 1.0435), where X is a random variable indicating the count of a word in the corpus.

respectively, for the first data set representing the salaries of football players, and the scale and shape parameters $x_m = 72.192$ and $\alpha = 1.0435$, respectively, for the second data set representing the counts of words. That is, $X \sim$ Pareto$(2.46, 0.13)$, where X is a random variable indicating the salary of a football player, and $X \sim$ Pareto$(72.192, 1.0435)$, where X is a random variable indicating the count of a word, respectively. The histograms and the PDFs (overlaid in red) for the probability of a salary of a football player (left) and for the count of a word (right) are shown in Figure 2.8.

A *population*, in the statistical sense, is the set of all items of interest to the data scientist carrying out some data analysis, for example, the population of all people living in England this year, the set of all 36 outcomes of rolling two dice, or the collection of all Twitter feeds from this month with a given hashtag. Even though a population may be infinite, such as the population of stars in the universe (at least from a practical perspective) or the populations of all integers, we will, in most cases, be dealing only with finite populations.

A *sample* is a subset of the population chosen to represent the population in data analysis. A sample is chosen using a well-defined procedure, for example, randomly, using a *Monte Carlo sampling* method. In a Monte Carlo method, a sampling distribution is chosen, for example, uniform sampling when all members of the population have the same chance of being chosen. The size of the sample is often important should we wish to make inferences from the sample relating back to the whole population being analysed. Sampling may be carried out without replacement—a chosen item can appear only once in the sample—or with replacement allowing for a chosen item to be selected again and thus to appear more than once in the sample. We will use uppercase letters such as N and M to denote the size of populations and lowercase letters such as n and m to denote the size of samples, where in most cases the sample size is much less than the population size, that is, $n \ll N$ and $m \ll M$.

Suppose that we have a sample $x_1, x_2, \ldots, x_n$ of n values from some population with cumulative distribution F_X. The *empirical distribution function* (EDF; also known as the *empirical cumulative distribution function* or ECDF), denoted by F_n, is defined as

$$F_n(x) = \frac{\#(x_i \leq x)}{n},$$

where x is a value of X and $\#(x_i \leq x)$ is the number of x_i in the sample such that $x_i \leq x$.

A *parameter* is a quantity that characterises some aspect of a population, while a *statistic* is a quantity that is computed from a sample of the population; so, for example, the mean or variance of a sample is a statistic. On the other hand, an *estimator* is a rule for computing a statistic based on a sample that has been observed by the data scientist. (Note the subtle difference between a statistic that is a "quantity" and an estimator that is a "rule.")

2.2 Expectation

The *expected value* $E(X)$ of a discrete random variable X with PMF p_X is the sum of all possible outcome values x of X each multiplied by the probability $p_X(x)$. Symbolically, it is written as

$$E(X) = \sum_x p_X(x) = \sum_x P(X = x) = \sum_x P(x),$$

where, as before, Σ denotes summation; the expected value of X is also known as the first moment of X.

For a continuous random variable Y with PDF f_Y, the sum is replaced by an integral from minus infinity to plus infinity of the PDF. The expectation $E(X)$ is commonly known as the *mean* of X, often written as μ_X or simply μ whenever X is understood from context. We also mention the useful concept of an *unbiased estimator*, which is an estimator that is equal in expectation to the actual value of the statistic being evaluated.

Intuitively, the expected value of a random variable is a weighted average of its possible values. When the distribution is uniform, the expected value is reduced to the average of the values. As a simple example, X could represent the outcome of rolling a fair die, leading to the expected value:

$$E(X) = \frac{1 + 2 + 3 + 4 + 5 + 6}{6} = 3.5.$$

Given a discrete random variable X with PMF p_X, a *mode* of X is a value x, where the distribution $p_X(x)$ is at its maximum value. Similarly, for a continuous random variable Y with PDF f_Y, a mode of Y is a maxima of its distribution f_Y. Note that the mode of a random variable may not be unique.

A *median* value of a random variable X is a value x that splits the distribution into two equal halves, and can thus be thought of as a "middle" value of the distribution. More formally, when the population is either odd or infinite, a median of X is a value x such that $P(X \leq x) \geq 0.5$ and $P(X \geq x) \geq 0.5$. When X is a discrete random variable over an even finite population, then the median of the distribution is the average of the two "middle" values of the distribution—one with cumulative probability just less than 0.5 and the other with cumulative probability just greater than 0.5. Note that, in general, the median of a random variable may not be unique. The median is thus at the 50th *percentile* of the distribution, and the four *quartiles* divide the distribution into four equal parts, from the first quartile to the fourth quartile.

Example 2.9. A *boxplot* visualisation summarising the salaries of different educational backgrounds for 5,000 individuals recorded by a survey run by a popular programming peer support website (see Table 2.10) is shown in Figure 2.9.

Table 2.10 Sample from a popular programming peer support website survey data on salary (in US dollars), professional programming experience in years (years-code-pro), and highest qualification (education), where LT stands for Less Than, MA stands for master's degree, and BA stands for bachelor's degree in any subject.

Salary	Years-code-pro	Education
180,000	20	MA
55,000	3	BA
77,000	2	BA
67,017	1	BA
90,000	4	LT BA

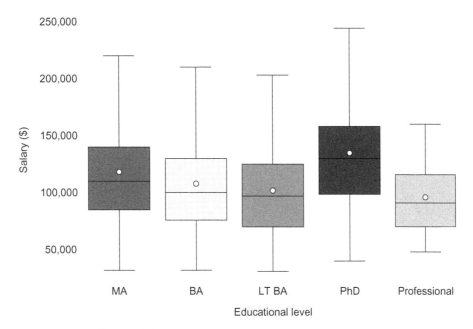

Figure 2.9   Boxplot of the salary and qualification data set.

The height of the box in the boxplot is the difference between the third (75th percentile) and first (25th percentile) quartiles, called the *interquartile range* (IQR). The median is represented by a horizontal line across each box and can be supplemented with further statistics, such as the mean, shown here as a white dot. In addition, each boxplot displays the minimum value (bottom whisker) and maximum value (top whisker).

Often we wish to single out values that differ significantly from others in the data set, called *outliers*, when, typically, the bottom whisker will represent the lowest value outside 1.5 times the IQR below the lower bound of the box and the top whisker will represent the highest value outside 1.5 times the IQR above the upper bound of the box; all values below and above the whiskers are considered to be outliers.

A method for estimating a statistic that relies on random resampling with replacement from a given sample of the population is the *bootstrap*. Resampling means that we repeatedly sample from the original sample, each time creating a new sample; in particular, in the bootstrap, each resample is taken with replacement. In its basic form, the *bootstrap percentile method* can be used to estimate the distribution of the population mean (or another statistic) by computing sample means over a large number of bootstrap resamples taken from the original sample. It is common to take at least 1,000 and often up to 10,000 resamples to form the bootstrap distribution of the statistic at hand, and its percentiles can be used to form *confidence intervals*. For example, the 95% bootstrap confidence interval will be the interval between the 2.5 and 97.5 percentiles of the bootstrap sampling distribution. A confidence interval allows us to obtain a better approximation, rather than a point estimate such as the expected value, of what the true statistic, say the mean of the population, may be. When the confidence interval covers a larger percentage, our belief in the range of values of the true mean is strengthened.

Example 2.10. We carried out a bootstrap computation of the heights of women recorded in a telephone survey in the United States in 1990; see Table 2.1. In particular, 10,000 resamples of the data were generated with replacement, to compute 95% confidence intervals for the mean, median, and mode of the data; the results are shown in Figure 2.10.

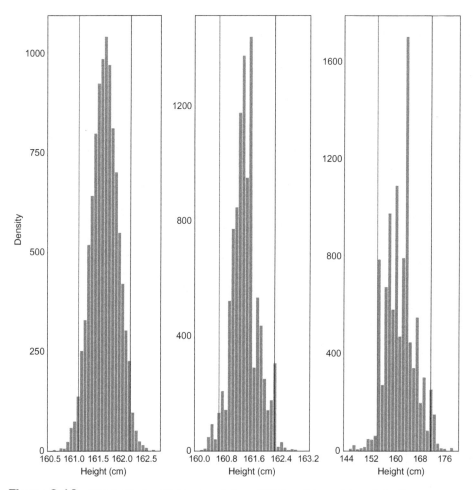

Figure 2.10   PDF for the bootstrap computation of 95% confidence intervals for the mean (left), median (middle), and mode (right) of the heights of women in the telephone survey data set.

Table 2.11 Sample of data recording the flights and
passenger counts on a monthly basis for international flights
leaving US airports on international flights (# denotes a
count, in this case the count of passengers).

Year	Month	#Passengers
2002	10	9,578,435
2002	11	9,016,535
2002	12	10,038,794
2003	1	9,726,436
2003	2	8,283,372

Example 2.11. Consider the number of passengers recorded on flights on a monthly
period from 2002 to 2020 departing from US airports on international flights; see
Table 2.11. Now, a *line plot* is a series of points that are joined by straight line fragments.
A line plot of the number of passengers on a yearly basis, together with 95% confidence
intervals for the mean and median, is shown in Figure 2.11. The confidence intervals are
computed from a bootstrap of 10,000 resamples of the passenger data over the months of
each year.

2.3 Variance

The spread of a random variable around the mean is measured with the *variance*. The
variance of a random variable X, written as σ_X^2 (or simply σ^2), is given by

$$\sigma^2 = E\left[(X - \mu)^2\right] = E(X^2) - E(X)^2,$$

recalling that $\mu = E(X)$; the variance of X is also known as the second moment of X.

Often, we are interested in the square root of the variance, σ_X (or simply σ), known as
the *standard deviation* (SD) of X. When discussing how far a value is from the mean, we use
the SD because its units are the same as those of the mean. The SD of a sample
population is called its *standard error* (SE) and is important in computing a confidence
interval around the mean, allowing us to obtain a better estimate of what the true mean
might be. For a population with SD σ_X, the SE of a sample of size n is $\sigma_X/\sqrt{n}$, and thus
it decreases by a factor of the square root of n when the sample size increases to n.

The concept of *covariance* gives a measure of the joint spread of two random variables
around their respective means. The covariance between two random variables, X and Y,
written as $cov(X,Y)$, is given by

$$cov(X,Y) = E\left[(X - E(X))(Y - E(Y))\right] = E(XY) - E(X)E(Y).$$

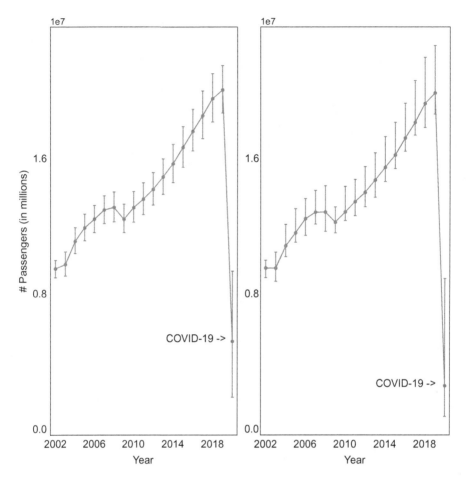

Figure 2.11   Two line plots with the mean number of passengers (left) and median number of passengers (right) on international flights leaving the US. The band represents the confidence intervals of the 2.5th and 97.5th percentiles computed from the monthly passenger count for each year.

As a special case, we have $\sigma^2_X = cov(X, X)$.

We often deal with time series data (introduced in Section 3.4 in Chapter 3), modelled as a sequence of random variables $X_1, X_2, \ldots$, where X_t, $t \geq 1$, is indexed by t denoting time. A *lag* is a fixed amount, say k, $t > k \geq 0$, so that the k-lag of X_t is X_{t-k}; that is, X_t and X_{t-k} are k time periods apart. Accordingly, we can measure the covariance between a time series and a k-lag of the time series as $cov(X_{t-k}, X_t)$; this measure is called *autocovariance* and is closely related to *autocorrelation*, mentioned later.

Skewness is a measure of how symmetric a distribution is. More formally, the *skewness* of a random variable X is defined as

$$\beta = E\left[\left(\frac{X-\mu}{\sigma}\right)^3\right],$$

where $\beta = 0$ when X is symmetric, $\beta < 0$ when X is negatively skewed, and $\beta > 0$ when X is positively skewed; the skewness of X is also known as the third moment of X.

Kurtosis is a measure of the "peakedness" and "tailedness" of a distribution relative to the normal distribution. More formally, the *excess kurtosis* (or simply the kurtosis) of a random variable X is defined as

$$\gamma = E\left[\left(\frac{X-\mu}{\sigma}\right)^4\right] - 3,$$

where $\gamma = 0$ when the tails of X are the same as the normal distribution, $\gamma < 0$ when the tails of X are thinner (i.e., decreasing at a faster rate) than those of the normal distribution, and $\gamma > 0$ when the tails of X are fatter (i.e., decreasing at a slower rate) than those of the normal distribution; the kurtosis of X is also known as the fourth moment of X.

Example 2.12. Consider the *Ames Housing* data set, recording 1,460 property sale prices in Ames, US, including the year sold, sale type, sale condition, and sale price in US dollars; see Table 2.12. In Figure 2.12 the histogram of the data set is shown, together with the PDF (overlaid in red) of a normal distribution with the same mean and SD as the original data set. Here, the data set is positively skewed.

Example 2.13. Consider a data set recording the age at death of notable individuals in 2016; see Table 2.13. This data set is composed of 6,839 notable deaths in 2016 published

Table 2.12 Sample of the data recording the sale prices of houses in US dollars in Ames.

Property	Sale price
1	208,500
2	181,500
3	223,500
4	140,000
5	250,000

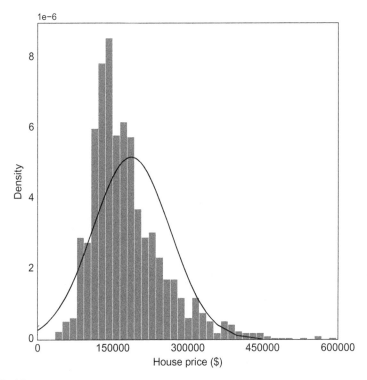

Figure 2.12   A histogram and PDF (overlaid in red) for the sale price of properties, demonstrating that the data set is positively skewed.

Table 2.13   Sample of the data recording the name and age at death of notable individuals in 2016.

Name	Age at death
Natasha Aguilar	45
George Alexandru	58
Fazu Aliyeva	83
Lennie Bluett	96
Dale Bumpers	90

on a monthly basis on Wikipedia, and includes, for each individual, the name, age, and reason for notability. In Figure 2.13 the histogram of the data set is shown, together with the PDF (overlaid in red) of a normal distribution with the same mean and SD as the original data set. Here, the data set is negatively skewed.

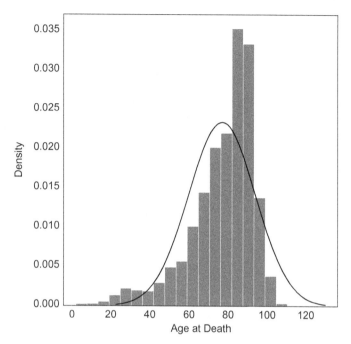

Figure 2.13 A histogram and PDF (overlaid in red) for age at death of notable individuals in 2016, demonstrating that the data set is negatively skewed.

Table 2.14 Sample of the data showing the first-order differences of Bitcoin values.

Time point	Difference
0	47.17
1	24.17
2	−23.34
3	−9.38
4	5.89

Example 2.14. Consider a Bitcoin cryptocurrency data set composed of the hourly recorded value of Bitcoin over the course of a year (from 01/01/2020 to 07/01/2021), totalling 8,929 rows; see Table 2.14 for a sample of the first-order differences, derived from the original data set by recording the change in value of Bitcoin at consecutive time points. In Figure 2.14 the histogram of the first-order differences of the data set is shown, together with the PDF (overlaid in red) of the maximum likelihood fit of a normal distribution to the data. Here, the kurtosis of the data set, calculated as 59.76, is high relative to the normal distribution, which is 0.

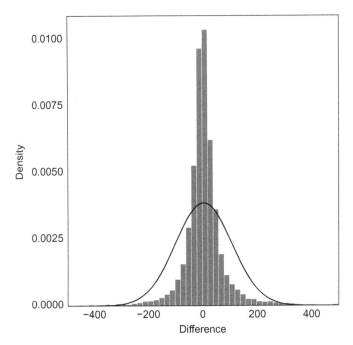

Figure 2.14 The histogram and PDF of the maximum likelihood fit of the normal distribution (overlaid in red) for the first-order differences of the value of Bitcoin, demonstrating that the excess kurtosis present in the data set is high.

2.4 Correlation

For random variables X and Y, let $(x_1, y_1), (x_2, y_2), \ldots, (x_n, y_n)$ be a sample of pairs of values, where for each pair (x_i, y_i), x_i is an X-value and y_i is Y-value, for $i = 1, 2, \ldots, n$. A *scatter plot* visualises such a sample of pairs, so that each (x_i, y_i) is plotted as a dot on the display; an example of six scatter plots is shown in Figure 2.15. A fitted regression line is a line that can be added to a scatter plot, as shown in Figure 2.15. It represents a possible linear relationship between X and Y; see Section 2.5 for more detail on regression. Informally, correlation measures the extent to which a scatter plot is concentrated around a regression line.

The correlation between random variables X and Y indicates an association between these random variables and, more precisely, the degree of linear association between them. It is a value between -1 and $+1$, where a value of 0 indicates that there is no linear relationship between X and Y, and the boundary values of $+1$ or -1 indicate, respectively, perfect positive and negative linear relationships between X and Y. If X and Y are independent, then their correlation is 0, but the correlation can be 0 without X and Y being independent; for example, this may be the case when the relationship between X and Y is nonlinear.

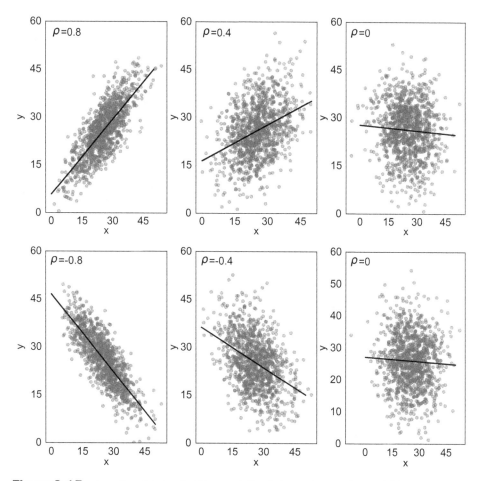

Figure 2.15 A scatter plot showing the correlation between two random variables X and Y on a synthetic data set with regression lines denoting the linear fit between X and Y. The reported Pearson correlation coefficient ρ appears in each subplot. The subplots in the top row illustrate positive correlation, while those in the bottom row illustrate negative correlation.

The correlation between two random variables, X and Y (also known as Pearson's correlation coefficient), written as $\rho_{X,Y}$ (or simply ρ), is given by

$$\rho_{X,Y} = \frac{cov(X,Y)}{\sigma_X \sigma_Y} = \frac{E\left[(X - E(X))\left(Y - E(Y)\right)\right]}{\sigma_X \sigma_Y}$$
$$= \frac{E(XY) - E(X)E(Y)}{\sqrt{E(X^2) - E(X)^2}\sqrt{E(Y^2) - E(Y)^2}}.$$

In the same manner as we have described autocovariance, we can also measure the correlation between a time series and a lag of the time series as ρ_{X_{t-k}, X_t}; this is called *autocorrelation*.

2.5 Regression

Correlation, as defined in Section 2.4, describes a linear relationship between the random variables X and Y. A linear relationship takes the form

$$Y = aX + b,$$

where a and b are the coefficients of the relationship, called the *slope* and *intercept*, respectively; the equation provides a *statistical model* for the linear relationship.

This model is one of the simplest and most intuitive relationships to determine visually, since it involves modelling the data in terms of a straight line, rather than as a more complex nonlinear model. We will use the convention that the Y values are plotted on the vertical axis against the X values on the horizonal axis. Now, although correlation is symmetric, that is, $\rho_{X,Y} = \rho_{Y,X}$, when fitting a line to data values, the roles of X and Y are important; X is called the *independent* variable (or the *explanatory* variable) and Y the *dependent* variable (or the *predictor* variable). When x is an X-value and y is a Y-value, $y = f(x)$, where f is a linear relationship between the independent random variable X and the dependent random variable Y, indicates that y is the output of applying the function f to x.

The process used for estimating the relationships between a dependent variable and an independent variable (or more generally multiple independent variables) is called *regression*. Frequently, in regression, the independent variable X is not random and can be viewed as a special case of a random variable, where no stochastic process is assumed; for example, in time series data of stock prices, the X values denote time and, in tabular data, the X values may denote level of education or age or advertising spend.

The standard method in regression of fitting a straight line through a data sample is the method of *least squares*. This method minimises the sum of squares of the *residuals*, with each residual being the difference between an observed value from the data and the corresponding fitted value from the least squares solution. We stress that a residual can be positive or negative, depending on whether the observed value is larger or smaller than the fitted value, and note that residuals are also known as *residual errors* to stress their magnitude. A data value with a large residual is called an *outlier*. Such extreme values are atypical relative to the other data values and reduce the goodness of fit to the model; a data scientist may consider removing outliers when they are thought to be erroneously present in the sample being used. The goodness of fit can be measured by the *coefficient of determination*, known as R^2, which is the square of the correlation coefficient between the observed values and the fitted values, thus taking on values between 0 and 1; the closer the fit, the closer R^2 is to 1.

Table 2.15 A sample of data from the Boston Standard Metropolitan Statistical Area in 1970, listing various attributes including crime per capita (CRIM), average number of rooms (RM), weighted distance to employment centres (DIST), teacher–student school ratios (PTRATIO), and price in units of 1,000 US dollars.

CRIM	RM	DIST	PTRATIO	Price
0.00632	6.575	4.0900	15.3	24.0
0.02731	6.421	4.9671	17.8	21.6
0.02729	7.185	4.9671	17.8	34.7
0.03237	6.998	6.0622	18.7	33.4
0.06905	7.147	6.0622	18.7	36.2

Example 2.15. Consider a data set from the Boston Standard Metropolitan Statistical Area (SMSA) in 1970, listing, for 506 properties drawn from the area, various attributes including crime per capita (CRIM), average number of rooms (RM), weighted distance to employment centres (DIST), teacher-student school ratios (PTRATIO), and price in units of 1,000 US dollars; see Table 2.15.

The independent variable RM is used to predict the dependent variable PRICE, using the method of least squares to fit the data, giving a coefficient of determination of $R^2 = 0.69$. In Figure 2.16 the fitted line is shown in red overlaid on the scatter plot of the data (left), together with the residual plot (right).

Of course not all relationships are linear. For example, the relationship between the dosage of a medical treatment and its effectiveness is generally nonlinear, as is the growth in the numbers of infected individuals over time in a pandemic. In this case, the methods used for fitting and measuring goodness of fit need to be extended to accommodate for the nonlinearity in the data. Logistic regression is a method used to predict the probability of a binary outcome as a nonlinear function of an independent variable, for example, giving the probability of a patient's survival after being administered a particular treatment.

The *logistic* function allows us to model this probability as a function of an independent variable (or more generally multiple independent variables). The *log-odds* or *logit* function, which is the inverse of the logistic function, provides us with a link from the nonlinear logistic function to modelling the logarithm of the *odds ratio* (or the ratio of the probabilities of success and failure) as a linear function of the independent variable. We formalise this as follows.

Suppose Y is a Bernoulli random variable and p is the probability that $Y = 1$, that is, $p = P(Y = 1)$. So, for an independent variable X, we can deduce that

$$logistic(aX + b) = \frac{1}{1 + \exp(-(aX + b))} = p,$$

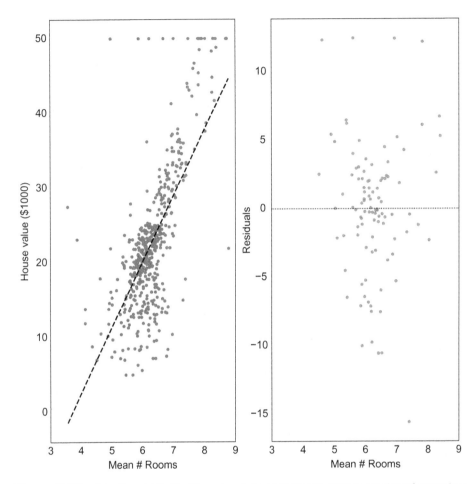

Figure 2.16   A scatter plot (left) of the price plotted against the average number of rooms in a property overlaid with a red line denoting the least squared linear fit and the corresponding residual errors (right).

implying that

$$logit(p) = \log\left(\frac{p}{1-p}\right) = aX + b,$$

where exp is the exponential function and log is the natural logarithm function, noting that both the logit and logistic functions have symmetry properties and are monotonically increasing, since log is monotonically increasing.

Example 2.16. Consider a data set used to predict the onset of diabetes based on medical predictors and a dependent variable representing the diagnostic outcome; see Table 2.16, where BMI stands for body mass index and DPF stands for diabetes pedigree function.

Table 2.16 A sample of data from the diagnostic data set used to predict the onset of diabetes for Pima women.

Glucose	Insulin	BMI	DPF	Age	Outcome
148	0	33.6	0.627	50	Diabetes
85	0	26.6	0.351	31	No Diabetes
183	0	23.3	0.672	32	Diabetes
89	94	28.1	0.167	21	No Diabetes
137	168	43.1	2.288	33	Diabetes

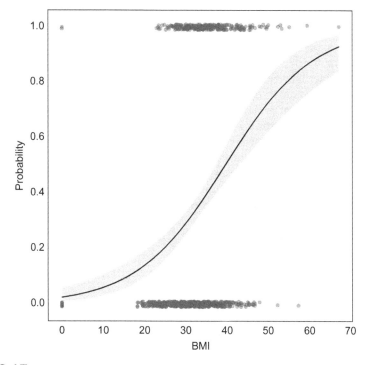

Figure 2.17 A logistic regression plot showing the classification of the data points into those with diabetes (top blue data points), and those without (bottom blue data points). A regression curve has been fit to the data with a 95% confidence interval computed from 10,000 bootstrap resamples.

In the data set, all patients in the data are female and at least 21 years of age and from Pima Indian heritage.

We use the independent variable BMI to predict the dependent variable $Outcome$, which has two possible values: Diabetes and No Diabetes. Logistic regression using the method of maximum likelihood estimation is applied to fit the parameters. In Figure 2.17

we show the plotted logistic regression together with a 95% confidence interval; the confidence interval representing the 2.5th and 97.5th percentiles was computed from a bootstrap of 10,000 resamples of the data.

It is worth mentioning that, in general, R^2 used for measuring the goodness of fit of a linear regression model is not appropriate for logistic regression, which fits a nonlinear model to the data, and thus needs to be modified. One such modification, called the coefficient of discrimination in logistic regression, suggests, as a replacement for R^2, using the difference between the average fitted probability of success and the average fitted probability of failure.

2.6 Chapter Summary

In this chapter we covered the basic statistical methods needed to grasp data science so that the reader can use the book as a self-contained resource.

We first introduced the basic notions leading to the definition of probability distribution and the common distributions that are used in subsequent chapters. We also introduced the concepts of expectation, variance, and correlation, all of which are of paramount importance for data science and machine learning. The methods presented can be used for summarising data, making inferences, and drawing conclusions based on the data available. We also covered some common graphical representations, including histograms and scatter plots, because visualising the data is often the key to understanding the data. Finally, we introduced regression analysis, an important topic in statistics that is central to the book and is commonly used for predicting, forecasting, and understanding the relationship between variables in the data.

3

Types of Data

Data is at the heart of data science, as the name suggests. We will now take an introductory look at the basic types of data that we need to be familiar with to be able to choose the appropriate storage structures and manipulation functions for the data set at hand. We concentrate on the elementary concepts with concise descriptions and explain their use by example, rather than a detailed computer science-oriented exposition of the technical programming aspects. We will also show, again in elementary fashion, how each data type can be visualised to enhance exploratory data analysis, which is a key activity of data science.

3.1 Tabular Data

Example 3.1. To illustrate tabular data, consider the data set capturing the hourly rainfall, temperature, and humidity in London recorded by the *UK Met Office* in 2015; see Table 3.1 for a sample of monthly summaries.

A stacked bar chart can be used to visually compare the magnitude of features such as temperature and humidity. To make the comparison meaningful, we divide the monthly averages by the yearly average. This gives rise to the stacked bar chart shown in Figure 3.1.

Table 3.1   A sample of the rainfall data set recording the average temperature and humidity in London summarised on a monthly basis.

Month	Temperature	Humidity
1	5.66	83.35
2	5.08	82.57
3	7.93	73.08
4	10.55	70.25
5	13.59	66.74

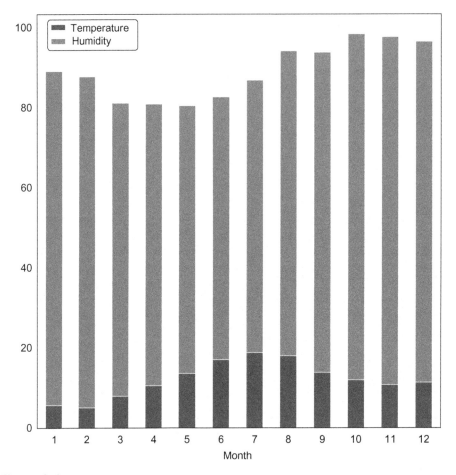

Figure 3.1   A stacked bar chart displaying the monthly temperature and humidity recorded in London in 2015 by the *UK Met Office*.

Tabular data is presented as a table with m rows and n columns, where each column is headed with the name of the feature (also known as a property or attribute) whose values are stored in the cells of the column. Such tabular data can also be viewed as an m-by-n *matrix*, which is called a *square matrix* when $m = n$. The square matrix with n rows and columns, whose main diagonal (i, i) entries are all equal to 1 and all other (i, j) entries, with $i \neq j$, are equal to 0, is called the n-by-n *identity matrix* and denoted by I_n; when n is understood from context, we refer to the identity matrix simply as I.

Features may have the following standard data types: *numeric* and *categorical*; numeric data is further divided into *interval* and *ratio* data, and categorical data is further divided into *nominal* and *ordinal* data. A numeric feature can be discrete (taking on a finite or infinite number of values) or continuous. Interval data allows distance between values to be measured, but the zero value is arbitrary. For example, temperature is an interval data type because it can be measured on different scales and, therefore, the zero value depends on the chosen scale. For ratio data, we have, in addition, a meaningful zero element, so, for example, length and weight are ratio data types. A categorical feature can take on only a fixed number of values, where each value represents a group. For example, blood type is categorical, as is binary data such as whether a flat has a garden or not. Nominal data only records the presence or absence of a property, whereas ordinal data has some ordering attached to it. So, blood type is nominal, whereas a feature recording income as low (coded as 1), middle (coded as 2), or high (coded as 3) is ordinal and allows it to be ranked. There are many examples of ranked data, as is demonstrated in Section 5.1 in Chapter 5 when introducing search engines and recommender systems.

Example 3.2. Consider a breakfast cereal data set, containing multiple features describing 77 commonly available breakfast cereals, with information captured on food labels including, amongst other features, protein, fat, sodium, fibre, carbohydrates (carbo), and potassium (potass); see Table 3.2 for a matrix describing the Pearson correlation between pairs of a sample of features from the data set.

A heatmap is a visual representation of the intensity of a relationship between variables in a data set. The heatmap, shown in Figure 3.2, reveals, for example, that there is a strong correlation between the amount of fibre and potassium contained in cereals, which promotes digestive health.

Table 3.2 A matrix of the Pearson correlation between each pair of a sample of features from the breakfast cereal data set. (The units for the features are as follows: protein, fat, fibre, and carbo are measured in grams, while sodium and potass are measured in milligrams.)

	Protein	Fat	Sodium	Fibre	Carbo	Potass
Protein	1.0000	0.2084	−0.0546	0.5003	−0.1308	0.5494
Fat	0.2084	1.0000	−0.0054	0.0167	−0.3180	0.1932
Sodium	−0.0546	−0.0054	1.0000	−0.0706	0.3559	−0.0326
Fibre	0.5003	0.0167	−0.0706	1.0000	−0.3560	0.9033
Carbo	−0.1308	−0.3180	0.3559	−0.3560	1.0000	−0.3496
Potass	0.5494	0.1932	−0.0326	0.9033	−0.3496	0.0216

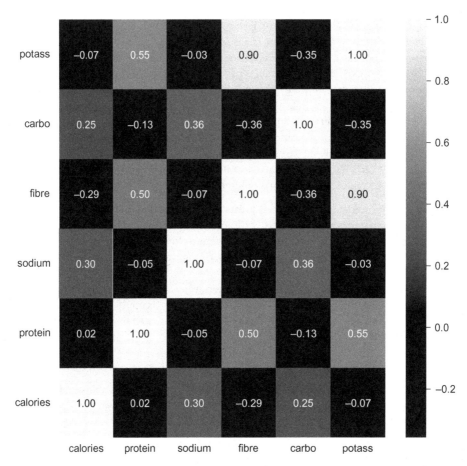

Figure 3.2 A heatmap of the pairwise Pearson correlation scores generated from the matrix
representation for the breakfast cereal data set. (The legend on the left of the
heatmap maps colour intensity to values.)

Example 3.3. Consider a data set of the time, location, depth (in km), and magnitude of
earthquakes (on the Richter scale) for the month of July recorded from sensor sites around
the world during 2021 and published by the *U.S. Geological Survey* (USGS); see Table 3.3.
The histogram depicting the distribution of recorded magnitudes of earthquakes is shown
in Figure 3.3; note that we already introduced histograms in Chapter 2 as a means to plot
the distribution of a numeric feature.

Table 3.3 Sample of the magnitude of earthquakes, on the Richter scale, recorded around the world during July 2021.

Time	Latitude	Longitude	Depth	Magnitude
2021-07-05T13:00:58.485Z	65.959200	−148.004700	7.40	1.50
2021-07-05T12:51:39.330Z	19.225166	−155.427673	31.77	1.98
2021-07-05T12:51:03.570Z	19.222834	−155.391998	31.30	1.98
2021-07-05T12:49:46.359Z	58.739400	−153.635500	11.20	1.50
2021-07-05T12:41:42.400Z	61.619800	−148.532000	33.40	1.00

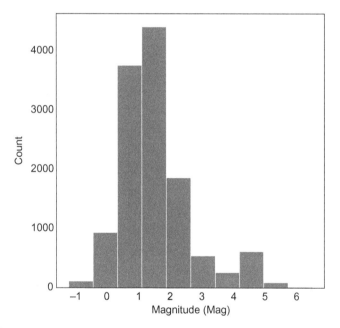

Figure 3.3 Histogram depicting the distribution of recorded magnitudes for earthquakes worldwide in July 2021.

Table 3.4 Years of experience against salary, in US dollars, for a sample of individuals in the data.

Experience	Salary
1.1	39,343
1.3	46,205
1.5	37,731
2.0	43,525
2.2	39,891

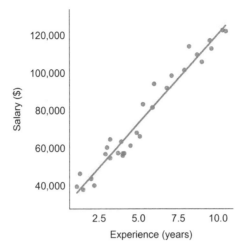

Figure 3.4   A scatter plot of the salary for 30 individuals against their years of experience, together with a linear regression line fitted to the data. The slope of the fitted line is 9,345, its intercept is 26,816, and the coefficient of determination of $R^2 = 0.97$.

Example 3.4. Consider a data set that contains the salary, in US dollars, of 30 individuals against their years of work experience; see Table 3.4. A scatter plot of salaries against years of experience, together with a linear regression line fitted to the data, is shown in Figure 3.4.

3.2   Textual Data

Large volumes of text are often organised in corpora, where each corpus is a collection of smaller textual units, called documents. A corpus may be multilingual, although the examples given throughout the book will be in English; there are, of course, some major differences between languages that merit lengthy discussion, but we will not include them in this introduction.

We will assume that each document can be broken up into words, which we will take as the lowest level semantically meaningful unit, although it is possible also to analyse textual data on the lower level of characters. We will also often make the simplifying assumption that the order of words in a document is not important, leading to the *bag-of-words* assumption (see Subsection 5.1.1 in Chapter 5). In this case, a document can be viewed as a matrix, where each row of the matrix represents a document in the corpus, and each column represents a word (or more generally a term) in the corpus. An element in such a document-term matrix is a numeric value, representing, say, the frequency of the term in the document or just the presence (1) or absence (0) of the term in the document; there are also other possible representation schemes for the values in the matrix that we do not discuss herein.

Example 3.5. A *word cloud* is a visual representation of a collection of words, where the size and font of words is displayed according to their importance in the text, which is often just their frequency of occurrence.

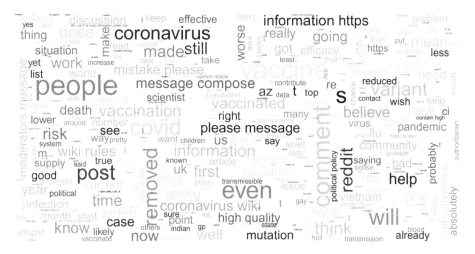

Figure 3.5 A word cloud summarising the most frequent words captured from Reddit posts published in 2021 on the topic of the coronavirus pandemic.

Table 3.5 A sample of the rank position and the total term frequency in thousands for the top ten words in the Reuters corpus of financial news documents.

Rank	Frequency
1	69,277
2	36,779
3	36,400
4	29,253
5	25,648
6	25,383
7	25,103
8	18,623
9	15,680
10	14,341

Figure 3.5 shows a word cloud summarising the Reddit posts during 2021 on the coronavirus pandemic. The word cloud is constructed from the most frequent 38,058 words from all posts with very common *stop words* such as "the," "it," and "at" removed.

Example 3.6. One way to visualise the distribution of words in a corpus is the *Zipf plot*, named after linguist George Kingsley Zipf, who studied the statistical properties of texts. A Zipf plot is constructed in two steps; see Section 3.7. In the first step, we apply a rank transformation to the data by ordering the words in the corpus according to frequency and

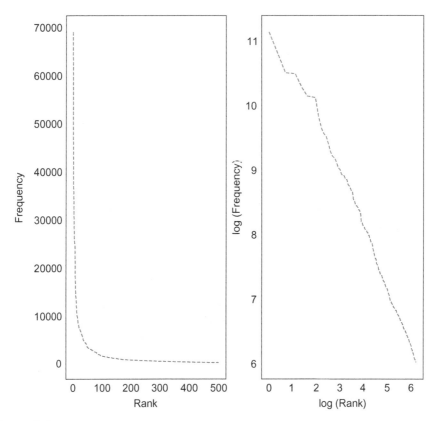

Figure 3.6   A rank-order distribution (left) and Zipf plot (right) of the 500 most frequent words
captured in the Reuters corpus.

ranking them from most frequent to least frequent, resulting in a distribution called a
rank-order distribution. Then, in the second step, we apply the log-log transformation to the
ranked data, and the plot of this transformation is called a Zipf plot.

Now, consider the Reuters ApteMod corpus for text categorisation, which is
composed of a collection of 10,788 documents from the Reuters financial news service;
see Table 3.5. The rank-order distribution of the top 500 words in the corpus is plotted on
the left of Figure 3.6, and the Zipf plot for this data is shown on the right of Figure 3.6.

3.3   Image, Video, and Audio Data

Image, video, and audio data are ubiquitous forms of unstructured data and, therefore,
machine learning methods are central in processing such data. Image recognition and its
subfield facial recognition have become important applications that demand
state-of-the-art machine learning techniques to perform accurately with large amounts of
data. Video also has numerous applications, many related to image processing, and others
distinct, such as closed-caption generation. A major application of audio data is speech

Figure 3.7 A sample of a collection of over three million images of cats and dogs for use as CAPTCHAs.

recognition, which again needs to perform accurately and scale to large data sets. We will not delve into these important types of data and their applications; however, most of the techniques we present in this introduction are applicable to all of them. Often the trick lies in the appropriate preprocessing on the input data to form a suitable format for the machine learning method to operate on.

Example 3.7. A contact sheet of thumbnails displaying a preview of the cat and dog image recognition data set is shown in Figure 3.7. This data set is used for the purpose of *Asirra* (Animal species image recognition for restricting access), which asks users to identify photographs of cats and dogs, acting as a CAPTCHA (Completely Automated Public Turing test to tell Computers and Humans Apart) for some websites requiring restricted access.

3.4 Time Series Data

A time series is a sequence of items $\mathbf{x} = \{x_1, x_2, \ldots, x_m\}$, $m \geq 1$, indexed by time, which is denoted by t; in general, a time series may be finite or infinite. Thus, in a time series $\mathbf{x}$, x_t precedes x_{t+1}, and either succeeds x_{t-1} if $t > 1$ or, if $t = 1$, is the first item

Table 3.6   A sample of the sunspot data showing the year and month, and the average count of sunspots observed.

Year-Month	Sunspots
1749—01	58.0
1749—02	62.6
1749—03	70.0
1749—04	55.7
1749—05	85.0

x_1 in the series. An item x_t is a numeric value that represents, at time t, for example, a stock price, a person's heartbeat, or the air temperature. A time series is modelled as a stochastic process, that is, as a sequence of random variables $\mathbf{X} = \{X_1, X_2, \ldots, X_m\}$, $m \geq 1$, where X_t is indexed by time.

Time series analysis is a big topic in its own right, and many books on this topic are available, including a large literature on time series forecasting. It is worth mentioning that machine learning methods such as neural networks (see Subsection 4.3.5 in Chapter 4) can be applied to time series forecasting problems.

Example 3.8. Consider a data set describing the monthly count of observed sunspots for over 230 years (1749–1983), with 2,820 total observations; see Table 3.6 for a sample of the data and the top of Figure 3.8 for the visualised time series. The moving average method smooths a time series by replacing each of the raw values in a time series by the average of several values within a window of a given size, where the centre of the window is positioned on the value being replaced. The moving average for the sunspot data, with a window of 12 months, is shown in the middle of Figure 3.8. A *corellogram*, or an autocorrelation (see Section 2.3) plot, shows the autocorrelation for range of time lags starting from zero when its value is 1. The correlogram for the sunspot data is shown at the bottom of Figure 3.8.

3.5   Geographical Data

Geographical data, more widely known as spatial data, provides information about locations (in the form of coordinates) and shapes (describing the topology of the space). The obvious way to analyse spatial data is through maps, where the landmarks of interest can be displayed on a map. We can, for example, compute the distance of routes between chosen landmarks, looking for the shortest or fastest route, assuming we have information about the mode of transport and the speed that can be travelled along the route. We may also wish to make use of other metrics in our analysis, such as the population sizes of various landmarks, which may represent cities, or the price of given commodities at those landmarks.

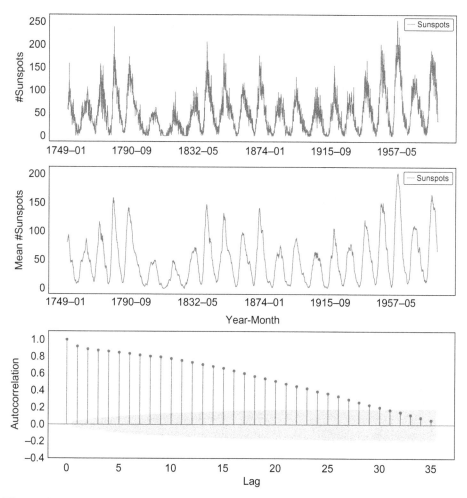

Figure 3.8 The count of monthly sunspots visualised as the raw time series (top), a moving average of the time series with a window size of 12 months representing a year of observations (middle), and a correlogram of the time series with a 95% confidence interval about 0, which represents no correlation (bottom).

Geostatistics deals with spatial random processes, whereby random variables (called spatial random variables) are associated with geographical locations. An important step in geostatistical analysis is that of estimating spatial autocorrelation, which measures the correlation between values of a spatial random variable, where each pair of values is weighted according to the distance between their associated locations: the closer they are in space, the higher the weight. This corresponds to the first law of geography, stated in 1969 by the geographer Tobler: "Everything is related to everything else, but near things are more related than distant things."

Table 3.7   The Longitude and Latitude columns represent map coordinates, and the third column records the topsoil copper concentration in parts per million.

Longitude	Latitude	Copper
181072	333611	85
181025	333558	81
181165	333537	68
181298	333484	81
181307	333330	48

Another major step in geostatistical analysis is that of interpolation of spatial random variables over a geographical region, which makes use of spatial autocorrelation to interpolate unknown values from existing ones, whilst minimising the prediction error as far as possible in some well-defined manner.

Example 3.9. The *variogram* is a function showing the degree of spatial continuity of spatial data; it calculates, for an input distance, the variability between pairs of data points separated by that distance. So, we expect the output of a variogram to grow with the distance; that is, we expect a monotonically increasing relationship between distance and variability. The smallest distance at which the variability is very close to the maximum variability is called the *range*, and the actual variability at the range (which is essentially the maximum variability) is called the *sill*. The *nugget* is the variability when the distance is close to zero; in practice it is greater than zero, which could be due to measurement error.

Consider a data set providing the locations and topsoil heavy metal concentrations recorded in a flood plain of the river Meuse, near the village of Stein in the Netherlands, where the survey of heavy metal concentrations was taken from composite samples of an area of 15 square metres; see Table 3.7. Figure 3.9 shows the variogram for this data set.

3.6 Social Network Data

We will discuss the concepts pertaining to social networks in Section 5.2 in Chapter 5, while here we touch upon the underlying network structure. A *network* (also known as a graph) is a collection of *nodes* (known as actors in the social network context) and *links* (or arcs) from one node to another. If the links are bidirectional, which is often the case in social networks, where links may denote friendship between two actors, then they are called *edges*. Edges (or links) may be weighted, where the weight may denote the strength of the tie between the nodes on both sides of the edge (or link).

Network data allows us to measure distance (see Subsection 5.2.1) between nodes, which is important in many applications, and to ascertain how central a node is in the network (see Subsection 5.2.2). The area in computer science that looks into the properties of networks is called *graph theory*, and many algorithmic problems can be recast in graph-theoretic terms.

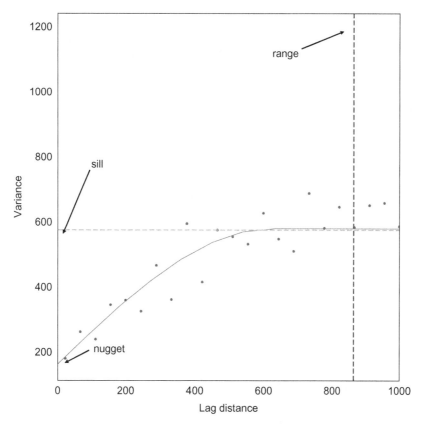

Figure 3.9   A variogram for the copper deposits with the range = 864.08, the sill = 574.90, and the nugget = 163.25.

The network data structure plays a central role in computer science and is thus also of prime importance to the data scientist. Apart from social networks, the internet is a global network of computing devices that is central to modern society and, more generally, a communication network can connect any number of computers—for example, across an organisation that may be geographically dispersed. There are many examples of networks, another being a transportation network, which can be viewed as a geospatial data structure.

Example 3.10. Consider the Karate Club social network data set composed of data collected by Wayne Zachary in 1977, from 34 members of a university karate club prior to the separation of the members after a dispute. In the network, each node represents a member of the club and each edge represents two members that were consistently observed to interact outside the normal activities of the club; see Table 3.8. A visualisation of the Karate Club social network is shown in Figure 3.10; the visualisation clearly shows the two factions of the club, although detailed analysis is still needed to establish the exact separation.

Table 3.8   Sample of the node ID and degree, that is, how many edges the node participates in, for members of the Karate Club social network.

Node	Degree
1	16
2	9
3	10
4	6
5	3
6	4

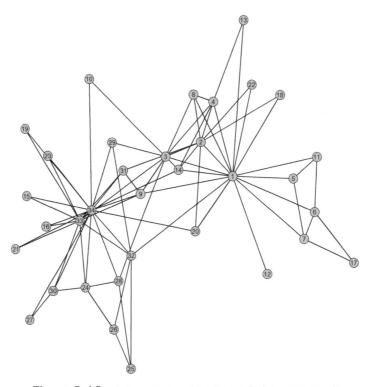

Figure 3.10   A visualisation of the Karate Club social network.

3.7 Transforming Data

Data transformation involves changing the values in a collection of data items in some well-defined way to facilitate data analysis.

Let $\mathbf{x} = \{x_1, x_2, \ldots, x_m\}$ be a collection of data items, which can be viewed as a *data set* or, more generally, a population.

Linear transformation is the process of scaling and shifting x_i into a value z_i, given by

$$z_i = ax_i + b,$$

where a and b are constants. Often a linear transformation is needed to achieve dimensional homogeneity, which is the requirement that we only compare quantities that have the same underlying unit.

Example 3.11. Conversion from degrees Celsius to Fahrenheit is a linear transformation, with $a = 9/5$ and $b = 32$, giving

$$\text{Fahrenheit} = 1.8 \ \text{Celsius} + 32.$$

Table 3.9 shows a sample of converted values between the two measures of temperature.

The *z-score* transforms x_i into a standardised score z_i, given by the linear transformation,

$$z_i = \frac{x_i - \mu}{\sigma},$$

where μ is the mean of the data set $\mathbf{x}$ and σ is its standard deviation. It is the number of standard deviations a value is above or below the mean. Converting a data set into z-scores is often referred to as *normalising* the data. Normalisation of the data set is analogous to converting a normally distributed (or Gaussian) random variable into a *standardised* normal variable with mean 0 and standard deviation 1.

Another typical linear transformation used to scale $\mathbf{x}$ to be between 0 and 1 is to transform each x_i in $\mathbf{x}$ to a value z_i, given by

$$z_i = \frac{x_i - \min(\mathbf{x})}{\max(\mathbf{x}) - \min(\mathbf{x})},$$

Table 3.9 A sample of values transformed from degrees Celsius to Fahrenheit, truncating all decimal values.

Celsius	Fahrenheit
15	59
16	60
17	62
18	64
19	66
20	68

where $\min(\mathbf{x})$ and $\max(\mathbf{x})$ are, respectively, the minimum and maximum of $\mathbf{x}$. More generally, if we wish to scale $\mathbf{x}$ to be between two constants a and b, where $a \leq b$, the transformation is given by

$$z_i = (b - a)\frac{x_i - \min(\mathbf{x})}{\max(\mathbf{x}) - \min(\mathbf{x})} + a.$$

Example 3.12. An example transformation converting between a five-star rating to the scale between 0 and 1 is shown in Table 3.10.

We may also allow nonlinear transformations, such as taking the square root, $\sqrt{x_i}$, of data values x_i. The *Box-Cox* transformation maps a value x_i to $z_i^{(\lambda)}$, defined as

$$z_i^{(\lambda)} = \begin{cases} \dfrac{x_i^\lambda - 1}{\lambda} & \text{if } \lambda \neq 0 \\ \log(x_i) & \text{if } \lambda = 0, \end{cases}$$

which is a more general transformation subsuming the square root transformation.

When we are performing regression (see Section 2.5 in Chapter 2), the data set is a collection of pairs (x_i, y_i) rather than single values x_i, and the task is to fit a curve (or a line as a special case), represented as a function f such that y_i is approximated by $f(x_i)$. We can apply a linear transformation to x_i, as shown here, if we are fitting a linear relationship, but it is also possible to apply nonlinear transformations to x_i or y_i or to both.

A common nonlinear transformation of pairs (x_i, y_i) is the *semi-log* transformation, which leaves x_i untransformed and maps y_i to $\log(y_i)$; this transformation maps exponential data to linear form. Another common transformation is the *log-log* transformation, which maps x_i to $\log(x_i)$ and y_i to $\log(y_i)$; this transformation maps power law data to linear form. An additional transformation on pairs (x_i, y_i) that is worth mentioning is the logit transformation on y_i defined in Section 2.5, which is the inverse of the logistic transformation.

Table 3.10 A five-star rating scheme (first column) transformed to the range 0 and 1 (second column).

Star rating	z
1	0.00
2	0.25
3	0.50
4	0.75
5	1.00

Table 3.11 Labour force survey 2010 showing the age groups and the number of working adults in the thousands.

Age	#Adults
18–24	3,553
25–29	2,943
30–34	2,754
35–39	3,140
40–44	3,395
45–49	3,167
50–54	2,650
55–64	3,130

Another type of transformation, called *binning*, groups data into ranges. For example, if we have customer data and one of the features (or properties) of its data items is age, we may wish to group customers into several groups or *bins*, say "young," "middle-aged," and "older." Each bin would contain the customers that fall into a range of ages defining the group, and the group's age may be represented by its average value within the group. As another example, when we are constructing a histogram, the number of bins to partition the data into may be specified by the user, but it is often determined automatically by some rule such as taking the square root of the number of data points, m, and rounding up to the closest integer value.

Example 3.13. Consider a data set describing the number of economically active adults in thousands, arranged into age groups, from a national UK labour force survey published by the Department for Business, Innovation, and Skills (BIS) in 2010; see Table 3.11. A histogram of binned data according to age groups is shown in Figure 3.11.

Finally, we mention the *rank* transformation, where we order the x_i's from the largest to the smallest (x_1 will be the largest value and x_m the smallest value) and replace x_i by its rank i. In case of ties, that is, when there are equal values, then the rank of these values can be determined by assigning the average of these ranks to all the tied values instead of the original ranks, or alternatively the tied ranks can be assigned at random to the tied values.

Here are two examples of the use of the rank transformation, the x_i's represent the number of occurrences of individual words within a corpus of text or the x_i's represent the proportional population size of cites. In such cases, the rank transformation will lead to a *rank-order* (or *rank-size* or *rank-frequency*) distribution of ranks.

Example 3.14. Consider the ranking of the most popular song streamed on a popular digital music service, on 1 January 2017, ranked by the number of user plays; see Table 3.12. A bar chart visualising the ranking is shown in Figure 3.12.

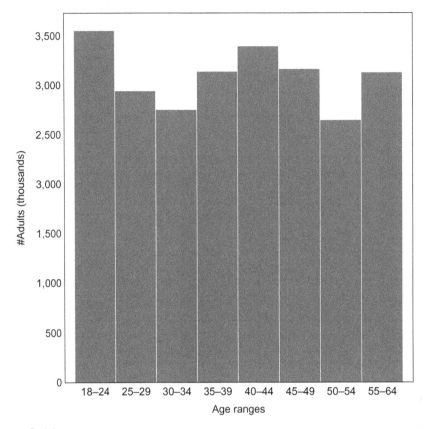

Figure 3.11   A histogram of the number of economically active adults in the UK recorded in a labour survey conducted by the Department for BIS in 2010.

Table 3.12   Ranking by count of streams of songs on a popular digital music service on 1 January 2017.

Rank	Artist	#Streams
1	CNCO	19,272
2	Shakira	19,270
3	Zion & Lennox	15,761
4	Ricky Martin	14,954
5	J Balvin	14,269
6	Carlos Vives	12,843
7	IAmChino	10,986
8	Chino & Nacho	10,653
9	Sebastian Yatra	9,807
10	Daddy Yankee	9,612

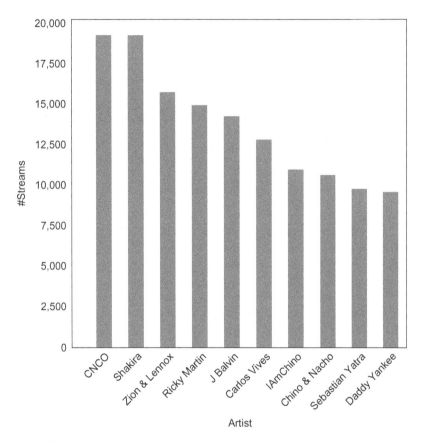

Figure 3.12 A bar chart of the top ten artists ranked by the number of streams recorded on a popular music digital service on 1 January 2017.

3.8 Chapter Summary

In this chapter we looked into the basic types of data we need to be familiar with as data scientists for effective processing and analysis. We first included the common types of tabular, textual, image, video, and audio data, which are often used in data science and machine learning applications. We then looked at time series, geographical, and social network data, which are more specialised in their application but important topics in their own right. Lastly, we covered data transformation, which can be used to accelerate data analysis.

Understanding these types of data is important in data science and machine learning to guide our choice of the appropriate tools and techniques for processing, analysing, and deriving insights from different data sources.

4

Machine Learning Tools

In this chapter we will introduce the most common machine learning tools used by data scientists. There are many books on the subject from the more theoretical to the very applied, some concentrating on the underlying mathematical theory and others on the techniques in the context of a specific programming language. In Section 4.1 we give an overview of what machine learning entails, including the introduction of some preliminary concepts a data scientist needs to know about to understand the topic. A fundamental property of a data set is whether it is labelled or not. A labelled data set input to a machine learning algorithm is a collection of pairs (x_i, y_i), where x_i is the input value and y_i is the output value, referred to as the *label*, that the algorithm is trained to predict. In an unlabelled data set, the format of pairs is $(x_i, ?)$, where the output value is not available. In Section 4.2 we introduce the notion of evaluation, which is central to machine learning, the objective being to assess the quality of the model output by the machine learning algorithm. In Section 4.3 we look at supervised machine learning algorithms, which build a statistical model (with a process called training) from labelled input data, while in Section 4.4 we look at unsupervised machine learning algorithms, where the model building has access only to unlabelled data. Finally, in Section 4.5 we look at semi-supervised machine learning algorithms that build models making use of only a small amount of labelled data.

4.1 What Is Machine Learning?

First, we discuss some general issues to do with machine learning and introduce some preliminary concepts that are needed in what ensues. Machine learning is central to the discipline of data science. The goal of machine learning is the automation of tasks that involve the discovery (or *learning*) of patterns from an input data set. A machine learning method is described by an algorithm, which is implemented in some coding language, that builds a statistical model from its input data, yielding predictions as its outputs. One aspect that distinguishes a machine learning algorithm from other types of algorithms is that a machine learning algorithm can automatically improve its performance when presented with additional data. For example, in an image classification machine learning task, where the algorithm is required to distinguish between the image of a cat and a dog, the more images of cats and dogs presented to the classification algorithm (often called the *classifier*) during its learning phase, the better we can expect its performance to be. The specification of the task is crucial here, since in this example we have described it as a binary classification task, and therefore, as specified, we cannot expect the machine learning algorithm to perform well when an image, say of a horse, which is neither a cat nor a dog, is presented to it. To distinguish between more than two type of images, we would need to harness a multiclass classification algorithm.

A *statistical model* constructed from a machine learning algorithm provides a mapping from the input data set to the outputs of the machine learning method used. A famous quote by the renowned 20th-century British statistician George Box is that "All models are wrong but some are useful." In algorithmic terms the computationally constructed statistical model is a *function* that, given an input, will yield a prediction as its output; the function is often referred to as a *decision function*.

To set the scene, assume random variables X and Y. A *labelled* data set is a collection of pairs (x_i, y_i), where the x_i's are X values and the y_i's are Y values. (As in a regression problem, which can itself be viewed as a supervised machine learning problem, X may not actually be random.) Each x_i is an input value, and each y_i is an output value, often referred to as the label of x_i; hence in this case, the data is said to be labelled. The data may also come in an *unlabelled* format as $(x_i, ?)$ pairs, where ? indicates that x_i does not have a label attached to it, and thus in this case, the data is said to be unlabelled.

A *feature* of a data set is an attribute or a property that is being measured. For example, recall from Section 3.1 that in tabular data the features are the column headers such as name, age, price, and time. In textual data, words are often the features being considered, which are represented by, for example, their counts, while in image data, an edge, corner, texture, or colour may be useful features, again represented by numerical values.

When introducing regression in Section 2.5, we mentioned that, in general, we could allow for multiple independent variables, say, $\mathbf{X} = X_1, X_2, \ldots, X_n$, with $n \geq 1$, $\mathbf{X}$ denoting a vector of random variables. Features can, in fact, be viewed as independent variables and, often, a vector of feature values is considered appropriate when modelling a data set for a machine learning task. Thus, the input $\mathbf{x}_i$ to a machine learning algorithm is generally a vector with $\mathbf{x}_i = \langle x_{i1}, x_{i2}, \ldots, x_{in} \rangle$, which we also call an *item*, an *instance*, or simply a *point*; for convenience we will often refer to an input simply as the value x_i, where in practice it may be a vector $\mathbf{x}_i$. (Note that we use a plain font for values such as x and a **bold** font for vectors such as $\mathbf{x}$.) The number of *dimensions* of an instance with n features is n.

When we are confronted with a large number of features, the *curse of dimensionality* problem arises, leading to a deterioration in performance. To counter this, *dimensionality reduction* aims to reduce the number of features in a machine learning task and, in particular, the process of reducing the number of features is called *feature selection*.

Machine learning algorithms generally fall into one of two categories: *supervised* or *unsupervised*. A supervised learning algorithm makes use of an input labelled data set to construct a statistical model of the data, while an unsupervised algorithm only uses unlabelled data to construct the model. The constructed model can then be used to *predict* the output value of an input x_i whose label has not been seen by the algorithm, to form a labelled pair (x_i, y_i). In a supervised algorithm, the label y_i may be the class or category x_i belongs to and, in an unsupervised algorithm, the label y_i may be the cluster or group x_i belongs to. We will also consider a third category of *semi-supervised* machine learning algorithms, when the amount of input labelled data is sparse, and employing a supervised algorithm on its own would not yield sufficiently good results.

The value y_i, which a machine learning algorithm is attempting to predict, is referred to as the *actual value*. Thus, in computational terms, the constructed model is a function f, whose objective is to predict the actual value y_i using $f(x_i)$, that is, by applying f to x_i. To distinguish between the predicted and actual value, we use the *hat* notation, $\hat{y}_i = f(x_i)$. In a regression problem, the predicted value $\hat{y}_i$ is a value that may be discrete or continuous, while in a classification or an unsupervised problem, the predicted value is normally an encoding of the class or cluster label. It is also possible that the predicted value $\hat{y}_i = f(x_i)$ is an estimate of the probability $P(y_i|x_i)$; for example, in a classification problem, we may wish to estimate the probability that an input value belongs to a particular class and then use a threshold value to decide which class the input value belongs to.

Before we delve into the actual machine learning algorithms, we will briefly describe the framework under which machine learning operates to be able to achieve acceptable performance in a real-world setting. The *parameters* of a model are the tunable variables being learnt by the algorithm while the model is being constructed. On the other hand, *hyperparameters* are model-independent parameters that are set before the model has been constructed and may be optimised as a further step after the initial model construction.

For a supervised learning algorithm, the machine learning process has three phases, all operating on disjoint subsets of the labelled data set. First, *training* for fitting the parameters of the model, then, an optional *validation* step for tuning the hyperparameters of the model, and finally, *testing* for evaluating the quality of the constructed model. Prior to executing these phases, the labelled data set is partitioned into three sets: (i) training, (ii) validation, and (iii) test (also referred to as *holdout*). A common method for training and testing, known as k-fold *cross-validation*, partitions the data set into $k > 1$ subsets, or folds, and then repeats the training and testing phases $k-1$ times, with the kth fold being the test set and the remaining folds being the training set. When the data set is unlabelled, we can only deploy an unsupervised machine learning algorithm to construct the model from the data. Once the model is constructed, it needs to be evaluated; methods of evaluation for both supervised and unsupervised learning algorithms are covered in Section 4.2.

Now, assume that a supervised machine learning algorithm has constructed a statistical model, represented by the function, say f, from the training data, $(x_1, y_1), (x_2, y_2), \ldots,$ (x_m, y_m), with $m \geq 1$, and that the pairs containing the values $\hat{y}_i$, predicted by the supervised learning algorithm during the training phase, are given by $(x_1, \hat{y}_1),$ $(x_2, \hat{y}_2), \ldots, (x_m, \hat{y}_m)$. A *loss function* (also known as a *cost function* or an *objective function*) provides us with a method of measuring how far $\hat{y}_i = f(x_i)$ is from the true value y_i, for $i = 1, 2, \ldots, m$. In particular, loss functions are used by supervised machine learning algorithms to improve their performance during training.

The four most common loss functions are *zero-one loss* (*L01*), *mean absolute error* (*MAE* or L1 loss), *mean squared error* (*MSE* or L2 loss), and *logarithmic loss* (*LOG*; also known as *cross-entropy loss*).

L01 is defined as

$$L01 = \frac{1}{m} \sum_{i=1}^{m} L01(y_i, \hat{y}_i),$$

where $L01(y_i, \hat{y}_i)$ is given by

$$L01(y_i, \hat{y}_i) = \begin{cases} 0 & \text{if } y_i = \hat{y}_i \\ 1 & \text{if } y_i \neq \hat{y}_i. \end{cases}$$

MAE is defined as

$$MAE = \frac{1}{m} \sum_{i=1}^{m} |y_i - \hat{y}_i|,$$

where $|y|$ is equal to the absolute value of y, that is,

$$|y| = \begin{cases} y & \text{if } y \geq 0 \\ -y & \text{if } y < 0. \end{cases}$$

MSE is defined as

$$MSE = \frac{1}{m} \sum_{i=1}^{m} (y_i - \hat{y}_i)^2,$$

noting that a variant of the *MSE*, called the *root mean squared error* (*RMSE*), is the square root of the *MSE*.

LOG is defined as

$$LOG = \sum_{i=1}^{m} -\log(\hat{y}_i),$$

where $\hat{y}_i$ in this case is the probability $P(y_i|x_i)$; that is, $\hat{y}_i$ is the estimate output by the machine learning algorithm of the probability that the correct class is y_i. In addition, log is the natural logarithm function, noting that we could replace the natural logarithm with the logarithm to the base 2 if we are interested in measuring the loss in bit units.

We can extend loss functions to unsupervised learning algorithms by assuming that the algorithm is computed over several iterations, where each iteration attempts to improve on the previous one by reducing the value of a loss function. In particular, in the preceding definitions, we set the y_i's to be the predicted values from the previous iteration of the algorithm (or from some initial values if it is the first iteration of the algorithm), while we set the $\hat{y}_i$'s to be the predicted values from the current iteration. In this manner the performance of the unsupervised algorithm can be monitored during the construction of the model.

An important optimisation technique used in machine learning algorithms is *gradient descent*, which is used to find local minima of a differentiable function. In machine learning the objective of gradient descent is to minimise the loss function used in the algorithm by updating the parameters being tuned in the direction of the steepest descent, taking steps proportional to the negative of the gradient of the loss function.

Overfitting and *underfitting* are characteristics of the statistical model, say f, constructed by a machine learning algorithm. Overfitting is the situation in which the predictions $\hat{y}_i = f(x_i)$ made by f fit the training data very closely (i.e., the loss is very small) and, as a result, the model does not generalise very well to the test data. Likewise, underfitting is the situation in which the model f does not perform well on the test data, due to an insufficient amount of training data or a misspecified learning algorithm—for example, when attempting to fit a linear model to a data set that is inherently nonlinear. An overfitted model is said to be one with *high variance*, while an underfitted model is one that has *high bias*.

As described, the concepts of overfitting and underfitting pertain to supervised algorithms because in unsupervised algorithms, we do not have test data. For unsupervised algorithms, we may frame the problem in terms of stability rather than in terms of overfitting or underfitting. By that, we mean that a clustering result is stable, that is, does not change much when new data becomes available.

We also mention *regularisation*, which is a technique to avoid overfitting. The idea is to add a *penalty term* to the loss function, making it harder for the algorithm to construct a more complex model with a very small loss. This method is consistent with Occam's razor, which states that, everything else being equal, a simpler model making fewer assumptions is preferable to a more complex one.

We now introduce *distance measures*, which are the opposite of similarity measures and play a major role in the formulation of both supervised and unsupervised methods.

Let $\mathbf{x} = \langle x_1, x_2, \ldots, x_n \rangle$ and $\mathbf{z} = \langle z_1, z_2, \ldots, z_n \rangle$ be two n feature vectors. Then the two most common distance measures are the *Euclidean* distance measure, D_E, given by

$$D_E(\mathbf{x}, \mathbf{z}) = \sqrt{\sum_{i=1}^{n}(x_i - z_i)^2},$$

and the *Manhattan* (or city block) distance measure, D_M, given by

$$D_M(\mathbf{x}, \mathbf{z}) = \sum_{i=1}^{n}|x_i - z_i|.$$

Two other useful distance measures, when the x_i and z_i are positive, that is, are non-negative and have at least one positive component, are the *cosine* distance measure, given by

$$D_C(\mathbf{x}, \mathbf{z}) = 1 - \frac{\sum_{i=1}^{n} x_i z_i}{\sqrt{\sum_{i=1}^{n} x_i^2}\sqrt{\sum_{i=1}^{n} z_i^2}},$$

and the *correlation* distance measure (see Section 2.4 in Chapter 2), given by

$$D_R(\mathbf{x}, \mathbf{z}) = 1 - \frac{\sum_{i=1}^{n} (x_i - \bar{\mathbf{x}})(z_i - \bar{\mathbf{z}})}{\sqrt{\sum_{i=1}^{n} (x_i - \bar{\mathbf{x}})^2} \sqrt{\sum_{i=1}^{n} (z_i - \bar{\mathbf{z}})^2}},$$

where $\bar{\mathbf{x}}$ and $\bar{\mathbf{z}}$ are the averages of the x_i's and z_i's, respectively. While the cosine distance is normalised, that is, it is bounded between 0 and 1, the correlation distance is bounded between 0 and 2.

Another useful distance measure is the *weighted Jaccard* distance, given by

$$D_J(\mathbf{x}, \mathbf{z}) = 1 - \frac{\sum_{i=1}^{n} min(x_i, z_i)}{\sum_{i=1}^{n} max(x_i, z_i)} = \frac{\sum_{i=1}^{n} |x_i - z_i|}{\sum_{i=1}^{n} max(x_i, z_i)},$$

where $min(x_i, z_i)$ is the minimum of x_i and z_i and $max(x_i, z_i)$ is the maximum of x_i and z_i. Both of these measures are normalised; that is, their values are between 0 and 1.

We close this section by referring to two important subareas of machine learning that are worthy of further exploration but are not explored herein due to space limitations. The first is *reinforcement learning*, which is a substantial subarea of machine learning. It is a general method, where the inputs to the algorithm are obtained through interactions with the environment. In reinforcement learning the algorithm is commonly referred to as a learning *agent*. The agent interacting with the environment performs some computation (referred to as an *action* in this context) and, as a result, receives a *reward* (or a *penalty*, which is a negative reward). The objective of the agent is to maximise the expected cumulative rewards that it has received over time. There are many applications of reinforcement learning; a few examples are training autonomous (or self-driving) cars, training drones to make them more autonomous, and learning how to play the game of Chess or Go.

The second subarea is *end-to-end* machine learning, which strives to minimise human intervention in the machine learning process so that the process is managed automatically from input to output. To a large degree, end-to-end machine learning is the ultimate goal and can encompass reinforcement learning, for example, in training autonomous cars so that they can adapt their behaviour to new situations that may occur as a result of interaction with the environment.

4.2 Evaluation

The goal of evaluation is straightforward: We wish to know the quality of the model constructed by the machine learning algorithm before putting it into practice. In addition, we would normally like to know the generalisation capabilities of the model on unseen data (also known as out-of-sample data).

As mentioned in Section 4.1, the machine learning process has three phases (i) *training* the model, (ii) *validation* for tuning the hyperparameters, and (iii) *testing* to evaluate the quality of the model. To simplify the exposition, we will not deal with phase (ii) and concentrate on phases (i) and (iii).

In Subsection 4.2.1 we will look into the evaluation of supervised machine learning algorithms, while in Subsection 4.2.2 we will focus on the evaluation of unsupervised algorithms. The differences in the evaluation methods for supervised and unsupervised methods are driven by the fact that for supervised models we train and test on labelled data, which acts as ground truth on which performance can be measured against, while for unsupervised models we train on unlabelled data and do not, in general, have labelled data for the testing phase.

4.2.1 Evaluation for Supervised Models

For supervised models, the input data set $\mathbf{S}$ is labelled. That is, $\mathbf{S} = \{(\mathbf{x}_1, y_1), (\mathbf{x}_2, y_2), \ldots, (\mathbf{x}_m, y_m)\}$, with $m \geq 1$, where each instance $\mathbf{x}_i$ is a vector of feature values $\mathbf{x}_i = \langle x_{i1}, x_{i2}, \ldots, x_{in} \rangle$. (We note that, in principle, an instance in a pair may have more than one label attached to it when it is assigned to multiple classes; however, we do not deal with this situation here.)

In Section 4.1 we mentioned k-fold cross-validation, which partitions the data set into $k > 1$ subsets and performs the evaluation on all the k-folds, taking the average evaluation of all the folds. In what follows we will concentrate on the simple train and test split regime rather than cross-validation. Assuming, as we have, that the data set is labelled, a split of 80% for training and 20% for testing (80-20 split) is common, but a 70-30 split is also widely used, and other splits cannot be discounted depending on the application.

Without loss of generality, we will assume for the rest of this section that $\mathbf{S}$ is the test data and, for simplicity of exposition, we will concentrate on the binary case when we have only two classes (the general case with more than two classes follows along the lines of the binary case, but there are some nuances to consider).

The *confusion matrix* (also known as the error matrix), shown in Figure 4.1 for a two-class problem, is the table that records the information needed for assessing the performance of a supervised method with respect to the data set $\mathbf{S}$. It is a square matrix, say $\mathbf{C}$, having one row and one column for each class, recording counts in each cell c_{ij}, denoting the number of instances from the test data for which the *actual* class is the row (i.e., i) and the *predicted* class is the column (i.e., j).

Let us call the first class 1 and the second class 0. For example, in an image classification task, the first class may correspond to images of cats and the second to images of dogs or any other animal. To make things clearer, we choose to call the first class (i.e., 1) the *positive* class and the second class (i.e., 0) the *negative* class. So there are four entries in the confusion matrix: (i) c_{11} counts how many times the actual class is 1 and the predicted class is 1, (ii) c_{12} counts how many times the actual class is 1 and the predicted class is 0, (iii) c_{21} counts how many times the actual class is 0 and the predicted class is 1, and (iv) c_{22} counts how many times the actual class is 0 and the predicted class is 0. Entry (i) corresponds to the number of *true positive* (TP) cases, entry (ii) corresponds to the number of *false negative* (FN) cases, entry (iii) corresponds to the number of *false positive* (FP) cases, and entry (iv) corresponds to the number of *true negative* (TN) cases. Thus, correct predictions are shown on the diagonal entries of the matrix, and incorrect predictions are shown on the off-diagonal entries. So, in general, the higher the diagonal entries and the lower the off-diagonal ones, the better the classification is.

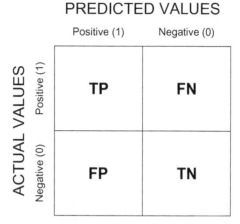

PREDICTED VALUES

Figure 4.1 The confusion matrix.

There are many ways to derive measures from the confusion matrix, but we concentrate on *accuracy*, *precision*, *recall*, and F1, which are the measures commonly used to evaluate supervised machine learning algorithms.

$$accuracy = \frac{TP + TN}{TP + TN + FP + FN}$$
$$precision = \frac{TP}{TP + FP}$$
$$recall = \frac{TP}{TP + FN}$$

Accuracy can be viewed as the overall success rate, that is, what proportion of correct classifications does the classifier output. This seems like a very sensible measure, but it does have a limitation in that it is biased toward the largest class; this is known as the accuracy paradox. For example, suppose we wish to classify email into *spam* (junk email) or *ham* (email that is not spam), with spam being the positive class and ham being the negative one. Now, assuming for argument's sake that most, say 80%, of email is spam, then a "dumb" classifier that always classifies an email as spam will have accuracy of 80%. The reason is that we will catch all the TPs but none of the TNs; however, if we use such a classifier, we will not see any email if all spam email is discarded. Note, in this case, that both the precision and recall are 0%.

Precision gives the proportion of emails correctly identified as spam (TP) out of all the emails that have either correctly identified as spam (TP) or incorrectly identified as spam (FP). On the other hand, recall gives the proportion of emails correctly identified as spam (TP) out of all the emails either correctly identified as spam (TP) or incorrectly identified as ham (FN). To make precision and recall more concrete, we can view the output of a classifier in terms of a search engine that presents the user with the true positive (TP) answers. Precision is then the proportion of correct answers the user sees (TP) out of all the answers that the search engine presented $(TP + FP)$, and recall is the proportion of correct answers the user sees (TP) out of all the answers that should have been presented $(TP + FN)$.

The $F1$ score combines precision and recall into a single measure by taking the harmonic mean of the two, giving

$$F1 = \frac{2}{\frac{1}{precision} + \frac{1}{recall}} = 2\frac{precision \cdot recall}{precision + recall} = \frac{2TP}{2TP + FP + FN}$$

It may seem a bit of a mystery why the harmonic mean is used rather than the arithmetic mean, which is the standard average. However, the harmonic mean is more intuitive when computing a mean of ratios, and precision and recall are indeed ratios. In particular, the harmonic mean gives more weight to smaller items being averaged than the standard average and is less than the average, unless all values in the mean are equal (in our case, precision being equal to recall).

It is worth mentioning that when we wish to combine the scores of several classifiers, binary or general multiclass, there are two variations of the F1 score: *micro-averaged* F1 and *macro-averaged* F1. Micro-averaged F1 is biased by the individual class frequencies, while in macro-averaged F1 all classes carry the same weight. To obtain the micro-averaged F1, we compute the precision and recall by summing up the values from the individual confusion matrices for each class and then normalise the result, while to obtain the macro-averaged F1, we compute the precision and recall for each confusion matrix of a class and take the average over all the classes. Micro-averaged F1 is, generally, not equal to macro-averaged F1, even for the binary case, when there is a class imbalance, that is, when there are more labelled data items from one of the classes. However, it can be seen that for binary classification, the micro-averaged F1 and accuracy are in fact equal.

Moreover, the F1 score based on the confusion matrix is an evaluation method tailored for classification problems. Regression problems can be evaluated using the mean absolute error, *MAE*, or mean squared error, *MSE*, loss functions introduced in Section 4.1.

Example 4.1. A real example of a confusion matrix evaluating the results of using logistic regression to identify individuals likely to develop diabetes is shown in Figure 4.2. The data employed for the logistic regression was curated by the National Institute of Diabetes and Digestive and Kidney Diseases; see Table 4.1 for a sample from the data set. The full data set is composed of 768 rows recording the number of pregnancies patients had, their plasma glucose concentration, blood pressure (BP), skinfold thickness, insulin levels, BMI, age, and outcome (label), among women in the Pima Indian society. We note that the data set is composed of female participants with an average age of 33 years. The precision, recall, and F1 for the logistic regression model are shown in stylised form in Table 4.2.

We close this subsection with a brief discussion on *calibrated* probabilities in the situation when the predicted value $\hat{y}_i = f(x_i)$ is an estimate of the probability $P(y_i|x_i)$. To illustrate the concept of calibration, let us assume a binary classification problem where we estimate the probability that an input value belongs to one of the classes. For example, we may wish to predict whether it will rain tomorrow or not. Accuracy, by definition, is the

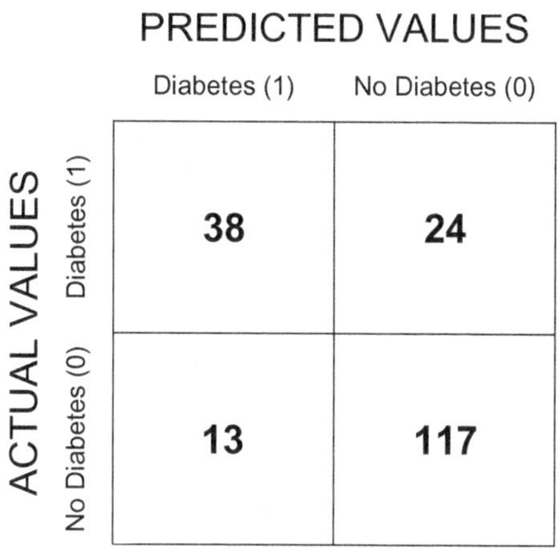

PREDICTED VALUES

Figure 4.2   The confusion matrix describing the model performance of a logistic regression model trained on the Pima Indian diabetes data set.

Table 4.1   A sample from the Pima Indian diabetes data set, where a class label with a value of 0 indicates that the individual does not have diabetes, while a value of 1 indicates that the individual has diabetes.

Pregnancies	Glucose	BP	Skin	Insulin	BMI	Age	Label
6	148	72	35	0	33.6	0.627	1
1	85	66	29	0	26.6	0.351	0
8	183	64	0	0	23.3	0.672	1
1	89	66	23	94	28.1	0.167	0
0	137	40	35	168	43.1	2.288	1

Table 4.2   The precision, recall, and F1 of the logistic regression model applied to the Pima Indian diabetes data set, with a 75–25 split between the training and test data.

Label	Precision	Recall	F1	Support
$Class_0$	0.83	0.90	0.86	130
$Class_1$	0.75	0.61	0.67	62
Total support:	192			
Micro-averaged F1:	0.81			
Macro-averaged F1:	0.77			

proportion of correct outcome predictions, while calibration tells us how likely the outcome is. Thus, a model is well calibrated if, when the prediction of rain is, say 0.8, it actually rains on 80% of the days when the weather conditions are similar to the input x_i. The proportion of days it actually rains is called the *empirical probability*. To assess how well calibrated the model is we can make use of a *reliability diagram*, which plots the empirical probabilities versus the predicted probabilities. The probabilities are well calibrated when they fall on the diagonal line of the reliability diagram or close enough to it.

4.2.2 Evaluation for Unsupervised Models

For unsupervised models, the input data set $\mathbf{U}$ is unlabelled. That is, $\mathbf{U} = \{(\mathbf{x}_1, ?),$ $(\mathbf{x}_2, ?), \ldots, (\mathbf{x}_m, ?)\}$, with $m \geq 1$, is unlabelled prior to the execution of the unsupervised method; as before, each instance $\mathbf{x}_i$ is a vector of feature values $\mathbf{x}_i = \langle x_{i1}, x_{i2}, \ldots, x_{in} \rangle$.

Once the machine learning algorithm has been run on the input data set $\mathbf{U}$, we obtain k clusters (or groups) having labels $1, 2, \ldots, k$, and we transform the unlabelled pairs $(\mathbf{x}_j, ?) \in \mathbf{U}$ into labelled pairs $(\mathbf{x}_j, \lambda(\mathbf{x}_j))$, where $y_i = \lambda(\mathbf{x}_j)$ is the cluster label of $\mathbf{x}_j$, resulting in the labelled data set,

$$\mathbf{S} = \{(\mathbf{x}_1, \lambda(\mathbf{x}_1)), (\mathbf{x}_2, \lambda(\mathbf{x}_2)), \ldots, (\mathbf{x}_m, \lambda(\mathbf{x}_m))\}.$$

$\mathbf{S}$ is thus partitioned into k clusters $\mathbf{S}_i$, for $i = 1, 2, \ldots, k$, in such a way that all instances in $\mathbf{S}_i$ have the same label i, that is, for all $\mathbf{x}_j \in \mathbf{S}_i, y_i = \lambda(\mathbf{x}_j) = i$. (We note that, in principle, an instance in a pair may have more than one label attached to it when it is assigned to multiple clusters; however, we do not deal with this situation here.)

Each cluster $\mathbf{S}_i$ may be represented by a *centroid* $\mathbf{c}_i$, which is an instance having n features, giving rise to k centroids, $\mathbf{C} = \{\mathbf{c}_1, \mathbf{c}_2, \ldots, \mathbf{c}_k\}$. The centroid $\mathbf{c}_i$ of a cluster $\mathbf{S}_i$ is computed as the average of all the instances in the cluster, that is

$$\mathbf{c}_i = \frac{1}{\#(i, \mathbf{S})} \sum_{(\mathbf{x}_j, i) \in \mathbf{S}_i} \mathbf{x}_j,$$

where $\#(i, \mathbf{S})$ is the number of instances in $\mathbf{S}$ having label i, that is, the number of instances in cluster $\mathbf{S}_i$, and the sum of two vectors is taken element-wise, that is,

$$\langle x_{j1}, x_{j2}, \ldots, x_{jn} \rangle + \langle x'_{j1}, x'_{j2}, \ldots, x'_{jn} \rangle = \langle x_{j1} + x'_{j1}, x_{j2} + x'_{j2}, \ldots, x_{jn} + x'_{jn} \rangle,$$

and thus the average of the vectors is also taken element-wise.

Another useful notation is the *norm* or length of a vector $\mathbf{x}$, written as $\|\mathbf{x}\|$. The most common norm is the *Euclidean norm* (or L2 norm), given by

$$\|\mathbf{x}\|_2 = \sqrt{x_1^2 + x_2^2 + \cdots + x_n^2},$$

which we often abbreviate to $\|\mathbf{x}\|$. The second most common norm is the *Manhattan norm* (or L1 norm, also known as the city block norm), given by

$$\|\mathbf{x}\|_1 = |x_1| + |x_2| + \cdots + |x_n|.$$

We concentrate on internal validation measures, that is, on evaluation methods that are based on the data set $\mathbf{U}$ that was clustered. An alternative is external validation, where the output clusters are compared to some ground truth, for example, labelled data, which is not always easy to obtain in the context of unsupervised learning.

A common basis for evaluating unsupervised methods is the *sum of squared error* (SSE), given by

$$\sum_{i=1}^{k} \sum_{\mathbf{x}_j \in \mathbf{S}_i} \|\mathbf{x}_j - \mathbf{c}_i\|^2,$$

where the difference between vectors is taken element-wise.

Example 4.2. An *elbow plot* depicting the number of clusters along the x-axis and the SSE on the y-axis is shown in Figure 4.3. In particular, such an elbow plot allows us to compare the SSE against the number of clusters to find the point after which the SSE drops and the curve bends; see Subsection 4.4.1 for more detailed motivation of the elbow heuristic in the context of k-means, where the number of desired clusters k is an input

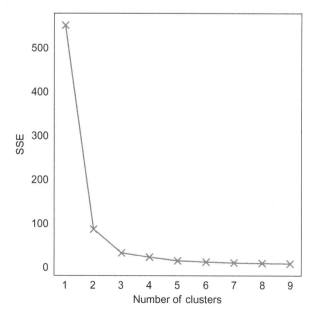

Figure 4.3   An elbow plot for the Iris data set, with the number of clusters along the x-axis and the SSE on the y-axis.

Table 4.3 A sample from the Iris data set, for two species, extracting two features representing the petal width and petal length of Iris flowers, both in centimetres.

Petal Length	Petal Width	Iris Species
1.4	0.2	setosa
1.3	0.2	setosa
4.7	1.4	versicolour
4.5	1.5	versicolour

parameter to the algorithm. The elbow plot was generated from the Iris data set by applying the k-means clustering algorithm (see Subsection 4.4.1) to label each row of the data with a cluster value based on the width and length of the petals of the Iris in centimetres; see Table 4.3 for a sample from the data set. The elbow plot in Figure 4.3 suggests that $k = 2$ is most likely (and this is indeed the case because the data set we used was generated from two species of flower, the Iris setosa and the Iris versicolour), although from the plot one may argue that $k = 3$ is also reasonable.

When we consider the data set to be one big cluster, that is, $k = 1$, then SSE is known as the *total sum of squared error* (SST); otherwise, when $k \geq 1$, it is known as the *within-cluster sum of squared error* (SSW). In addition, the *between-cluster sum of squared error* (SSB) is given by

$$\sum_{i=1}^{k} \#(i, \mathbf{S}) \, (\bar{\mathbf{c}} - \mathbf{c}_i)^2 \, ,$$

where $\bar{\mathbf{c}}$ is the average of all instances in the data set, that is, the centroid of the single cluster when computing the SST. It can be shown that the total sum of squared error is equal to the within-cluster sum of squared error plus the sum of the between-cluster sum of squared error, that is, SST = SSW + SSB.

The SSW measures intra-cluster *cohesion* or *compactness*, while the SSB measures inter-cluster *separation*. The smaller the cohesion and the larger the separation, the better the clustering. It is important to note that these measures are conditional on k being the "optimal" number of clusters, which is an important issue to address in unsupervised algorithms that require the number of clusters, k, to be input to the algorithm, as for example in the k-means introduced in Subsection 4.4.1.

Now, let $d(i, j)$ be the minimum distance between clusters $\mathbf{S}_i$ and $\mathbf{S}_j$, under a distance measure D; that is, $d(i, j)$ is the inter-cluster measure given by

$$d(i, j) = \min_{\mathbf{x} \in \mathbf{S}_i, \mathbf{z} \in \mathbf{S}_j} D(\mathbf{x}, \mathbf{z}),$$

and let $d(i)$ for cluster $\mathbf{S}_i$ be the maximum distance over all pairs of instances in $\mathbf{S}_i$; that is, $d(i)$ is the intra-cluster measure given by

$$d(i) = \max_{\mathbf{x},\mathbf{z}\in\mathbf{S}_i} D(\mathbf{x},\mathbf{z});$$

$d(i)$ is known as the *diameter* of $\mathbf{S}_i$.

The *Dunn index* can now be defined as

$$\frac{\min_{\mathbf{S}_i,\mathbf{S}_j,i\neq j} d(i,j)}{\max_{\mathbf{S}_i} d(i)}.$$

It follows that a high Dunn index is desirable, since an increase in the numerator will result in higher separation and a decrease in the denominator will result in higher cohesion.

Now, consider a pair $(\mathbf{x}_j, i)$, that is, the jth instance, which is in cluster $\lambda(\mathbf{x}_j) = i$, and distance measure D. We let $a[i](j)$ be the average distance under D of the jth instance to all other instances in the cluster $\mathbf{S}_i$. In addition, determine the average distance of the instance $\mathbf{x}_j$ to all instances in a cluster other than $\mathbf{S}_i$, and let $b[i](j)$ be the minimum of these averages. Now, the *silhouette coefficient* for the instance $\mathbf{x}_j$ in cluster $\mathbf{S}_i$, denoted by $s[i](j)$, is given as

$$s[i](j) = \begin{cases} \dfrac{b[i](j) - a[i](j)}{\max\left(a[i](j), b[i](j)\right)} & \text{if } k > 1 \\ 0 & \text{if } k = 1, \end{cases}$$

where $\max(a[i](j), b[i](j))$ is the maximum of $a[i](j)$ and $b[i](j)$; it follows that $s[i](j)$ is between -1 and 1. The silhouette coefficient, $s[i]$, for a cluster $\mathbf{S}_i$, called its *average silhouette width*, is the average over all instances $\mathbf{x}_j$ in $\mathbf{S}_i$ of the silhouette coefficients $s[i](j)$. The silhouette coefficient of the clustering of $\mathbf{S}$, called its *overall average silhouette width*, is the average over all instances $\mathbf{x}_j$ in $\mathbf{S}$ of the silhouette coefficients $s[i](j)$.

Overall, when $a[i](j)$ is small, the cluster is cohesive with respect to the jth instance, and when $b[i](j)$ is large, the clusters in $\mathbf{S}$ are well separated with respect to the instance. Thus, when $s[i](j)$ is close to 1, the data is well clustered with respect to the jth instance; when it is close to -1, it is badly clustered with respect to the instance; and when it is close to 0, it is on the boundary of two clusters.

Example 4.3. The Dunn index and silhouette coefficient values based on the clusters output by the k-means algorithm, for $k = 2$ to $k = 6$, operating on the Iris data set introduced earlier, are shown in Table 4.4; the corresponding *silhouette plot* is shown in Figure 4.4.

The silhouette plot displays $s[i](j)$ for each instance $\mathbf{x}_i$ in cluster $\mathbf{S}_j$, where each cluster is displayed in a different colour. It is a measure of how close each point in one cluster is to points in the neighbouring clusters. This provides a way to assess the number of clusters visually. The silhouette plot, in Figure 4.4, for a clustering parameter of $k = 6$, shows that

Table 4.4   A summary of the Dunn index and silhouette coefficients (i.e., the overall average silhouette width) for the clusters output by k-means, with $k = 2$ to $k = 6$, computed over the Iris data set.

k	Dunn Index	Silhouette Coefficient
2	0.546	0.765
3	0.220	0.660
4	0.141	0.612
5	0.115	0.583
6	0.095	0.571

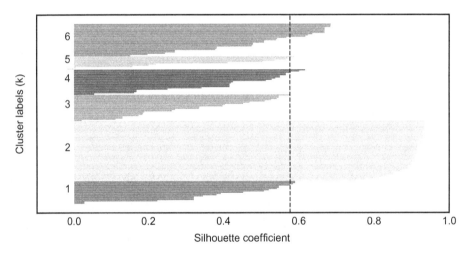

Figure 4.4   The silhouette plot for $k = 6$ clusters generated by k-means computed over the Iris data set. The vertical line represents the silhouette coefficient, which is 0.571 in this case (see Table 4.4).

this clustering is not a good one. This is mainly due to the below-average silhouette scores for clusters 4 to 6, which can be seen to decrease sharply for their instances.

Instead, a setting of $k = 2$ for the number of clusters will provide the best result shown by a higher silhouette score in the positive range (i.e., 0.765, which is much closer to 1 than 0.571; see Table 4.4). A score closer to 1 indicates that the data points are compact within the cluster that they belong to and separate from other clusters, whereas values nearer to 0 denote overlapping clusters. The setting of $k = 2$ is indeed appropriate in this case, where we have a two-class problem, because we have removed the rows of data related to the third species of Iris.

We now turn to topic modelling, which concentrates on clustering textual data, where we assume that the data set is a corpus consisting of m instances called *documents*.

Each document in the corpus is represented by a vector of n features, one for each word from a vocabulary of words V. In particular, the ith feature value x_i of a document $\mathbf{x} = \langle x_1, x_2, \ldots, x_n \rangle$ is the number of occurrences of word i in document $\mathbf{x}$, which is zero if the word is not in the document. This method of representing documents is based on the *bag-of-words* assumption, where the order of words in a document is not considered to be important. To gain a better understanding of the corpus, we assume that there are k latent *topics*, $\mathbf{T} = \{t_1, t_2, \ldots, t_k\}$, which best describe a corpus $\mathbf{U}$, and are to be discovered by the topic modelling algorithm. The topics may be considered to be clusters; however, in topic modelling, we consider distributions rather than points estimates, and thus in this probabilistic setting of topic modelling, each document is a distribution of topics and each topic is a distribution of words. Topic modelling is introduced in more detail in Subsection 4.4.4. To evaluate topic models, we turn to *topic coherence*, a measure that allows us to quantify the interpretability of topics.

Now a document $\mathbf{x}$ is said to *contain* a word, w_i, if $x_i > 0$. The number of documents in $\mathbf{S}$ containing w_i is denoted by $\#(w_i, \mathbf{S})$, and the number of documents in $\mathbf{S}$ containing both w_i and w_j is denoted by $\#(w_i, w_j, \mathbf{S})$. So, for two words w_i and w_j, we define $p(w_i)$ and $p(w_i, w_j)$, as

$$p(w_i) = \frac{\#(w_i, \mathbf{S})}{m}$$

and

$$p(w_i, w_j) = \frac{\#(w_i, w_j, \mathbf{S})}{m},$$

respectively, recalling that m is the number of documents (or instances) in the corpus. The *pointwise mutual information* between w_i and w_j, denoted as $PMI(w_i, w_j)$, is given by

$$PMI(w_i, w_j) = \log\left(\frac{p(w_i, w_j) + \epsilon}{p(w_i)p(w_j)}\right),$$

where ϵ is a small positive constant, added to avoid the logarithm being zero.

In a nutshell, $PMI(w_i, w_j)$ measures the co-occurrence strength between w_i and w_j. PMI is an information theoretic measure of the divergence between the joint probability of w_i and w_j and their individual probabilities assuming they are independent. Topic coherence for a given topic can now be defined as the average PMI between the top-h (i.e., the h most probable) words in the topic.

We conclude this section by introducing the *Hopkins* statistic, which is a measure of clustering tendency that is constructed as follows:

(i) Generate a small random sample (without replacement) of h instances $\mathbf{X} = \{\mathbf{x}_1, \mathbf{x}_2, \ldots, \mathbf{x}_h\}$ from $\mathbf{S}$;

(ii) Generate uniformly a random set of h instances $\mathbf{Y} = \{\mathbf{y}_1, \mathbf{y}_2, \ldots, \mathbf{y}_h\}$ from the feature space that the data set $\mathbf{S}$ comes from. For example, if $n = 2$ (i.e., there are two features), where the first feature represents the age of a person and the second the gender of a person, then a random instance will be one with a uniform random age and gender;

(iii) We let $\mathbf{u}_i$ be the distance of $\mathbf{y}_i \in \mathbf{Y}$ from its nearest neighbour $\mathbf{x}_j \in \mathbf{S}$ for $i = 1, 2, \ldots, h$, that is, $D(\mathbf{y}_i, \mathbf{x}_j)$, where D is a reference distance; and

(iv) We let $\mathbf{w}_i$ be the distance of $\mathbf{x}_i \in \mathbf{X}$ from its nearest neighbour $\mathbf{x}_j \in \mathbf{S}$ for $i = 1, 2, \ldots, h$, that is, $D(\mathbf{x}_i, \mathbf{x}_j)$.

Given the $\mathbf{u}_i$ and $\mathbf{w}_i$, the Hopkins statistic is defined as

$$H = \frac{\sum_{i=1}^{h} \mathbf{u}_i}{\sum_{i=1}^{h} \mathbf{u}_i + \mathbf{w}_i}.$$

Now it can be seen that if H is approximately 0.5, then $\mathbf{S}$ is uniformly distributed, since both the $\mathbf{u}_i$ and $\mathbf{w}_i$ values contribute equally to the sum, and so the clustering tendency of $\mathbf{S}$ is very low. On the other hand, the clustering tendency of the data is high when H is close to 1, since the sum of the $\mathbf{w}_i$ values will be low compared to the contribution of the $\mathbf{u}_i$ values. Finally, when H is close to 0, then the data set is regularly spaced; that is, it is neither clustered nor random, since in this case the $\mathbf{u}_i$ values are small relative to the $\mathbf{w}_i$ values.

4.3 Supervised Methods

As we are dealing with supervised methods, we will assume a labelled data set $\mathbf{S} = \{(\mathbf{x}_1, y_1), (\mathbf{x}_2, y_2), \ldots, (\mathbf{x}_m, y_m)\}$, with $m \geq 1$, where each input $\mathbf{x}_i$ is a vector of feature values $\mathbf{x}_i = \langle x_{i1}, x_{i2}, \ldots, x_{in} \rangle$. To train and test a model, the data set will be partitioned into training, validation (optional), and test sets, or into k-folds for cross-validation. However, generally, we will not consider these details in this section and often simply refer to $\mathbf{S}$ as the training set.

4.3.1 K-Nearest Neighbours

K-nearest neighbours (KNN) is a simple yet powerful classification algorithm based on measuring the *distance* between two data vectors, $\mathbf{x} = \langle x_1, x_2, \ldots, x_n \rangle$ and $\mathbf{z} = \langle z_1, z_2, \ldots, z_n \rangle$, each having n features. We assume that $(\mathbf{x}, y)$ is in the labelled data set $\mathbf{S}$ and that the goal of the classification task is to predict the label of the unseen instance $\mathbf{z}$, not present in the training set.

In KNN terminology, $\mathbf{x}$ and $\mathbf{z}$ are called *neighbours*, and the distance between them, under a distance measure D, is $D(\mathbf{x}, \mathbf{z})$; see Section 4.1 for the definition of some of the common distance measures used in machine learning. The KNN algorithm has a single input parameter k, with $k \geq 1$, resulting in a k-NN classifier, so that an instance $\mathbf{z}$ is classified by the majority class (i.e., label) of its k nearest neighbours as determined by D.

In other words, let $\mathbf{x}_1', \mathbf{x}_2', \ldots, \mathbf{x}_k'$ be the k nearest neighbours of $\mathbf{z}$ under D, that is, the closest k instances to $\mathbf{z}$ under D, and $(\mathbf{x}_1', y_1'), (\mathbf{x}_2', y_1'), \ldots, (\mathbf{x}_k', y_1')$ the corresponding pairs in **S**. We then take a vote amongst the classes y_i', for $i = 1, 2, \ldots, k$, represented by k labels of the neighbours in the data set, counting how many votes each class has within these k instances. The class $\hat{y}$ with the most votes, called the *majority class*, is declared the winner and is paired with **z**. In particular, the pair $(\mathbf{z}, ?)$ becomes $(\mathbf{z}, \hat{y})$, that is, $\hat{y}$ is the prediction made by the KNN algorithm. Pseudocode for KNN is given in Algorithm 4.1.

Algorithm 4.1 KNN

Input: k, D, **S**, $(\mathbf{z}, ?)$,
  1: **for** $i = 1 : k$ **do**
  2:     Let $\mathbf{x}_i'$ be the ith nearest neighbour to **z** according to D
  3: **end for**
  4: Let $\hat{y}$ be the majority class of the k labels y_i', for $i = 1, 2, \ldots, k$,
          where ties are resolved if they exist
  5: **return** $(\mathbf{z}, \hat{y})$

A problem that may occur is a tie between two or more classes; that is, they all receive the same number of votes. In the case of a binary classifier, when there are only two classes, it is easy to verify that when k is an odd number, say 3, then there will be no ties. Otherwise, there are several schemes for breaking ties. The simplest methods are either to make a random choice among the tied classes or to use a 1-NN classifier to break the tie, that is, setting $k = 1$. Another method to break ties is to choose the largest class, that is, the one with the most instances in the labelled data set. Yet another method is to sum up the distances to the neighbours in each of the tied classes and choose the closest class. Finally, a rule of thumb on how big k should be is to set k to the square root of m, where m is the size of the training set **S**.

KNN can also be used to solve regression problems by replacing the majority rule with the average of the k nearest neighbours; that is, $(\mathbf{z}, ?)$ becomes $(\mathbf{z}, \hat{y})$, where the prediction $\hat{y}$ is given by

$$\hat{y} = \frac{1}{k} \sum_{i=1}^{k} y_i'.$$

Example 4.4. An exoplanet (also known as an extrasolar planet) is a planet that orbits a star outside the solar system; data on exoplanets is available for download from the NASA Exoplanet Archive.

The data set describes the characterisation of exoplanets and their host stars. The data includes exoplanet parameters including masses and orbital parameters and characterisation data, including radial velocity curves, photometric light curves, images, and spectral analyses; see Table 4.5 for a sample from the data set, where planets that are considered extrasolar are labelled by a 1 and those that are not by a 0.

The confusion matrix is shown in Figure 4.5 and the precision, recall, and F1 for the KNN model are shown in stylised form in Table 4.6.

Table 4.5   A sample from the exoplanet data set recording attributes of the candidate exoplanets, where the label column records a 1 for exoplanets and a 0 otherwise.

Stellar Radius	Right Ascension	Declination	Kepler-band	Label
−0.061	291.934	48.141	15.347	1
−0.067	285.534	48.285	15.597	0
−0.078	297.004	48.134	15.436	1
−0.133	288.754	48.226	15.509	1
−0.483	298.864	42.151	12.660	0

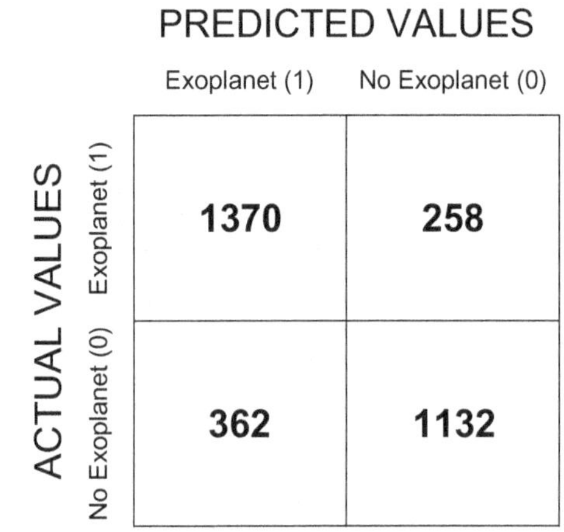

Figure 4.5   The confusion matrix describing the model performance of a KNN model computed on the exoplanet data set.

Table 4.6   The precision, recall, and F1 for a KNN model applied to the exoplanet data set, with a 67–33 split between the training and test data.

Label	Precision	Recall	F1	Support
$Class_0$	0.81	0.76	0.79	1494
$Class_1$	0.79	0.84	0.82	1628
Total support:	3122			
Micro-averaged F1:	0.80			
Macro-averaged F1:	0.80			

KNN is a simple algorithm that makes no assumptions about the data; for example, it may well be nonlinear. Even if it does not produce results as accurate as state-of-the-art machine learning algorithms, it is still competitive. However, the main disadvantage of KNN is that it is relatively slow due to high memory requirements because it does not learn in the traditional manner and simply consults the data each time it needs to make a decision.

4.3.2 Naive Bayes

Naive Bayes is another simple yet powerful machine learning algorithm based on Bayes' theorem, which was defined in Section 2.1 in Chapter 2, and can be written as

$$P(A|B) = \frac{P(A)P(B|A)}{P(B)},$$

where A and B are events; $P(A|B)$ is called the *posterior*, $P(A)$ is called the *prior*, $P(B|A)$ is called the *likelihood*, and $P(B)$ is called the *normalising constant*, making sure that the probabilities sum up to 1.

For the purpose of classification, we may assume k classes $c_1, c_2, \ldots, c_k$, with labelled pairs such as $(\mathbf{x}, y)$ in $\mathbf{S}$, where $\mathbf{x} = \langle x_1, x_2, \ldots, x_n \rangle$, n is the number of represented features, and each label is one of the k classes. Thus, given a class c_i and the instance $\mathbf{x}$, we can recast Bayes' theorem as

$$P(c_i|\mathbf{x}) = \frac{P(c_i)P(\mathbf{x}|c_i)}{P(\mathbf{x})},$$

and since $P(\mathbf{x})$ is a constant, we may write

$$P(c_i|\mathbf{x}) \propto P(c_i)P(\mathbf{x}|c_i),$$

where the symbol $\propto$ means proportional to. Moreover, by assuming that all features are conditionally independent of each other given the class c_i, we obtain

$$P(c_i|\mathbf{x}) \propto P(c_i)P(x_1|c_i)P(x_2|c_i)\cdots P(x_n|c_i),$$

which is the essential building block of the naive Bayes classifier.

Now the task of the classifier is to predict the class of an instance $\mathbf{z} = \langle z_1, z_2, \ldots, z_n \rangle$ in the pair $(\mathbf{z}, ?)$, whose class label is unknown. The prediction made by naive Bayes is $\hat{y}$; that is, $(\mathbf{z}, ?)$ becomes $(\mathbf{z}, \hat{y})$ and is given by

$$\hat{y} = \underset{i \in \{1,2,\ldots,k\}}{\arg\max} \ P(c_i)P(z_1|c_i)P(z_2|c_i)\cdots P(z_n|c_i),$$

where an $\in$ stands for member of (or *in*) and "arg max" returns the index i of the class $\hat{y} = c_i$ such that $P(c_i|\mathbf{z})$ is maximal; this is known as the *maximum a posteriori* decision rule or simply *MAP*.

To describe a common problem of naive Bayes and its solution, let us consider its application to email spam filtering. To recall the terminology, "spam" email is junk email that is unsolicited, while "ham" email is the opposite; that is, it is email that is not spam and is generally desirable. Typical spam email may attempt to sell something to an unsuspecting user, offer the user some reward out of the blue, be a phishing scam that attempts to deceive the user to hand over sensitive information, or any number of sophisticated ploys to make a profit from the user. So, spam filtering is a binary text classification problem, with two classes: spam and ham. We will make a simplification in considering only the textual body of an email, its features being the words in the text. Examples of spam words may be "cheap," "free," and "cash," while examples of ham words may be "data," "student," and "meeting." In general, other parts of the email can also contain features as well as images or other attachments.

Recall that the training set S contains m instances. Each instance $\mathbf{x} = \langle x_1, x_2, \ldots, x_n \rangle$ represents the text in the body of an email containing n words x_j, for $j = 1, 2, \ldots, n$, with j being the position of the word in the text. Two email instances will, in general, be of different lengths and therefore contain a different number of words; however, in what follows we will use n as a generic document length and ignore the fact that a word x_j may appear in several positions in a single email and in different positions in different emails.

We first need to estimate the probability $P(c_i)$ of class c_i, where $i \in \{1, 2, \ldots, k\}$; we will assume that $P(c_i) > 0$, that is, that there is at least one email in each class. Intuitively, $P(c_i)$ is proportional to the number of instances in S that are in each class c_i. In the case of spam filtering, each instance is an email, which is labelled as being in one of the spam or ham classes. To formalise this, let $\#(c_i, S)$, for $i = 1, 2, \ldots, k$, be the number of emails in the training set whose label is c_i. Then, $P(c_i)$ is given by

$$P(c_i) = \frac{\#(c_i, S)}{m}.$$

Recall that $P(x_j | c_i)$ is a shorthand for $P(X_j = x_j | C_i = c_i)$, denoting the probability of the word x_j given the class c_i. In the context of spam filtering, we expect $P(X_j = \text{cheap} | C_i = \text{spam})$ to be greater than $P(X_j = \text{cheap} | C_i = \text{ham})$, while we expect $P(X_j = \text{data} | C_i = \text{ham})$ to be greater than $P(X_j = \text{data} | C_i = \text{spam})$.

The probability $P(x_j | c_i)$ comes in two forms: *multinomial*, where we count the number of occurrences of the word x_j in an email represented by $\mathbf{x}$ independently of its position j in the body of the email, or *Bernoulli*, where we record 0 or 1 depending on whether the word x_j appears in the email or not. Multinomial naive Bayes is also known as the *bag-of-words* model, while Bernoulli naive Bayes is also known as the *binary independence* model.

To approximate the conditional probability $P(x_j | c_i)$, assume $(\mathbf{x}, y)$ is a labelled pair in the training set S whose label y is c_i. We then let $\#(x_j, c_i, S)$ be the number of occurrences of the word x_j, over all labelled pairs in S whose label is c_i, independently of its position j. That is, under the bag-of-words model $\#(x_j, c_i, S)$ is the number of occurrences of the word x_j in *all* emails represented by training pairs $(\mathbf{x}, y)$, whose label y

is c_i, while under the binary independence model $\#(x_j, c_i, \mathbf{S})$ is the number of emails having label c_i that contain the word x_j. Then, $P(x_j|c_i)$ is given by

$$P(x_j|c_i) = \frac{\#(x_j, c_i, \mathbf{S})}{\sum_{w \in V} \#(w, c_i, \mathbf{S})},$$

where V is the vocabulary of all the words that appear in an email text and w is a word in V.

Using this formalism, we can predict the class $\hat{y}$ of an instance $\mathbf{z}$, using the maximum a posteriori decision rule given here, by plugging in our estimates for $P(c_i)$ and $P(z_j|c_i)$ for the words z_j.

However, a problem with the current method of approximating $P(z_j|c_i)$ for a word z_j in the jth position in $\mathbf{z} = \langle z_1, z_2, \ldots, z_n \rangle$ is that z_j may not have appeared in any of the emails in the training set and, therefore, $P(z_j|c_i)$ will be 0 for all classes c_i. *Additive smoothing* addresses this problem of zero counts by redefining $P(x_j|c_i)$ as

$$P(x_j|c_i) = \frac{\#(x_j, c_i, \mathbf{S}) + \alpha}{\left(\sum_{w \in V} \#(w, c_i, \mathbf{S}) \right) + \alpha N},$$

where $\alpha \geq 0$ and N is the number of words in the vocabulary V; when $\alpha = 1$, additive smoothing is known as Laplace smoothing. Pseudocode for naive Bayes is given in Algorithm 4.2.

Algorithm 4.2 Naive Bayes

Input: $V, \alpha, \mathbf{S}, (\mathbf{z}, ?)$,
1: $P(c_i) = \frac{\#(c_i, \mathbf{S})}{m}$ % Train the class probabilities
2: $P(x_j|c_i) = \frac{\#(x_j, c_i, \mathbf{S}) + \alpha}{\left(\sum_{w \in V} \#(w, c_i, \mathbf{S}) \right) + \alpha N}$ % Train the word probabilities
3: Let $\hat{y} = \underset{i \in \{1,2,\ldots,k\}}{\arg\max} \ P(c_i) P(z_1|c_i) P(z_2|c_i) \cdots P(z_n|c_i)$
4: **return** $(\mathbf{z}, \hat{y})$

One useful extension of naive Bayes is when we have a continuous feature, say X, and we wish to approximate the conditional probability $P(X = x|C = c)$ for a class variable C. Assuming that the distribution of the X values can be approximated by a normal distribution with mean μ and standard deviation σ, we can then estimate this probability using its PDF; this extension to naive Bayes is called *Gaussian naive Bayes*.

Example 4.5. In Table 4.7 we show a sample from an SMS (short message service) data set that has been collected for SMS spam research containing SMS messages in English labelled according to whether they are *ham* (legitimate email) or *spam* (junk mail).

We first apply Bernoulli naive Bayes to categorise the SMS messages into one of two classes: spam or ham. The confusion matrix summarising the performance of trained model is shown in Figure 4.6. The precision, recall, and F1 for the Bernoulli naive Bayes model are shown in stylised form in Table 4.8. Second, we apply multinomial naive Bayes

Table 4.7   A sample from the spam or ham SMS messages data set, where the label column records a 0 for ham messages and a 1 for spam messages.

SMS text	Label
Go until jurong point, crazy.. Available only ...	0
Ok lar... Joking wif u oni...	0
U dun say so early hor... U c already then say...	0
Free entry in 2 a wkly comp to win FA Cup fina...	1
WINNER!! As a valued network customer you have...	1
Had your mobile 11 months or more? U R entitle...	1

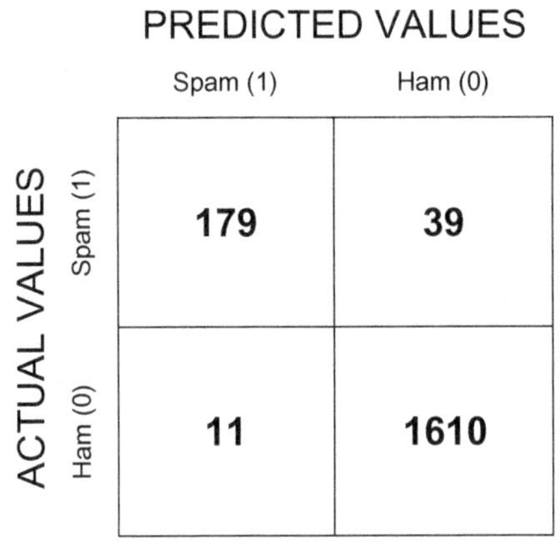

PREDICTED VALUES

Figure 4.6   The confusion matrix for the Bernoulli naive Bayes model trained on the SMS data set.

to categorise the SMS messages; the confusion matrix summarising the performance of trained model is shown in Figure 4.7. The precision, recall, and F1 for the multinomial naive Bayes model are shown in stylised form in Table 4.9.

Table 4.8   The precision, recall, and F1 score for a Bernoulli naive Bayes classifier used to classify email messages into ham (labelled as 0) or spam (labelled 1) using a training set of examples, with an 85–15 split between the training and test data.

Label	Precision	Recall	F1	Support
$Class_0$	0.98	0.99	0.98	1621
$Class_1$	0.94	0.82	0.88	218
Total support:	1839			
Micro-averaged F1:	0.97			
Macro-averaged F1:	0.97			

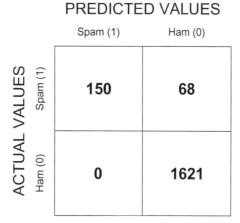

Figure 4.7   The confusion matrix for the multinomial naive Bayes model trained on the SMS
data set.

Table 4.9   The precision, recall, and F1 score for a multinomial
naive Bayes classifier used to classify email messages into ham
(labelled as 0) or spam (labelled 1) using a training set of
examples, with an 85–15 split between the training and test data.

Label	Precision	Recall	F1	Support
$Class_0$	0.96	1.00	0.98	1621
$Class_1$	1.00	0.69	0.82	218
Total support:	1839			
Micro-averaged F1:	0.96			
Macro-averaged F1:	0.96			

In Table 4.10 we show a sample from a data set recording 23 species of gilled
mushrooms in the Agaricus and Lepiota family. Each species is identified as being either
edible (labelled as 0) or as being definitely poisonous or of unknown edibility and not
recommended (labelled as 1). Third, we apply the Gaussian naive Bayes to categorise the
mushrooms; the confusion matrix summarising the performance of trained model is
shown in Figure 4.8. The precision, recall, and F1 for the Gaussian naive Bayes model are
shown in stylised form in Table 4.11.

Table 4.10   A sample from the mushroom data set recording various physical attributes of mushrooms, with a target label where a 0 means it is safe to consume and a 1 means the mushroom is poisonous.

Shape	Colour	Bruises	Odour	Label
5	4	1	6	1
5	8	1	6	1
0	8	1	3	0
5	9	1	0	0
5	3	0	5	0

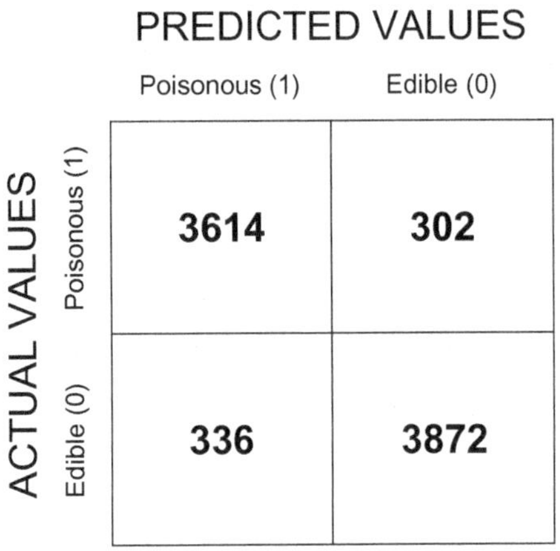

PREDICTED VALUES

Figure 4.8   The confusion matrix for the Gaussian naive Bayes model trained on the mushroom data set.

Table 4.11   The precision, recall, and F1 score for a Gaussian naive Bayes classifier used to classify mushrooms as safe (labelled as 0) or poisonous (labelled 1) using a training set of examples, with an 85–15 split between the training and test data.

Label	Precision	Recall	F1	Support
$Class_0$	0.93	0.92	0.92	4208
$Class_1$	0.91	0.92	0.92	3916
Total support:	8124			
Micro-averaged F1:	0.92			
Macro-averaged F1:	0.92			

Despite the assumption of conditionally independent features, which is clearly not satisfied in many if not most applications, naive Bayes is surprisingly effective in practice. One reason why naive Bayes performs well is that as a result of the conditional independence assumption, fewer features are needed than in methods that attempt to model dependencies between features.

4.3.3 Support Vector Machines

Support vector machines (SVM) are a powerful and elegant machine learning classification algorithm. They provide a solid and well-understood classification algorithm that works in practice and has notably been applied for classifying text, image, and bioinformatics data. We concentrate on SVM for binary classification, but the algorithm has also been extended to deal with the classification of multiple, greater than two, classes. It is interesting to note that the development of SVM started from its theoretical aspects and only then moved to their implementation, while neural networks, discussed later, have been widely driven by their successes in practice.

Next, we introduce some notation that will enable us to present the ideas underlying the theory behind SVM. The *dot product*, $\mathbf{x} \cdot \mathbf{z}$, between two n feature vectors $\mathbf{x} = \langle x_1, x_2, \ldots, x_n \rangle$ and $\mathbf{z} = \langle z_1, z_2, \ldots, z_n \rangle$ is an important operation in machine learning, defined as

$$\mathbf{x} \cdot \mathbf{z} = x_1 z_1 + x_2 z_2 + \cdots + x_n z_n = \sum_{i=1}^{n} x_i z_i.$$

Often we identify vectors such as $\mathbf{x}$ and $\mathbf{z}$ as column matrices when $\mathbf{x} \cdot \mathbf{z}$ is written as $\mathbf{x}^T \mathbf{z}$, where $\mathbf{x}^T$ is the *transpose* of $\mathbf{x}$; that is, the row and column indices are switched, and the column vector $\mathbf{x}$ becomes a row vector $\mathbf{x}^T$. (We will be quite relaxed regarding the notation and use both forms interchangeably.)

A fundamental equality relating the dot product of two vectors to the product of its norms (see Subsection 4.2.2 for the definition of the norm of a vector) is given by

$$\mathbf{x} \cdot \mathbf{z} = \|\mathbf{x}\| \, \|\mathbf{z}\| \cos \theta,$$

where $\cos \theta$ is the cosine of the angle θ between $\mathbf{x}$ and $\mathbf{z}$. Note that $\cos \theta$ can be interpreted as the *similarity* between $\mathbf{x}$ and $\mathbf{z}$ and $1 - \cos \theta$ as the distance between them, as in Section 4.3.1.

The decision boundary separating the two classes is called a *hyperplane*, and its dimensionality is one less than the number of features, that is, $n - 1$. For the purpose of displaying the separating hyperplane, the cases of interest are restricted to $n \leq 3$. So, if we have a single feature, $n = 1$, then the separating hyperplane is simply a point. When there are two features, $n = 2$, then the hyperplane is a line. With three features, $n = 3$, the separating hyperplane is a two-dimensional surface.

Let $(\mathbf{x}_i, y_i)$, for $i \in \{1, 2, \ldots, m\}$, be a labelled pair in the training set $\mathbf{S}$, where $\mathbf{x}_i$ is a vector of n feature values $\mathbf{x}_i = \langle x_{i1}, x_{i2}, \ldots, x_{in} \rangle$. We assume that the class label of y_i is either 1 or -1, depending on which of the two classes $\mathbf{x}_i$ belongs to. So the objective of SVM is to find a hyperplane that linearly separates $\mathbf{S}$ into the two classes.

In SVM the decision function f to be learnt, predicting $\hat{y}_i = f(\mathbf{x}_i)$, is given by

$$f(\mathbf{x}_i) = sgn\,(\mathbf{w} \cdot \mathbf{x}_i + b),$$

where $\mathbf{w}$ is a vector of n values called *weights* in this context and b is a *bias* term, that is, the offset of the hyperplane from the origin in the input space, and for a number v, $sgn(v)$, is defined as

$$sgn(v) = \begin{cases} -1 & \text{if } v < 0 \\ 0 & \text{if } v = 0 \\ 1 & \text{if } v > 0. \end{cases}$$

Given the specification of the decision function f, the goal of SVM is to find the largest separation, or *margin*, between the two classes. Maximising the margin is also described using the metaphor of finding the largest "street-width" between the *support vectors* $\mathbf{x}_i$ that are closest to the separating hyperplane. This leads to the following optimisation problem,

$$\arg\min_{\mathbf{w},b} \frac{1}{2} \|w\|^2 \text{ such that for all } i, \ y_i\,(\mathbf{w} \cdot \mathbf{x}_i + b) \geq 1,$$

where "arg min" returns $\mathbf{w}$ and b such that half the norm of $\mathbf{x}$ squared is minimal. We note that the optimisation is specified as a minimisation problem, since using linear algebra, the distance between the two hyperplanes is shown to be $2/\|w\|$, and the square of the norm is used for convenience.

The margin resulting from the preceding optimisation problem is a *hard margin* in the sense that a separating hyperplane can be found only if $\mathbf{S}$ is linearly separable; see Figure 4.9.

We may wish to relax this and allow a small number of training instances, such as $\mathbf{x}_i$, to be misclassified, that is, on the wrong side of the margin, causing the classes to overlap and resulting in a *soft margin*; see Figure 4.10.

A soft margin is achieved by introducing non-negative *slack* variables, ξ_i, corresponding to each labelled pair $(\mathbf{x}_i, y_i)$, for $i = 1, 2, \ldots, m$, and modifying the preceding equation for finding a hard margin, leading to

$$\arg\min_{\mathbf{w},b,\xi} \frac{1}{2} \|w\|^2 + C \sum_{i=1}^{m} \xi_i \text{ such that for all } i, \ y_i\,(\mathbf{w} \cdot \mathbf{x}_i + b) \geq 1 - \xi_i,$$

where $\xi = \langle \xi_1, \xi_2, \ldots, \xi_m \rangle$, C is positive *penalty* term, and $C \sum_{i=1}^{m} \xi_i$ is bounded by a constant. Note that a large value of C will force the slack variables to be small and the soft margin will be closer to the hard margin.

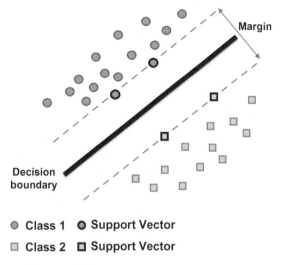

Class 1 ● Support Vector ○

Class 2 ▢ Support Vector ◻

Figure 4.9 Example of an SVM hard margin.

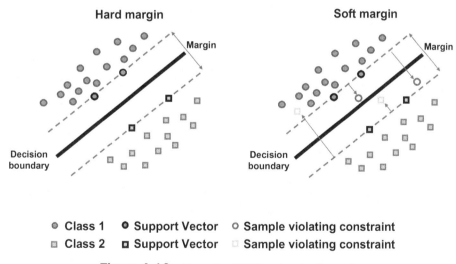

● Class 1   ● Support Vector   ○ Sample violating constraint
▢ Class 2   ◼ Support Vector   ◻ Sample violating constraint

Figure 4.10 Example of SVM hard and soft margins.

Subtracting ξ_i from 1 on the left-hand side of the equation leads to a relaxation of the hard margin and can be tuned using the penalty term C. The preceding optimisation problem is typically solved numerically using quadratic programming algorithms.

Example 4.6. A sample from the Iris data for two species, Iris setosa and Iris versicolour, is shown in Table 4.3, and a scatter plot exhibiting the hard margin between the two classes is shown Figure 4.11. To demonstrate soft margin classification, we used an alternative data set for the two species, Iris versicolour and Iris virginica. A scatter plot exhibiting the soft margin between these two classes is shown Figure 4.12.

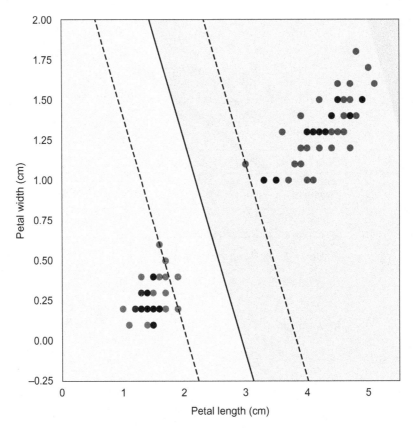

Figure 4.11   A scatter plot of the Iris data set for the two classes representing the species Iris setosa and Iris versicolour. The decision boundary was computed using hard margin SVM classification and shows the hard margin between the two classes.

The confusion matrix summarising the performance of the hard margin SVM classifier trained on the Iris setosa and versicolour data set is shown in Figure 4.13, and the precision, recall, and F1 for the hard SVM classifier are shown in stylised form in Table 4.12. Correspondingly, the confusion matrix for the soft margin SVM classifier trained on the Iris versicolour and virginica data set is shown in Figure 4.14, and the precision, recall, and F1 for the soft margin SVM classifier are shown in stylised form in Table 4.13.

Although a soft margin relaxes the linear separability constraint to deal with noisy data, it does not generalise well for inherently nonlinear data. SVM deals with this problem by transforming the data into a higher dimension with the expectation that in the higher dimensional space the classes will be linearly separable using SVM as presented previously. So, for example, if the data is not linearly separable in two-dimensional space by a line, as shown on the left-hand side of Figure 4.15, we could apply a nonlinear transformation to the data to a three-dimensional space, whereby the data becomes linearly separable by a two-dimensional hyperplane, as shown on the right-hand side of Figure 4.15.

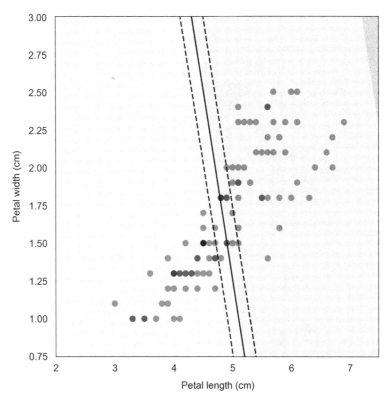

Figure 4.12 A scatter plot of the Iris data set for the two classes representing the species Iris versicolour and Iris virginica. The decision boundary was computed using soft margin SVM classification and shows the soft margin between the two classes.

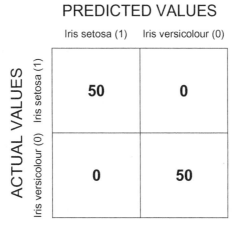

Figure 4.13 The confusion matrix for a hard margin SVM binary classifier trained on the Iris data with classes Iris versicolour and Iris setosa.

Table 4.12 The precision, recall, and F1 score for a hard margin SVM binary classifier trained on the Iris data with classes Iris versicolour (labelled as class 0) and Iris setosa (labelled as class 1), with a 67–33 split between the training and test data.

Label	Precision	Recall	F1	Support
$Class_0$	1.00	1.00	1.00	50
$Class_1$	1.00	1.00	1.00	50
Total support:	100			
Micro-averaged F1:	1.00			
Macro-averaged F1:	1.00			

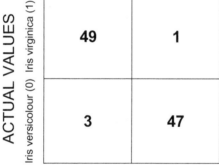

Figure 4.14 The confusion matrix for a soft margin SVM binary classifier, with $C = 100$, trained on the Iris data with classes Iris versicolour and Iris virginica.

This is exactly what a *kernel* function achieves. To explain how this works, consider the two n feature vectors $\mathbf{x}$ and $\mathbf{z}$, and assume they are in the training set $\mathbf{S}$. In particular, we may apply a nonlinear transformation ϕ to the instances in $\mathbf{S}$, resulting in $\phi(\mathbf{x})$ and $\phi(\mathbf{z})$ when applied to $\mathbf{x}$ and $\mathbf{z}$. A low-order polynomial transformation may do the trick, as in Figure 4.15, but there are many transformations available in the bag of tricks of a data scientist.

When we are solving the SVM optimisation problem in terms of the training data set $\mathbf{S}$, instances such as $\mathbf{x}$ and $\mathbf{z}$ crucially appear as dot products such as $\mathbf{x} \cdot \mathbf{z}$, where the dot

Table 4.13 The precision, recall, and F1 score for a soft margin SVM binary classifier, with $C = 100$, trained on the Iris data with classes Iris versicolour (labelled as class 0) and Iris virginica (labelled as class 1), with a 67–33 split between the training and test data.

Label	Precision	Recall	F1	Support
$Class_0$	0.98	0.94	0.96	50
$Class_1$	0.94	0.98	0.96	50
Total support:	100			
Micro-averaged F1:	0.96			
Macro-averaged F1:	0.96			

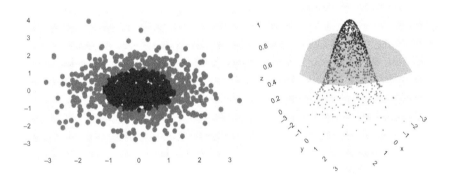

Figure 4.15 Example of SVM nonlinear kernel, showing a dense circle of data points surrounded by a ring of data points (left plot) and its nonlinear kernel transformation (right plot).

product can be viewed as computing a similarity measure between pairs of instances. Thus, if we can avoid computing the dot products directly, we could solve the SVM optimisation problem as before, but in the higher dimensional space, without directly applying the nonlinear transforming to the original space. This is exactly what is achieved by *kernels*, which can be viewed as similarity measures between vectors that can potentially reduce the complexity of solving SVM for nonlinear data. A kernel K is thus defined as a function that satisfies

$$K(\mathbf{x}, \mathbf{z}) = \phi(\mathbf{x}) \cdot \phi(\mathbf{z}),$$

where ϕ may be a nonlinear transformation; that is, we allow ϕ to be either linear or nonlinear.

This equation is also known as the *kernel trick*, to emphasise that the kernel may be computed directly on $\mathbf{x}$ and $\mathbf{z}$ without computing the dot product in the transformed space. As a special case, the *linear kernel*,

$$K(\mathbf{x}, \mathbf{z}) = \mathbf{x} \cdot \mathbf{z},$$

that is, with $\phi(\mathbf{x}) = \mathbf{x}$ and $\phi(\mathbf{z}) = \mathbf{z}$, results in *linear support vector machines* (LSVM), which are equivalent to SVM with a hard or soft margin, as developed earlier, before introducing kernels.

One of the most commonly used kernels is the *Gaussian kernel* (also known as the *radial basis function kernel*), which has the shape of a normal distribution. It is defined as

$$K(\mathbf{x}, \mathbf{z}) = \exp\left(-\frac{\|\mathbf{x} - \mathbf{z}\|^2}{2\sigma^2}\right),$$

where σ is a positive parameter, which controls the spread of the kernel.

The value of the Gaussian kernel depends on the squared Euclidean distance, $\|\mathbf{x} - \mathbf{z}\|^2$, between $\mathbf{x}$ and $\mathbf{z}$. If this distance is small, then the instances are considered to be similar, and dissimilar if the distance is large. Moreover, if σ^2 is small compared to the distance between $\mathbf{x}$ and $\mathbf{z}$, then the value of the kernel tends to 0, while if it is large, then the kernel tends to 1. It follows that if σ^2 is too small, then SVM will tend to overfit the data, while if it is too large, then it will tend to underfit the data. Therefore, when we are using a Gaussian kernel, tuning σ is important.

SVM maintains its competitiveness in the landscape of machine learning algorithms. However, it is generally considered an inefficient method for large data sets when using nonlinear kernels. Despite this, LSVM is considered to be scalable and performs well in practice even when nonlinearity is present. Pseudocode for SVM is given in Algorithm 4.3, where C is a penalty term.

Algorithm 4.3 SVM

Input: C, $\mathbf{S}$, $(\mathbf{z}, ?)$

  1: Choose the transformation ϕ to be applied to training instances in $\mathbf{S}$

  2: Choose the kernel K to be used when solving the optimisation problem

  3: Solve:

$$\underset{\mathbf{w}, b, \xi}{\arg\min} \tfrac{1}{2}\|w\|^2 + C\sum_{i=1}^{m}\xi_i$$

such that for all i, $y_i(\mathbf{w} \cdot \phi(\mathbf{x}_i) + b) \geq 1 - \xi_i$

  4: Let $\hat{y} = sgn(\mathbf{w} \cdot \phi(\mathbf{z}) + b)$

  5: **return** $(\mathbf{z}, \hat{y})$

4.3.4 Decision Trees and Random Forests

Decision trees are a very popular and well-established classification technique in machine learning. In particular, they are relatively simple to understand and construct for large data sets. They are also interpretable and transparent to nonexperts; that is, they are "white box" models, as opposed to neural networks, which are generally considered to be "black box" models, since studying their structure will not necessarily inform us about the problem being addressed. As before, to simplify the presentation, we will concentrate on binary classification.

To understand the intuition behind decision trees, consider a series of questions and answers, where, for simplicity, we consider binary, *yes* or *no* answers. Consider an example from the medical domain, more specifically, predicting whether a person will have a heart attack. Some of the explanatory features that could be used to predict whether someone is susceptible to a heart attack are age, gender, smoking, drinking, family history, and medical history such as cholesterol levels, chest pain, hypertension, and diabetes. The data set holding the information may be organised in tabular form, with a column for each explanatory feature and an additional yes/no column for the predictor feature. Each row in the table represents the data pertaining to a single person, with the predictor feature being the label; a "yes" label means the person has the disease, and a "no" label means the person does not have the disease. Decision trees lend themselves well to such tabular data where n, the dimensionality of the data, is relatively low. Using our terminology, we will assume, as before, a labelled data set $\mathbf{S} = \{(\mathbf{x}_1, y_1), (\mathbf{x}_2, y_2), \ldots, (\mathbf{x}_m, y_m)\}$, having $m \geq 1$ instances, where each input $\mathbf{x}_i$ is a vector of feature values, and an instance $\mathbf{z}$ in a pair $(\mathbf{z}, ?)$, whose class label is unknown and to be predicted by the algorithm.

An example of a decision tree derived from heart attack data, illustrating a possible series of questions and yes/no answers leading to whether a person is susceptible to a heart attack, is shown in Figure 4.16.

We now will explain what a *tree* is in this context. A tree data structure resembles an upside-down tree (perennial plant) with the *root* node at the top of the tree. The tree items beneath the root are called *nodes*, and the branches connecting the nodes are called *links* (or arcs). Thus, a tree is a hierarchical structure, with each node having zero or more *child* nodes; if the tree is binary, as in our case, where we concentrate on binary classification with yes and no questions, a node will have either zero or two child nodes. In a tree structure, each node has a unique *parent* node unless it is the *root* node, which has no parent. When a node has no child nodes, it is called a *leaf* node; otherwise, it is called an *internal* node; *sibling* nodes are those that share the same parent node. (See Figure 4.17 for an illustration of the node types in a tree data structure.)

A *path* from one node to another in the tree is a sequence of links that join a distinct sequence of nodes to each other; if n_1 is the first node on the path and n_2 is the last node on the path, we say that the path is from node n_1 to node n_2. In a tree there is a unique path connecting any two nodes n_1 and n_2 in the tree. (See Figure 4.18 for an illustration of the concept of a path in a tree data structure. The interpretation of this path in the context of a decision tree is that an individual between 30 and 39 years of age with no symptoms of hypertension is not at risk of a heart attack compared to others in the data set.)

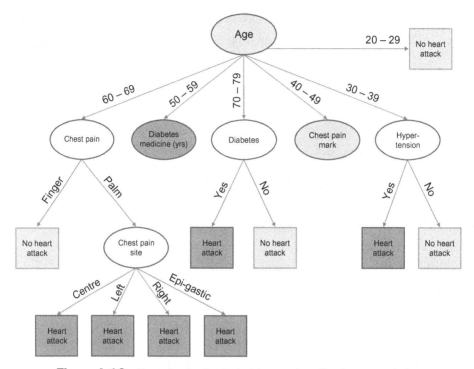

Figure 4.16   Example of a simple decision tree based on heart attack data.

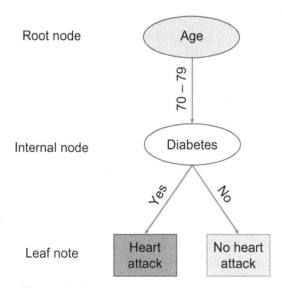

Figure 4.17   Node types in a tree data structure.

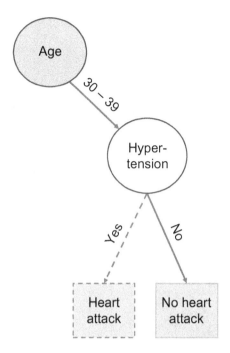

Age --> 30 – 39 --> Hypertension --> No heart attack

Figure 4.18   A path taken from the root node (labelled "Age") through the internal node (labelled "Hypertension") leading to the leaf node (labelled "No heart attack").

In a decision tree, each internal node is labelled by a feature, each leaf node is labelled by a class, and each link is labelled by a binary yes/no test condition leading from the parent node feature to the child node feature (when the child is an internal node) or class (when the child is a leaf node). Thus, each leaf node is labelled by the class output by the decision tree algorithm, for an instance that *satisfies* all the answers from the root to that leaf. For our heart attack example, assume we have two classes *YHA* (yes, will get a heart attack) and *NHA* (no, will not get a heart attack). Then, we may have the following self-explanatory paths from the root *Age* to a leaf labelled *YHA*:

$$Age \xrightarrow{>60} Smoking \xrightarrow{yes} Chest-Pain \xrightarrow{yes} YHA$$

and from the root *Age* to a leaf labelled *NHA*:

$$Age \xrightarrow{>60} Smoking \xrightarrow{no} Chest-Pain \xrightarrow{no} NHA$$

The decision tree construction algorithm starts from an initial tree containing only a single chosen node, its *root* node, with which we associate the full training set **S**.

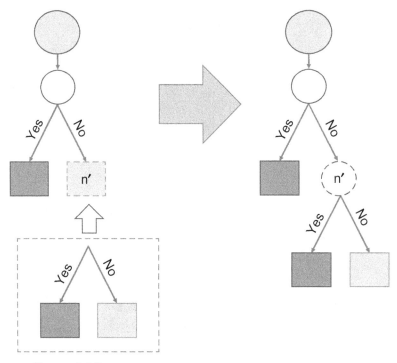

Figure 4.19   Crucial step of the decision tree construction algorithm.

The underlying idea behind the algorithm is that at each stage it operates on an intermediate decision tree, where all nodes in the tree, such as a node n', are associated with a subset $\mathbf{S}'$ of $\mathbf{S}$ in such a way that all the instances $\mathbf{x}'_i$ contained in the subset $\mathbf{S}'$ that are associated with n' satisfy all the answers from the root to this node. The crucial step at each stage of the algorithm is to choose one of the leaf nodes, say n', in the intermediate tree according to some criterion and *splitting* it into two further nodes, as follows. The split occurs by adding to the tree two new leaf nodes, and creating links with the appropriate binary test condition (either yes or no) from n' to these new leaf nodes, which will become children nodes of n'. The chosen leaf node n' then becomes an internal node, and the subset $\mathbf{S}'$ is partitioned accordingly into two disjoint subsets to be associated with the new leaf nodes in such a way that instances comply with the test outcomes; see Figure 4.19 for an illustration of the crucial step. When no more splitting occurs, the intermediate decision tree becomes the final one output by the algorithm. The class label of a leaf node with associated subset $\mathbf{S}'$ is determined according to the majority of class labels in $\mathbf{S}'$.

Node splitting as described here is based on the criteria of *Gini impurity* and the gain in purity from a parent node to a child node. The Gini impurity of a node n' in the decision tree is intuitively the probability that when randomly drawing, with replacement, two instances from the subset $\mathbf{S}'$ of $\mathbf{S}$ associated with n', their labels differ. It is given by

$$G(n') = 1 - \left(P(c_1|n')^2 + P(c_2|n')^2 \right),$$

where $P(c_i|n')$ is the probability of class c_i given a node n' in the decision tree, recalling that we have assumed binary classification: c_1 could be the probability of the "yes" class and c_2 the probability of the "no" class. To compute $P(c_i|n')$, for $i = 1, 2$, we assume that $\mathbf{S}'$ contains m' instances. Then, $P(c_i|n')$ is given by

$$P(c_i|n') = \frac{m'_i}{m'},$$

where m'_i is the number of instances in $\mathbf{S}'$ having class label c_i. It follows that for binary classification, the lower bound of the Gini impurity is $G(n') = 0$, which occurs when $P(c_i|n') = 1$ for $i = 1$ or 2, and its upper bound is $G(n') = 0.5$, which occurs when $P(c_i|n') = 0.5$ for $i = 1$ and 2. When $G(n') = 0$, n' is a *pure* node and no splitting is necessary.

Suppose that we are considering splitting a leaf node n' and linking to it two new leaf nodes n'_1 and n'_2 with associated subsets $\mathbf{S}'_1$ and $\mathbf{S}'_2$, which partition $\mathbf{S}$ according to some binary test condition on a candidate feature that will label n' after the split occurs. Then, the *gain* in impurity in splitting n' with respect to the chosen feature, denoted by ΔG, is given by

$$\Delta G = G(n') - \left(\frac{\#\mathbf{S}'_1}{m'} G(n'_1) + \frac{\#\mathbf{S}'_2}{m'} G(n'_2) \right),$$

where $\#\mathbf{S}'_i$ is the number of instance in $\mathbf{S}'_i$, for $i = 1, 2$.

The underlying idea of the decision tree algorithm is to choose the feature that maximises the gain when splitting the node. Obviously if $G(n') = 0$, then n' is pure and no split will lead to any gain. Moreover, it has been shown that the gain is always non-negative, implying that if the gain is higher, then the split will lead to less impurity in the new children nodes. Pseudocode for the decision tree algorithm, which we call DT, is given in Algorithm 4.4, where θ is a non-negative threshold value.

A known disadvantage of decision trees is their instability to changes in the training data set, so a relatively small change in the input may lead to a significant change in its predictions. Another disadvantage is that their output may produce complex trees that do not generalise well to correctly classify new unseen instances. This is especially true if we

---

Algorithm 4.4 DT

Input: θ, $\mathbf{S}$, $(\mathbf{z}, ?)$

1: Let T be the decision tree, initialised as a single node, n', its root,
    with which we associate the full training set $\mathbf{S}$
2: Let ΔG, the gain in impurity, be the maximum gain from splitting n'
3: **while** $\Delta G > \theta$ **do**
4:     Split n' by adding two new leaves n'_1 and n'_2 to T as described above
5:     Let ΔG be the maximum gain in impurity from splitting a leaf,
       say n' in T, according to a binary test condition on some feature
6: **end while**
7: Let $\hat{y}$ be the label of the leaf node in T that is satisfied by $\mathbf{z}$
8: **return** $(\mathbf{z}, \hat{y})$

---

set the threshold θ in Algorithm 4.4 to 0, when the resulting decision tree will perfectly classify the training set, most likely resulting in overfitting the data and a loss in generalisation capability. One simple way of reducing overfitting is to increase θ, but if the increase is excessive, then the output tree will result in underfitting; thus, tuning the hyperparameter θ for this purpose is required as a further validation step in the decision tree algorithm. Another method to combat these problems is *pruning* the tree before it is finally output, by removing branches of the tree that may cause overfitting. Let us call a parent of a leaf node a *frontier* node. Then, a simple yet effective bottom-up pruning method, called *reduced error pruning*, considers the removal of a frontier node in the tree output by Algorithm 4.4, if the performance of the pruned tree on a further validation set of instances is no worse than its performance prior to pruning the frontier node. This process is repeated on the pruned tree until further pruning of frontier nodes reduces the performance of the resulting tree.

To further address the shortcomings of decision trees as a learning technique, the *random forest* method has been proposed. In a nutshell, the idea is to construct multiple decision tree learners, employing randomness in doing so, and using a *majority vote* of the tree learners to decide on the class of an unseen instance. The method of employing multiple learners, who may be or may not be using the same learning algorithm to make a decision, is called *ensemble learning*. The expectation is that by employing multiple learners, as in a random forest, the ensemble would improve the performance of the learning task relative to what it may have done with an individual learner; this can be viewed as a form of the wisdom of crowds. In general, ensemble methods tend to work well when there is diversity among the multiple learners; in the case of the random forest method, the diversity manifests itself in the training set used for each decision tree learner and in the chosen hyperparameters of the algorithm (we give more detail in the following paragraphs).

The main steps of the random forest method can be summarised as follows. In the first step, multiple bootstrap samples (see Section 2.2 in Chapter 2) are taken from the training set **S**, where each bootstrap sample has m instances, noting that due to resampling with replacement, the same instance may appear more than once in any of the samples. In this case, there are diminishing returns in having more than $N = 100$ bootstrap samples. In the second step, a decision tree is constructed for each of the bootstrap samples, resulting in a forest. However, when we split a node in the construction of a tree in the forest, only a random subset of $\sqrt{n}$ features are considered. Finally, when the constructed forest is presented with an unseen instance, its class is predicted according to a majority vote among the trees in the forest. This general process of building an ensemble from a collection of bootstrap samples and then building a classifier from each sample is called *bootstrap aggregation* or simply *bagging*.

Example 4.7. The heart disease data set, known as the Cleveland database, was compiled by several medical institutions. The data records 76 attributes about 303 patients, but published work has only referred to using a subset of 14 of them. These include, amongst others, age; gender, where 0 is female and 1 is male; chest pain type (CP) experienced by the patient, using a range of integer values from 1 to 4 (1 = typical angina, 2 = atypical angina, 3 = nonanginal pain, and 4 = asymptotic); resting blood pressure (RBP) in millimeters of mercury (mmHg); cholesterol in milligrams per 100 millilitres (mg/dl); and diagnosis of whether the patient is suffering from heart disease or not, where 0 indicates absence (label= 0) and presence is indicated on a range from 1 to 4 (label> 0). See Table 4.14 for a sample from the data set.

The confusion matrix summarising the performance of the decision tree model trained on the heart disease data set is shown in Figure 4.20 and the precision, recall, and F1 for the decision tree model are shown in stylised form in Table 4.15. Correspondingly, the confusion matrix for the random forest model applied to the heart disease data set is shown in Figure 4.21 and the precision, recall, and F1 for the random forest model are shown in stylised form in Table 4.16.

Table 4.14 A sample from the heart disease data set, where the diagnosis is made on a range of 0 to 4, with 0 indicating absence and 1 to 4 indicating presence in increasing severity; the class label is a binary variable, where 0 indicates absence of heart disease (i.e., diagnosis = 0) and 1 indicates presence (i.e., diagnosis > 0).

Age	Gender	CP	RBP	Cholesterol	Diagnosis	Label
35	1	2	122	192	0	0
37	1	3	130	250	0	0
41	0	2	130	204	0	0
41	1	4	110	172	1	1
56	1	2	120	236	0	0
57	0	4	120	354	0	0
57	1	4	140	192	0	0
60	1	4	130	206	4	1
62	0	4	140	268	3	1
63	1	4	130	254	2	1

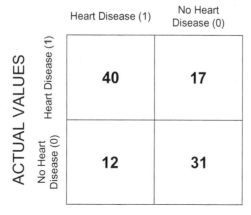

Figure 4.20 The confusion matrix for the decision tree classifier trained on the heart disease data set.

Table 4.15   The precision, recall, and F1 score for a decision tree classifier applied to the heart disease data set, with a 67–33 split between the training and test data.

Label	Precision	Recall	F1	Support
$Class_0$	0.72	0.65	0.68	43
$Class_1$	0.70	0.77	0.73	57
Total support:	100			
Micro-averaged F1:	0.71			
Macro-averaged F1:	0.71			

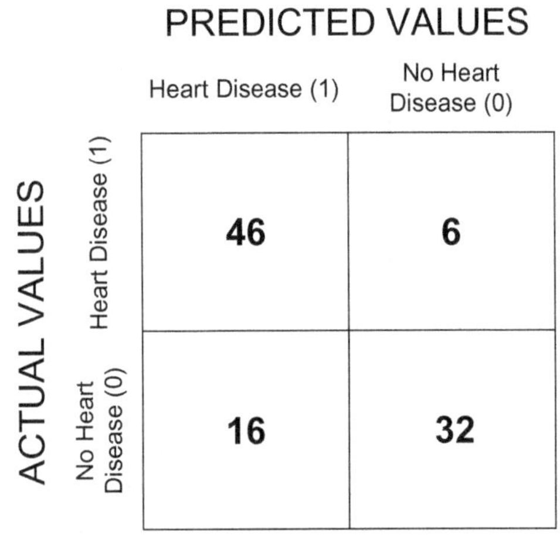

PREDICTED VALUES

Figure 4.21   The confusion matrix for the random forest classifier trained on the heart disease data set.

The F1 score for both the decision tree and random forest classifiers is higher for $Class_1$ than for $Class_0$. However, of the two classifiers, the random forest model performed better than the decision tree model, with an F1 of 0.79 compared to 0.71.

Random forests have proven to be a more effective method than using just a single decision tree, as we obtain a variety of trees that, taken as a whole, address the problem of individual trees overfitting the training data. Another aspect is that by reducing the number features for each tree, when n is large, random forests deal with the problem of

Table 4.16 The precision, recall, and F1 score for a random forest classifier applied to the heart disease data set, a 67–33 split between the training and test data.

Label	Precision	Recall	F1	Support
$Class_0$	0.86	0.67	0.75	48
$Class_1$	0.75	0.90	0.82	52
Total support:	100			
Micro-averaged F1:	0.79			
Macro-averaged F1:	0.79			

high-dimensional data. Pseudocode for the random forest algorithm, which we call RF, is given in Algorithm 4.5, where N is the number of bootstrap samples taken from the training data set, $\mathbf{S}$, and θ is the threshold value for the decision tree algorithm.

Algorithm 4.5 RF

Input: N, θ, $\mathbf{S}$, $(\mathbf{z}, ?)$
1: Take N bootstrap samples $\mathbf{B}_i$ from $\mathbf{S}$
2: Let $(\mathbf{z}, \hat{y}_i) = \text{DT}(\theta, \mathbf{B}_i, \mathbf{z}, ?)$, for $i = 1, 2, \ldots, N$, where in DT
   $\sqrt{n}$ out of n features are chosen randomly as candidates for node splitting
3: Let $\hat{y}$ be the majority class label out of $\hat{y}_1, \hat{y}_2, \ldots, \hat{y}_N$.
4: **return** $(\mathbf{z}, \hat{y})$

Decision trees and random forests are widely deployed by data science practitioners due to their simplicity, effectiveness, and interpretability. However, random forests are not a panacea, since scaling them to large data sets (when m is large) has been challenging due to the potentially prohibitive size of the bootstrap samples. Moreover, the complexity is exacerbated when there are a large number of decision trees to construct (i.e., when N is large). It is also worth pointing out that for data that is not inherently tabular, such as time series data, random forests may not be suitable.

4.3.5 Neural Networks and Deep Learning

Neural networks (NNs, or in full *artificial neural networks*) are a very popular machine learning method with data scientists. This may seem surprising given that NNs are inherently black box models; that is, there is a dichotomy between their structure, as seen by the data scientist, and the semantics of the problem being solved. The bottom line is that the performance of NNs has proven to be very competitive on a wide range of applications, such as image classification, speech recognition, natural language processing, and time series forecasting. There is also an element of what is fashionable, and this, of course, changes over time.

The structure underlying a NN is a *network* comprising *nodes*, which in this context are simple processing units (or artificial neurons), and weighted links connecting the nodes, the *weights* indicating the strength of connection between two linked nodes. We will generally assume that the network is *directed*; that is, a link from n_1 to n_2 does not necessarily imply that there is a link from n_2 to n_1. Many of the NN architectures, such as *feedforward* NNs, are *acyclic*, while others, such as *recurrent* NNs, are *cyclic*. A network is *cyclic* if it contains one or more cycles; otherwise, it is *acyclic*, where a *cycle* is defined as a sequence of nodes $\langle n_1, n_2, \ldots n_k, n_1 \rangle$, with links from n_i to n_{i+1}, for $i = 1, 2, \ldots, k-1$, and a further link from n_k to n_1, where the only repeated node in the sequence is n_1, which is the first and last node.

A NN is normally organised in *layers*, where a layer is a collection of sibling nodes operating at a particular depth of the network; see Figure 4.22. In a feedforward NN, the *input* layer is a collection of nodes, none of which have any parents, while none of the nodes in the *output* layer have any children. There can be zero or more *hidden* layers, which come in between the input and output layers, each having both parents and children; note that the network may not be a tree, in which case a node may have more than one parent node. If the network is cyclic, such as a recurrent NN, we still have these three types of layers, with additional links between them producing cycles in the network.

NNs are thus very flexible in the sense that a variety of architectures can be used and, within any architecture, such as feedforward networks, a choice is to be made on the number of layers and nodes within each layer. Moreover, varying operational semantics are attached to different network architectures, and we are barely able to touch the surface here. In fact, many books have been written on the many aspects of NNs, both in terms of

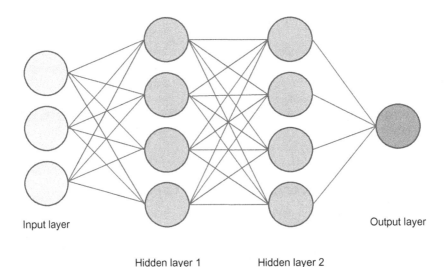

Input layer

Output layer

Hidden layer 1   Hidden layer 2

Figure 4.22   Example of a feedforward NN with two hidden layers.

how they operate as a machine learning method and on their application in a variety of domains.

It is worth mentioning that setting aside the neural hype, several robust software packages are available for nonexperts to construct NNs, which are both scalable and allow for flexibility in training and testing the constructed networks. On the other hand, tuning NNs can be an arduous task, with many parameters to tune, so it is unlikely that the budding data scientist will achieve the best possible results without gaining some expertise and experience in the art of deploying NNs.

To confuse the issue, there is also *deep learning* for NNs, which is essentially the ability to train NNs with many hidden layers, where the data is transformed from one layer to the next one. Deep learning was made possible due to advances in hardware, such as the availability of GPUs (graphical processing units) for accelerating the computation, and many ingenious heuristics that have been developed over the years both to speed up computation and improve the accuracy of training NNs. As a result of the concerted effort in NN technology in the context of deep learning, NNs have overshadowed other methods due to their impressive performance, when tuned properly and trained with sufficient computing resources. However, at the end of the day, the choice of which machine learning method to use is guided by the specific task to be solved, and NNs are not a panacea for all machine learning tasks.

We start our short journey into the land of NNs by introducing the simplest NN, the *perceptron*, which is a feedforward NN (see Figure 4.22) with no hidden layers (see Figure 4.23). As before, we will assume a labelled training data set $\mathbf{S}$ having $m \geq 1$ instances, where $(\mathbf{x}, y)$ in $\mathbf{S}$, with each instance $\mathbf{x} = \langle x_1, x_2, \ldots, x_n \rangle$ having n features,

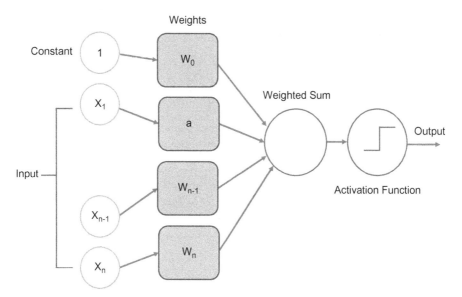

Figure 4.23 Example of a perceptron, that is, a feedforward NN with no hidden layers.

and another instance $\mathbf{z} = \langle z_1, z_2, \ldots, z_n \rangle$ in a pair $(\mathbf{z}, ?)$, whose class label is unknown and to be predicted as $\hat{y}$ by the machine learning algorithm.

In Figure 4.23 we see that the instance $\mathbf{x}$ is fed into the perceptron's network, together with an additional fixed constant, x_0, which is independent of $\mathbf{x}$ and normally set to 1. We have $n+1$ weights connecting the input and output layers, resulting in a single output being computed; there is one weight per feature and an additional weight, w_0, determining a *bias* term $b = w_0 x_0$. The single output is computed via a pipeline of two nodes comprising the output layer. The first computes the weighted sum, $\mathbf{w} \cdot \mathbf{x} + b$, and the second applies an activation function to this sum.

In a perceptron, the decision function f to be learnt, predicting $\hat{y} = f(\mathbf{x})$, is thus given by

$$f(\mathbf{x}) = \phi\left(\mathbf{w} \cdot \mathbf{x} + b\right),$$

where $\mathbf{w} = \langle w_1, w_2, \ldots, w_n \rangle$ is a vector of n weights, $b = w_0 x_0$ is a bias term computed via an additional weight w_0 and the constant input x_0, normally set to 1, and ϕ is an *activation function*, as discussed in the following paragraphs.

Activation functions allow us to add nonlinearity to the output of a node in the network. It is important to note that if we do not use activation functions (i.e., we assume the activation function is the identity mapping), then a multilayer NN reduces to a linear regression model. Introducing nonlinearity into the activation function of a multilayer network allows NNs to approximate any continuous function to any level of precision; this is called the *universal approximation theorem*. It is also desirable for the activation to be differentiable to allow the use of gradient descent, introduced in the following paragraphs, in training the network.

Two of the most common activation functions, apart from the identity function $\phi(v) = v$ for a value v, are the sigmoid and rectifier functions. The *sigmoid* (or *logistic*) function, σ, is given by

$$\sigma(v) = \frac{1}{1 + \exp(-v)},$$

noting that we have already used σ to denote the standard deviation and will therefore make sure that no confusion occurs. It is worth mentioning the *hyperbolic tangent* (tanh), which is a rescaled version of the sigmoid function such that it is between $+1$ and -1 and centred at 0. It is given by

$$tanh(v) = \frac{\exp(v) - \exp(-v)}{\exp(v) + \exp(-v)}.$$

The *rectifier* function, $RELU$, is given by

$$RELU(v) = max(0, v),$$

where $max(0, v)$ is the maximum of 0 and v, also written in this case as x^+. Note that although $RELU$ is close to being linear, it is not linear. In addition, $RELU$ is not differentiable at the single point 0; however, for practical purposes, one can set the derivative at 0 to be 0, and gradient descent, described next, will be well behaved.

The sigmoid function introduces nonlinearity into the output by squashing it to be between 0 and 1; therefore, the sigmoid function can be interpreted as a probability. On the other hand, the $RELU$ function is easy to compute and performs well within deep networks with many layers. A problem with the sigmoid function in the presence of many layers is known as the *vanishing gradient* problem. Essentially, since the sigmoid function is exponential, when the gradient is less than 1, it will decay very fast and get close to 0 over a chain of multiplications, and thus have a detrimental effect on gradient descent, leading to poor learning. (The converse problem, when the gradient is larger than 1, is called the exploding gradient problem.) The $RELU$ activation function can be seen to resolve this problem because its derivative is 1 as long as $v > 0$, although its derivative drops to 0 when v is negative, in which case it will lead to a "dead" neuron and the weight will remain unchanged at that point. This can be resolved with a variant of $RELU$, called *leaky RELU*, which is defined as $max(0.01x, x)$, whose derivative is always positive; the constant 0.01 is empirical and may be replaced by another small positive constant less than one.

Returning to the perceptron whose decision function f, given by

$$\hat{y} = f(\mathbf{x}) = \phi\left(\mathbf{w} \cdot \mathbf{x} + b\right),$$

we now introduce the *delta rule*, which is a gradient descent optimisation method for modifying the weights in the network to approximate f, providing the basic building block for training a multilayer NN using the backpropagation method described later.

The intuition behind the delta rule is to minimise the error, $y - \hat{y}$, between the prediction $\hat{y} = f(\mathbf{x})$ and the label y from the training pair $(\mathbf{x}, y)$ by moving, in proportional steps, in the opposite direction of the gradient. We will assume that we are minimising the MSE (mean squared error),

$$E = \frac{1}{2}\left(y - \hat{y}\right)^2,$$

although other loss functions may be used; the factor of $1/2$ is introduced to simplify the derivative.

On using the chain rule from calculus,

$$\frac{\partial E}{\partial w_i} = \frac{\partial E}{\partial \hat{y}}\frac{\partial \hat{y}}{\partial w_i} = -\left(y - \hat{y}\right)\frac{\partial \hat{y}}{\partial w_i} = -\left(y - \hat{y}\right)\phi'\left(\mathbf{w} \cdot \mathbf{x} + b\right)\frac{\partial w_i x_i}{\partial w_i}$$
$$= -\left(y - \hat{y}\right)\phi'\left(\mathbf{w} \cdot \mathbf{x} + b\right)x_i,$$

where ∂ is the partial derivative symbol and ϕ' is the derivative of the activation function.

Now, the *learning rate* α is a hyperparameter between 0 and 1, which affects the rate at which the delta rule modifies the weights during the learning process. If it is set to a value that is too small, the learning may take a long time, whereas if the learning rate is too high, then the resulting model may be suboptimal, since gradient descent may not converge. The learning rate can be tuned, but we will not go into this issue here.

We can now present the delta rule, for the weight w_i in $\mathbf{w}$, denoted as Δw_i, by

$$\Delta w_i = -\alpha \frac{\partial E}{\partial w_i} = \alpha \left(y - \hat{y} \right) \phi' \left(\mathbf{w} \cdot \mathbf{x} + b \right) x_i,$$

noting that this also applies to the bias term on setting $w_i = w_0$ and $x_i = x_0$.

Pseudocode for learning the weights in a perceptron is given in Algorithm 4.6, where we assume $x_0 = 1$. In the algorithm, T is a hyperparameter defining the number of *epochs*, that is, the number of times the machine learning algorithm will loop through the training set. To distinguish between the weights in each epoch, they are superscripted with the epoch number. We have assumed that we update the weights for each training pair; however, it is also possible to update the weights in *batches*, that is, only after several training pairs have been processed, depending on the batch size. To avoid overfitting, we may evaluate the model after each epoch on the validation set and stop training if the performance of the model has degraded. It is also possible to stop training if the MSE drops below a threshold, but it is not always clear how to set the threshold.

Algorithm 4.6 Perceptron

Input: S, $(\mathbf{z}, ?)$

  1: Initialise $\mathbf{w}$ to small positive random values and set $w_0 = 0$

  2: **for** $t = 0 : T-1$ **do**   % T is the number of epochs

  3:     **for** all pairs $(\mathbf{x}, y) \in \mathbf{S}$ **do**   % Loop over all pairs in the training set

  4:         **for** $i = 0 : n$ **do**   % Loop over all the weights

  5:              $w_i^{t+1} = w_i^t + \Delta w_i^t$ % Update the weights with the delta rule

  6:         **end for**

  7:     **end for**

  8: **end for**

  9: Let $\hat{y} = \phi \left(\mathbf{w} \cdot \mathbf{z} + b \right)$

 10: **return** $(\mathbf{z}, \hat{y})$

The backpropagation method extends gradient descent, as implemented by the delta rule, from perceptrons to feedforward networks with one or more hidden layers. In the backpropagation algorithm, the weight parameters in the NN are updated iteratively, layer by layer, employing the delta rule at each stage, starting from the output layer and working back to the input layer. To understand the iterative step, assume that the weights between two layers have been updated using the delta rule. In the first instance, the weights between the last hidden layer and the output layer have just been updated and, more generally, the weights between the $(i-1)$th layer and the ith layer are the ones that have just been updated. The algorithm now has to update the weights between the $(i-2)$th and $(i-1)$th layer; in the second instance, after the first update of weights, these will be the weights between the last hidden layer and the layer that came before it. The trick to get the job done is to treat the $(i-1)$th layer as if it were the output layer and proceed as before using the delta rule. There is, of course, some bookkeeping to take care of, since the $(i-1)$th layer may contain several nodes, and we thus may need to compute a sum to obtain the current output from a node in the $(i-2)$th layer. Otherwise, we proceed in the same manner. We encourage readers to fill in the details themselves, or look it up and carefully follow the derivation, since the backpropagation method has been highly influential and is widely used in training NNs.

Example 4.8. The *Titanic* data set describes the survival status of individual passengers on this tragic voyage. The data set contains records of the passengers who embarked on the voyage, including their passenger class (pclass), gender, age, the amount they paid for the fare (fare), and their cabin location, if known (cabin). The class label, survived, indicates whether the passenger survived the disaster, labelled as class 1, or did not survive, labelled as class 0; see Table 4.17 for a sample from the data set.

We first apply a perceptron (a feedforward NN with no hidden layers) to categorise the survival status of the *Titanic* passengers; the confusion matrix summarising the performance of trained model is shown in Figure 4.24. The precision, recall, and F1 for the NN model are shown in stylised form in Table 4.18. Second, we apply a feedforward NN with a

Table 4.17 A sample from the *Titanic* data set recording attributes of the passengers who embarked on the voyage, including their passenger class, gender, age, amount paid in fares, and their cabin location, if known. The class label, Survived, is a binary variable, where 1 means the passenger survived the disaster and 0 means they did not survive.

Pclass	Gender	Age	Fare	Cabin	Survived
1	female	38.0	71.2833	C85	1
3	female	26.0	7.9250	N/A	1
1	female	35.0	53.1000	C123	1
3	male	22.0	7.2500	N/A	0
3	male	35.0	8.0500	N/A	0

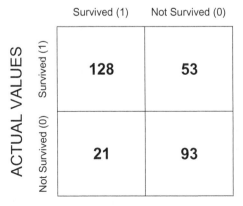

Figure 4.24 The confusion matrix for the perceptron trained on the *Titanic* data set.

Table 4.18 The precision, recall, and F1 score for the perceptron with a 67–33 split between the training and test data, which was used to classify those passengers who survived (labelled as class 1) and those who did not survive (labelled as class 0) the *Titanic* voyage.

Label	Precision	Recall	F1	Support
$Class_0$	0.64	0.82	0.72	114
$Class_1$	0.86	0.71	0.78	181
Total support:	295			
Micro-averaged F1:	0.74			
Macro-averaged F1:	0.75			

PREDICTED VALUES

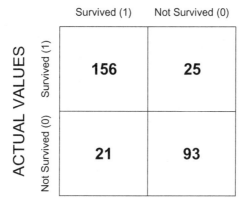

Figure 4.25 The confusion matrix for a feedforward neural network with one hidden layer trained on the *Titanic* data set.

single hidden layer to categorise the survival of the *Titanic* pasengers; the confusion matrix summarising the performance of the trained model is shown in Figure 4.25. The precision, recall, and F1 for the feedforward NN with a single hidden layer are shown in stylised form in Table 4.19. Third, we apply a feedfoward NN with two hidden layers to categorise the survival status of the *Titanic* passengers; the confusion matrix summarising the performance of the trained model is shown in Figure 4.26. The precision, recall, and F1 for the feedforward NN with two hidden layers are shown in stylised form in Table 4.20.

Table 4.19 The precision, recall, and F1 score for a feedforward neural network with a single hidden layer, with 12 neurons with a 67–33 split between the training and test data, which was used to classify those passengers who survived (labelled as 1) and those who did not survive (labelled as class 0) the *Titanic* voyage.

Label	Precision	Recall	F1	Support
Class$_0$	0.76	0.68	0.72	114
Class$_1$	0.81	0.86	0.84	181
Total support:	295			
Micro-averaged F1:	0.79			
Macro-averaged F1:	0.78			

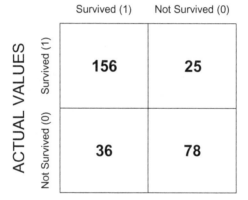

PREDICTED VALUES

Figure 4.26 The confusion matrix for a feedforward neural network with two hidden layers trained on the *Titanic* data set.

We briefly mention several neural architectures that go beyond feedforward networks. In particular, we introduce convolutional NNs, recurrent NNs, long short-term memory networks, and attention mechanisms. Many other heuristics and variations aim to improve some aspect of NNs, and these are being documented as they are invented. Because NNs are a modular architecture, there seems to be no end to the possibilities of extending their capabilities.

Convolutional neural networks (CNNs) are specifically designed for tasks that involve processing multidimensional data and spatially oriented inputs such as image data presented as a two-dimensional grid of pixel data; the two-dimensional input, which we will assume for simplicity, also lends itself to other applications, notably board games such as Go and

Table 4.20   The precision, recall, and F1 score for a feedforward
neural network with two hidden layers, each with 12 neurons with a
67–33 split between the training and test data, which was used to
classify those passengers who survived (labelled as class 1) and those
who did not survive (labelled as class 0) the *Titanic* voyage.

Label	Precision	Recall	F1	Support
$Class_0$	0.97	0.50	0.66	114
$Class_1$	0.76	0.99	0.86	181
Total support:	295			
Micro-averaged F1:	0.80			
Macro-averaged F1:	0.76			

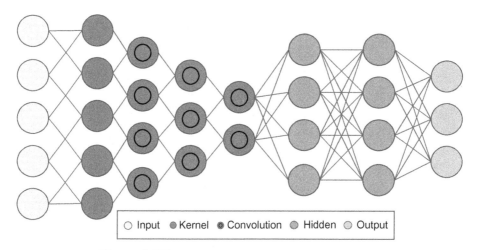

○ Input ● Kernel ◉ Convolution ● Hidden ○ Output

Figure 4.27   Example of a convolutional neural network.

Chess. CNNs distinguish themselves from other architectures by the provision of
convolutional layers, which comprise a collection of *filters* (also known as *kernels*); see
Figure 4.27 for an example of the CNN architecture. Each filter learns a specific feature or
pattern, such as an edge, a corner, a simple shape, or more complex features in deeper
convolutional layers, composed from simpler features from shallower convolutional layers.
Each filter in a convolutional layer is specified as a matrix of numbers, say a 3-by-3 matrix.
Operationally, in a forward pass of the convolutional network, each filter slides over every
3-by-3 block of pixels in the input, computing the dot product of the filter with the block
and storing it. The output of the convolutional layer, pertaining to its filters, results in a
new *stacked* representation of the input consisting of the convolutions of the filters with the
input image. This representation is then passed to the next convolutional layer, resulting in
yet another representation of the input, resulting from the convolution of the filter from

the next layer and the representation passed to it from the previous layer. To reduce the size of the stack passed on to the next layer, *max pooling* is deployed, which reduces each 3-by-3 slice to its maximum value. Other "tricks" (or if you prefer, heuristics) such as weight sharing, to make sure that a filter uses the same weights when computing the dot product with a convolutional layer, are employed to make the process more efficient. This process is then iterated across further convolutional layers of the CNN. Note that the filters are learnt as part of the CNN's learning algorithm through backpropagation.

Recurrent neural networks (RNNs) allow cycles in the network architecture to enable the modelling of sequential information of varying length such as time series. Typically, in an RNN, previous outputs can be fed back into the network as inputs; see Figure 4.28 for an example of the RNN architecture. The additional expressivity of RNNs compared to feedforward networks is that they possess internal memory; that is, they can remember information that they processed in the past. To train RNNs, we deploy a variant of the backpropagation algorithm, called *backpropagation through time* (BPTT). The intuition behind BPTT is straightforward: When applying a forward pass through the network and a backward link leading to a previously visited node is encountered, the network is unfolded by copying revisited nodes, resulting in a feedfoward NN to which backpropagation can be applied. Of course, there is some housekeeping to keep track of when computing BPTT, such as sharing weights between copied parts of the network. However, for long sequences, BPTT suffers from the vanishing gradient problem, mentioned previously. One solution to this problem, alluded to earlier, is to replace sigmoid activations with RELU activations, which are designed to address this problem. However, the performance of the RNN is sensitive to the network's initial weights. A proposed solution that has proven to be effective is to initialise the recurrent weight matrix (which is a square matrix) to be the identity matrix.

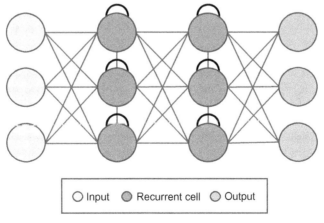

Figure 4.28   Example of a recurrent neural network.

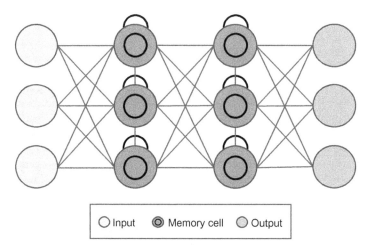

Figure 4.29 Example of a long short-term memory NN.

Another method for dealing with the vanishing gradient problem is to use a special kind of RNN, called *long short-term memory* (LSTM) networks, where nodes in hidden layers are replaced by LSTM memory units; see Figure 4.29 for an example of the LSTM architecture. An LSTM unit has the capability of long-term memory, which is useful, for example, in text where there may be long-term dependencies between passages. Technically, an LSTM unit is composed of a cell, which is responsible for storing the information; that is, it is the memory part of the unit, with three gates controlling the flow of information: input, output, and forget. The input gate is responsible for adding information to the cell state, the output gate is responsible for selecting the information from the cell state to show as an output, and the forget gate is responsible for removing information from the cell state. The training of LSTM networks can now proceed along the lines of RNNs using BPTT.

Lastly, we mention the *attention* mechanism in NNs, which enable the network to focus on relevant subsets of an input sequence when constructing an output sequence. For example, when the input is textual and words are presented to the network one by one, only several words may be relevant to the task when presented with the next word. Here, we concentrate on *sequence to sequence* (seq2seq) models, used, for example, in machine translation and image captioning, where an input sequence is transformed into an output sequence. In seq2seq models, the two key components are an *encoder* network and a *decoder* network. The role of the encoder is to convert each item in the input into a vector representation and, after the input sequence has been processed, the resulting internal vector representation is passed on to the decoder, which reverses the process and restores the original items from this representation. *Attention weights* are formed from subsets of the input to decide on which part of the input sequence the decoder should pay attention to when producing the output. At each stage the attention weights tell the decoder what relevant *context* it should be looking at, thus avoiding considering the whole sequence as its current context, which would lead to memory problems, since NNs find larger sequences harder to memorise.

As a final thought, the input to a NN may be more complex than a sequence and come in the form of a graph or a network, in which case we are in the realm of *graph neural networks* (GNNs). Graphs were introduced in Section 3.6 in the context of social network data, but they are prevalent in many areas that are naturally couched in terms of graphs, such as transportation, communication networks, biology, chemistry, and computer vision. In a nutshell, the underlying idea of GNNs is to map the input graph to an internal representation that allows classification or prediction tasks of graph properties at either the graph level, the node level, or the edge level.

To summarise, NNs are scalable, very flexible, and well performing and there are many architectures to choose from. On the flip side, NNs are a black box model, can be complex, and are generally hard to tune. There is, however, a grand goal to achieve in what is called *end-to-end* learning, where a single NN will provide a model for the whole system pipeline from the input data to the final output.

Due to the broadness of the NN literature, it is possible to cover only the fundamental notions and give a sense of how NNs work and what purpose they may be used for. We close this section with a famous quote from Donald Hebb, a famous 20th-century neuropsychologist: "Neurons that fire together wire together," referred to as Hebb's law, which provided inspiration for the field of artificial NNs. It succinctly summarises how NNs work.

Finally, we note that it is useful to distinguish between two types of models constructed by supervised methods, that is, discriminative and generative models. For an input, output pair $(\mathbf{x}, y)$ from a labelled data set $\mathbf{S}$, a model that estimates $P(y|\mathbf{x})$ is called *discriminative*, while one that estimates $P(\mathbf{x}, y) = P(y)P(\mathbf{x}|y)$ is called *generative*. Thus, a discriminative model tells how likely the output y is given the input $\mathbf{x}$, as, for example, is done by SVMs. On the other hand, a generative model tells us how to generate sample outputs such as y from inputs such as $\mathbf{x}$, as, for example, is done by naive Bayes.

4.4 Unsupervised Methods

Because we are dealing with unsupervised methods, we will assume an unlabelled data set $\mathbf{U} = \{(\mathbf{x}_1, ?), (\mathbf{x}_2, ?), \ldots, (\mathbf{x}_m, ?)\}$, with $m \geq 1$, where, as for supervised models, each input instance $\mathbf{x}_i$ is a vector of n feature values $\mathbf{x}_i = \langle x_{i1}, x_{i2}, \ldots, x_{in} \rangle$; when convenient we will not distinguish between $\mathbf{U}$ and its instances $\{\mathbf{x}_1, \mathbf{x}_2, \ldots, \mathbf{x}_m\}$, and refer to both simply as $\mathbf{U}$. In unsupervised learning, the task of the machine learning algorithm is to assign an output label y_i to $\mathbf{x}_i$, corresponding to the cluster or group $\mathbf{x}_i$ belongs to, so $(\mathbf{x}_i, ?)$ becomes the pair $(\mathbf{x}_i, y_i)$. Once the labels are assigned to instances in $\mathbf{U}$, it becomes a labelled data set, and we will refer to it as $\mathbf{S}$ according to our previous convention. Because distance measures play a key role in many unsupervised learning algorithms, we refer readers to Subsection 4.1, where we defined some commonly used distance measures.

The two main methods employed in unsupervised learning are *cluster analysis* and *dimensionality reduction*. The goal of clustering is to group the input data set into clusters, which are subsets of the data, in such a way that, in some well-defined sense, instances within clusters are more similar to each other than to instances across clusters. On the other hand, the goal of dimensionality reduction is to reduce the number of features in multivariate instances such as $\mathbf{z} = \langle z_1, z_2, \ldots, z_n \rangle$, having $n > 1$ dimensions or features, especially if n is much greater than 1. In particular, the goal of the reduction is to transform the n-dimensional space into a lower dimensional one whilst preserving the original space as far as possible, thus addressing the curse of dimensionality problem and making it easier to analyse and visualise the data.

4.4.1 K-Means

The k-means algorithm, where k is a parameter specifying the number of clusters to produce, can be viewed as the workhorse of clustering algorithms due its ease of use and relative effectiveness. As with KNN, distance measures (see Section 4.1) are critical to the formulation of k-means.

Assuming k clusters having labels $1, 2, \ldots, k$, as described in Subsection 4.2.2, we transform the unlabelled pairs $(\mathbf{x}_j, ?) \in \mathbf{U}$ into labelled pairs $(\mathbf{x}_j, \lambda(\mathbf{x}_j))$, where $y_i = \lambda(\mathbf{x}_j)$ is the cluster label of $\mathbf{x}_j$, resulting in the labelled data set,

$$\mathbf{S} = \{(\mathbf{x}_1, \lambda(\mathbf{x}_1)), (\mathbf{x}_2, \lambda(\mathbf{x}_2)), \ldots, (\mathbf{x}_m, \lambda(\mathbf{x}_m))\}.$$

$\mathbf{S}$ is thus partitioned into k clusters $\mathbf{S}_i$, for $i = 1, 2, \ldots, k$, in such a way that all instances in $\mathbf{S}_i$ have the same label i, that is, for all $\mathbf{x}_j \in \mathbf{S}_i, y_i = \lambda(\mathbf{x}_j) = i$. Each cluster $\mathbf{S}_i$ is represented by a *centroid* $\mathbf{c}_i$, as defined in Subsection 4.2.2, giving rise to k centroids, $\mathbf{C} = \{\mathbf{c}_1, \mathbf{c}_2, \ldots, \mathbf{c}_k\}$. Thus, in k-means the centroid $\mathbf{c}_i$ of cluster $\mathbf{S}_i$ is computed as the average of all the instances in the cluster. In addition, we have a reference distance measure D such that the centroids $\mathbf{c}_i$ satisfy the property that

$(\mathbf{x}_j, i)$ belongs to cluster $\mathbf{S}_i$, if $\mathbf{c}_i$ is the closest centroid to $\mathbf{x}_j$ under D,

that is, the distance (or dissimilarity), $D(\mathbf{x}_j, \mathbf{c}_i)$, between $\mathbf{x}_j$ and $\mathbf{c}_i$ is the smallest over all centroids in $\mathbf{C}$; if a tie occurs and $\mathbf{x}_j$ has the same smallest distance to two or more centroids, then one of the clusters is chosen randomly as the target cluster.

The k-means algorithm, whose pseudocode is given in Algorithm 4.7, proceeds in an iterative fashion, improving the distribution of instances to clusters until the algorithm converges.

An important property of the k-means algorithm, assuming D is the squared Euclidean distance, is that it minimises the loss function given by the sum of squared error (SSE; introduced in Subsection 4.2.2),

$$\sum_{i=1}^{k} \sum_{\mathbf{x}_j \in \mathbf{S}_i} \|\mathbf{x}_j - \mathbf{c}_i\|^2,$$

Algorithm 4.7 k-means

Input: k, D, $\mathbf{U}$,

1: Select k instances $\mathbf{C} = \{\mathbf{c}_1, \mathbf{c}_2, \ldots, \mathbf{c}_k\}$ from $\mathbf{U}$ as initial centroids

2: Let $\mathbf{S}$ become $\mathbf{U}$ % The output will be labelled

3: **repeat**

4:      Assign each $\mathbf{x}_j \in \mathbf{S}$ to the cluster $\mathbf{S}_i$

5:         such that $\mathbf{c}_i$ is the closest centroid to $\mathbf{x}_j$ under D

6:      Assign label $y_i = \lambda(\mathbf{x}_j) = i$ to instance $\mathbf{x}_j$, resulting in the pair $(\mathbf{x}_j, i)$

7:      Recompute the centroid for each of the k clusters, that is,

$$\mathbf{c}_i = \frac{1}{\#(i, \mathbf{S})} \sum_{(\mathbf{x}_j, i) \in \mathbf{S}} \mathbf{x}_j,$$

8: **until** the cluster labels in $\mathbf{S}$ do not change

9: **return** $\mathbf{S} = \{(\mathbf{x}_1, y_1), (\mathbf{x}_2, y_2), \ldots, (\mathbf{x}_m, y_m)\}$

---

recalling that $\mathbf{c}_i$ is the centroid of cluster $\mathbf{S}_i$ and the difference between vectors is taken element wise. We note that if we divide the SSE by m, the number of instances in the data set that is constant for the data set, we get the MSE loss function. (Moreover, the result would be the same if $D = D_E$ is the Euclidean distance, since square root is a monotone function.) At each repetition step of k-means, apart from the last step, the SSE decreases.

Example 4.9. We reuse the heart disease data set, with the sample data shown in Table 4.14. The elbow plot or k-means applied to this data set is shown in Figure 4.30, indicating that $k = 3$ is the optimal number of clusters for this data set.

The k-means algorithm is sensitive to the method by which the initial of k centroids are selected. Apart from the simple method used in line 1 of Algorithm 4.7, we could also assign each point randomly to one of the k clusters and then use the centroids of the resulting initial clusters as the initial centroids. A more sophisticated method for choosing the initial seed centroids is called *maxmin*. It first chooses a random instance from $\mathbf{S}$ as the first centroid, and then at each step the next centroid is chosen from the remaining instances in $\mathbf{S}$, as the furthest (i.e., max) from the nearest (i.e., min) instance to an existing centroid chosen at a previous step. A further step often taken to improve the clustering result is to run k-means multiple times and choose the clustering whose SSE is the minimum.

Now how do we determine the parameter k input to the k-means algorithm? We mention a couple of methods to determine a reasonable value for k that could resolve one of the drawbacks of k-means in that k needs to be known in advance.

One method is the *elbow* heuristic, which runs k-means on a range of k values starting from 1 and looks for the value of k when the SSE drops and an "elbow" in the curve is identified, that is, the position where the curve bends. A typical plot of the SSE against the number of clusters is shown in Figure 4.30; in this case, the elbow is at $k = 3$, which is

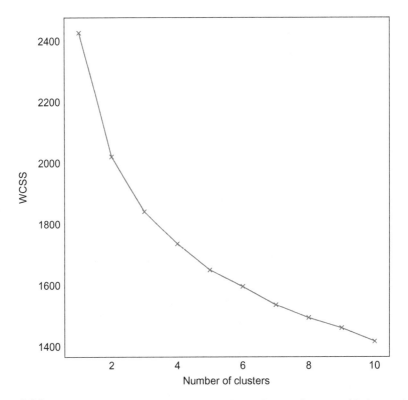

Figure 4.30 Elbow plot for *k*-means applied to the heart disease data set, with the number of clusters along the x-axis and the SSE on the y-axis.

seen to be the optimal number of clusters. However, the elbow heuristic is somewhat ambiguous, since it does not have a precise mathematical definition.

Another method makes use of the silhouette coefficient (as defined in Section 4.2.2) for the clustering of **S** induced by *k*-means. More specifically, for each value of *k*, we run *k*-means and determine the silhouette coefficient for the resulting clustering and choose the *k* for which the coefficient is the maximum. This method has an advantage over the elbow method in giving a definitive answer and, moreover, it combines cohesion (distances within clusters) and separation (distances between clusters), while the elbow method is based on cohesion alone.

One limitation of *k*-means is its sensitivity to outliers due to the way centroids are computed. An algorithm addressing this issue is *k-medoids*, which replaces centroids by medoids as exemplars of the centres of clusters. More specifically, a medoid for a cluster is an instance in the data set acting as the centre of the cluster, and the *k*-medoids algorithm will choose these centres so as to minimise the distance between each medoid and other instances in the cluster it represents. Therefore, since medoids are actual instances in the data set, it is highly unlikely that a medoid is an outlier.

While k-means minimises the SSE, the k-medoids typically minimises the sum of absolute errors (SAE), given by

$$\sum_{i=1}^{k} \sum_{\mathbf{x}_j \in \mathbf{S}_i} |\mathbf{x}_j - \mathbf{m}_i|,$$

where $\mathbf{m}_i \in \mathbf{S}_i$ is the medoid for cluster $\mathbf{S}_i$ and $\mathbf{M} = \{\mathbf{m}_1, \mathbf{m}_2, \dots, \mathbf{m}_k\}$ are the k-medoids, one for each cluster. If we divide the SAE by m the number of instances in the data set, which is constant for the data set, we get the MAE loss function.

The k-medoids algorithm, whose pseudocode is given in Algorithm 4.8, proceeds in an iterative fashion improving the distribution of instances to clusters until the algorithm converges; we will assume that in the algorithm $D = D_M$, the Manhattan distance, which is consistent with the SAE criterion.

Algorithm 4.8 k-medoids

Input: k, D, $\mathbf{U}$,

1: Select k instances $\mathbf{M} = \{\mathbf{m}_1, \mathbf{m}_2, \dots, \mathbf{m}_k\}$ from $\mathbf{U}$ as initial medoids
2: Let $\mathbf{S}$ become $\mathbf{U}$ % The output will be labelled
3: **repeat**
4:    Assign each $\mathbf{x}_j \in \mathbf{S}$ to the cluster $\mathbf{S}_i$
5:        such that $\mathbf{m}_i$ is the closest medoid to $\mathbf{x}_j$ under D
6:    Assign label $y_i = \lambda(\mathbf{x}_j) = i$ to instance $\mathbf{x}_j$, resulting in the pair $(\mathbf{x}_j, i)$
7:    **for** $i = 1 : k$ **do**
8:        **for** each $\mathbf{x}_j \in \mathbf{S}_i$ **do**
9:            Compute the SAE resulting from swapping $\mathbf{m}_i$ with $\mathbf{x}_j$
10:       **end for**
11:       Assign $\mathbf{m}_i$ to the instance $\mathbf{x}_j$ with the lowest SAE
12:   **end for**
13: **until** the cluster labels in $\mathbf{S}$ do not change
14: **return** $\mathbf{S} = \{(\mathbf{x}_1, y_1), (\mathbf{x}_2, y_2), \dots, (\mathbf{x}_m, y_m)\}$

The k-means and k-medoids are *hard clustering* methods, where each instance belongs to exactly one cluster, and thus the clusters partition the data set. Relaxing the condition that an instance belongs to a single cluster results in *soft clustering*, where each instance is assigned a probability, or more generally, a non-negative weight, of belonging to a cluster. An example of a soft clustering method is the *Gaussian mixture model* (GMM), which is a weighted sum of k Gaussian distributions. When we employ a GMM to cluster data, the mixture weights of the k clusters are probabilities that sum up to 1 as expected, and each instance is thus assigned a probability of belonging to each of the k clusters represented by a Gaussian distribution according to the cluster probability. A simple example illustrating soft clustering is that of pursuing a hobby, where instances represent people and each of the k clusters represents a hobby a person may pursue.

4.4.2   Hierarchical Clustering

In hierarchical clustering the number of clusters is not specified in advance. As with k-means, hierarchical clustering is a popular, versatile, and well-understood clustering method. It comes in two flavours:

Agglomerative: Bottom-up clustering, where the initial clusters contain single instances, and thereafter clusters are iteratively merged to create higher levels in the hierarchy.

Divisive: Top-down clustering, where initially there is only one cluster containing all the instances, and these are split to create multiple clusters at lower levels of the hierarchy.

We will concentrate on agglomerative clustering but also briefly mention divisive clustering, which proceeds in reverse order to agglomerative clustering. We will also assume without loss of generality that clusters are merged or split two at a time, which is the standard binary case.

To construct an hierarchical agglomerative clustering (HAC), which is by far the most common hierarchical clustering mechanism, we iteratively merge the two closest (or most proximate) clusters. HAC's initial configuration is m singleton clusters, one for each instance in the data set. The measure deployed for defining the distance (also referred to as dissimilarity) between clusters is called the *linkage* criteria, denoted as $L(i, j)$, for clusters $\mathbf{S}_i$ and $\mathbf{S}_j$. The most common ones are (i) *single-link* clustering (L_S), (ii) *complete-link* clustering (L_C), and (iii) *average-link* clustering (L_A).

Single-link, L_S, defines the distance between two clusters to be the minimum distance between any two instances, one in each cluster. On the other hand, complete-link, L_C, defines the distance between the two clusters as the maximum distance between any two instances. Finally, average-link, L_A, defines the distance between the clusters to be the average distance between all pairs of instances one in each cluster.

When clusters are represented by centroids, we may employ *Ward's linkage criterion* (or *Ward's minimum variance criterion*), which measures the distance between two clusters as the increase in SSE resulting from merging the two clusters. More precisely, for two distinct clusters $\mathbf{S}_i$ and $\mathbf{S}_j$ with centroids, $\mathbf{c}_i$ and $\mathbf{c}_j$, Ward's linkage criterion is given by

$$L_W(i, j) = \frac{\#(i, \mathbf{S})\#(j, \mathbf{S})}{\#(i, \mathbf{S}) + \#(j, \mathbf{S})} \|\mathbf{c}_i - \mathbf{c}_j\|^2,$$

recalling that $\#(i, \mathbf{S})$ is the number of instances in $\mathbf{S}_i$.

The single link criterion can detect irregularly shaped clusters naturally but is sensitive to outliers. On the other hand, the complete link criterion is less sensitive to outliers but has the tendency to split large clusters. The average link criterion can be viewed as a compromise between the single and complete linkage methods. Finally, Ward's criterion is analogous to the k-means SSE criterion in the context of hierarchical clustering and is quite similar to the average link method.

The pseudocode for computing hierarchical agglomerative clustering is given in Algorithm 4.9. It proceeds in an iterative fashion by merging two clusters at each iteration, according to the chosen linkage criterion, until a single cluster containing all the instances

---

Algorithm 4.9 HAC

Input: L, **U**,

1: Initialise the dendrogram **T** to be **U**, i.e., **T** contains m leaves all of which are singleton clusters

2: Let the number of remaining clusters **R** become **T**

3: **while R** contains more than one cluster **do**

4:     Choose the two distinct clusters, $\mathbf{S}_i$ and $\mathbf{S}_j$, in **R** that have the smallest distance under L; ties are broken randomly

5:     Remove $\mathbf{S}_i$ and $\mathbf{S}_j$ from **R** and add a new cluster $\mathbf{S}'$ to **R** having all the instances in either $\mathbf{S}_i$ or $\mathbf{S}_j$

6:     Add a new node to **T** labelled $\mathbf{S}'$

7:     Create two new links in **T**, one from $\mathbf{S}'$ to $\mathbf{S}_i$ and the other from $\mathbf{S}'$ to $\mathbf{S}_j$; the length of the links are proportional to the distance $L(\mathbf{S}_i, \mathbf{S}_j)$

8:     % Note that we do not distinguish between a node and its label

9: **end while**

10: **return T**

---

remains; at most m iterations of the loop are possible. The algorithm outputs a dendrogram summarising the resulting clustering, whose root node is a single cluster equal to **U**.

Example 4.10. We illustrate HAC by clustering the Iris data set, this time with classes for three species—the Iris setosa, Iris versicolour, and Iris virginica—employing the Euclidean distance measure. For each Iris species, the discovered clusters are based on four features: petal length and width and sepal length and width. In doing, so we will also demonstrate the use of the *dendrogram* to display the resulting clustering in a tree format.

In Figure 4.31 we show the dendrogram resulting from the single-link method, while in Figure 4.32 the dendrogram resulting from the average-link method and in Figure 4.33 the dendrogram resulting from Ward's linkage method.

Horizontal lines in the figures define where clusters merge, and vertical lines indicate which clusters or data points were merged to form new clusters. The heights of the horizontal lines indicate the distance required to enable a cluster to form. Starting from each label at the bottom, we can follow a vertical line upward and observe where it joins with a horizontal line. The height of this horizontal line tells us the distance at which a data point was merged with another data point to form a new cluster or merge with an existing cluster. The three clusters corresponding to the horizontal line across each of the three figures act as a threshold cutting each tree and show the three clusters below it, corresponding to the three Iris species mentioned above.

Divisive hierarchical clustering essentially proceeds in reverse order. It starts from a single cluster containing all the data set and, thereafter, it iteratively splits one chosen cluster according to some criterion until there are no more clusters to split; that is, all the leaf clusters are singletons. A criterion often used to choose which cluster to split is to pick the one with the largest *diameter*, that is, the one whose distance between the furthest points in the cluster is the largest. Three methods that can then be deployed for splitting a cluster once chosen are (i) use k-means with $k = 2$ to split the cluster; (ii) select the two

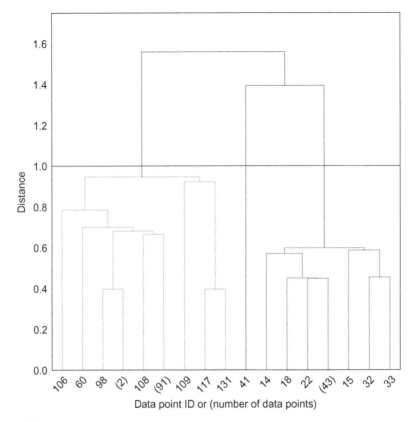

Figure 4.31   A dendrogram of HAC applied to the Iris data set using the single-link method. The x-axis is labelled with the data point ID (if it is an initial cluster) or the number of data points in the cluster (in brackets), and the y-axis represents the distance between two clusters being merged.

most distant instances in the cluster as seeds to form two new clusters, and then assign each instance from the old cluster to the most proximate of the two new clusters; or (iii) select the most distant instance from the cluster, that is, the instance that is on average most dissimilar to all other instances in the cluster, as a seed to form a new cluster, and then move to the new cluster all instances from the old cluster that are closer to the new cluster than to the old one.

Hierarchical clustering is quite attractive, since it is conceptually simple and flexible and does not require the number of clusters to be known in advance. Moreover, the dendrogram can be used to determine the number of clusters output, given that a distance threshold between the clusters is decided upon; the tree is cut horizontally at the threshold level, as shown in Figures 4.31, 4.32, and 4.33, where in this case the thresholds result in three clusters being output. On the flip side, the computational complexity of hierarchical clustering is much larger than that of k-means and therefore is not considered to be suitable

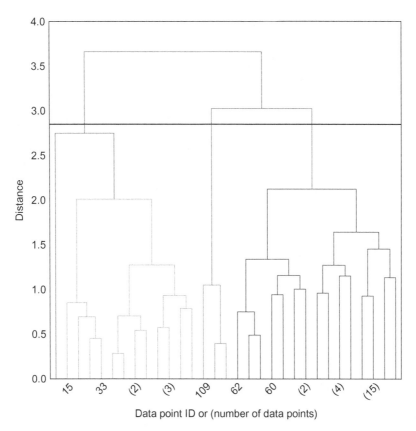

Figure 4.32 A dendrogram of HAC applied to the Iris data set using the average-link method. The x-axis is labelled with the data point ID (if it is an initial cluster) or the number of data points in the cluster (in brackets), and the y-axis represents the distance between two clusters being merged.

for large data sets. Another disadvantage of hierarchical clustering is that once instances have been assigned to a cluster, they cannot be separated at a later step of the algorithm.

4.4.3 Principal Components Analysis

Principal components analysis (PCA) is probably the best known method for dimensionality reduction. The goal of PCA is to find a low-dimensional representation of the feature space whilst preserving as much of the variation in the data as possible. PCA has applications in many domains where large high-dimensional data sets are processed. Examples are image processing, bioinformatics data such as gene expression data, and in quantitative finance.

We now give some basic mathematical intuition behind PCA as a linear transformation technique that maps the data into a lower dimensional space. The data set for PCA is represented in tabular form with one row per instance, $\mathbf{x} = \langle x_1, x_2, \ldots, x_n \rangle$, out of the m

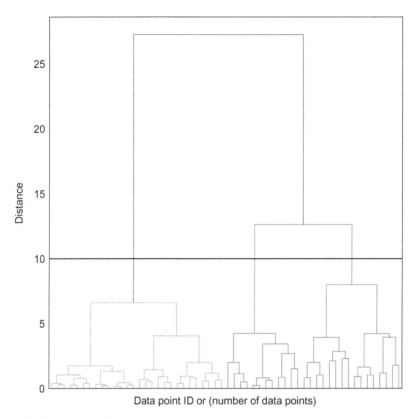

Figure 4.33 A dendrogram of HAC applied to the Iris data set using Ward's linkage method. The x-axis is labelled with the data point ID (if it is an initial cluster) or the number of data points in the cluster (in brackets), and the y-axis represents the distance between two clusters being merged.

instances in the data set $\mathbf{U}$, and one column for each of the n features in the instances of $\mathbf{U}$. For the sake of explaining the intuition behind the mathematics of PCA, we refer to the data set $\mathbf{U}$ as an m-by-n matrix, where each of the m row vectors, say i, is the ith instance in $\mathbf{U}$, and each of the n columns vectors, say j, is the vector of the jth feature values. We also make use of the concept of a unit vector, which is vector whose norm is 1; any vector, such as $\mathbf{x}$, can be *normalised* to a unit vector in the same direction as $\mathbf{x}$ by the transformation $\mathbf{x}/\|\mathbf{x}\|$; see Subsection 4.3.3 for the definition of the norm of a vector.

The *covariance matrix* of an m-by-n matrix such as $\mathbf{U}$, denoted by $COV(\mathbf{U})$, is an n-by-n square matrix whose i,j elements are the covariances between the ith and jth dimensions (or columns) of $\mathbf{U}$, for $i, j = 1, 2, \ldots, n$; see Subsection 2.3 in Chapter 2 for the definition of covariance, noting that the diagonal of the covariance matrix holds the variances of each dimension of $\mathbf{U}$.

PCA lowers the dimensionality of the data set by discovering new features, which are linear combinations of the existing features, such that given any instance $\mathbf{x} \in \mathbf{U}$ a combined feature is given by

$$\mathbf{u} \cdot \mathbf{x} = u_1 x_1 + u_2 x_2 + \cdots + u_n x_n,$$

where $\mathbf{u} = \langle u_1, u_2, \ldots, u_n \rangle$ is a unit vector. The variance of the linear combination induced by $\mathbf{u}$ with respect to the covariance matrix of $\mathbf{U}$ is given by

$$\mathbf{u}^T COV(\mathbf{U})\mathbf{u},$$

where the transpose $\mathbf{u}^T$ of the column vector $\mathbf{u}$ is a row vector, and multiplication is given by its standard extension to matrices. The role of PCA is to identify the unit vector that maximises the preceding variance, which reduces to solving the equation given by

$$COV(\mathbf{U})\mathbf{u} = \lambda\mathbf{u},$$

for some scalar value λ. In technical terms λ is called an *eigenvalue* of $COV(\mathbf{U})$, and $\mathbf{u}$ is called its *eigenvector*.

Actually a matrix, such as the covariance matrix, will have n eigenvalues $\lambda_1 \geq \lambda_2 \geq \ldots \geq \lambda_n$ and corresponding eigenvectors $\mathbf{u}_1, \mathbf{u}_2, \ldots, \mathbf{u}_n$. The largest eigenvalue is $\lambda = \lambda_1$, with its corresponding eigenvector $\mathbf{u} = \mathbf{u}_1$. Similarly, the second largest eigenvalue is $\lambda = \lambda_2$, with its corresponding eigenvector $\mathbf{u} = \mathbf{u}_2$, and so on for the rest of the eigenvalues and eigenvectors. From the derivation of PCA, it follows that the first eigenvector is the direction in which the data varies the most, the second eigenvector is the direction in which the data varies the second most, and so on for the other eigenvectors. It is important to note that these eigenvectors are orthogonal; that is, their dot product is zero, implying that they are linearly independent. The vector $\mathbf{U}\mathbf{u}_i$ holding the linear combinations of the features induced by PCA is called the ith *principal component*, and the elements of the ith eigenvector $\mathbf{u}_i$ are called the *loadings* of the ith principal component.

The amount of variance explained by the ith eigenvector is given by

$$\frac{\lambda_i}{\lambda_1 + \lambda_2 + \ldots \lambda_n},$$

so we aim to choose the fewest number of eigenvectors, say k, to summarise the data set $\mathbf{U}$, starting from $\mathbf{u}_1$, in such a way that

$$\frac{\lambda_1 + \lambda_2 + \ldots \lambda_k}{\lambda_1 + \lambda_2 + \ldots \lambda_n} \geq \theta,$$

where θ is a threshold less than 1.

The principal components can also be displayed visually, as in Figure 4.34, which is a visualisation of the first two principal components, requiring only a two-dimensional display space.

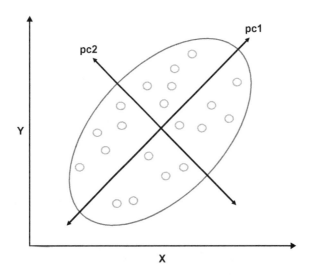

Figure 4.34   Example of PCA in two dimensions. The x-axis is labelled by pc1, the first principal component, while the y-axis is labelled by pc2, the second principal component.

Table 4.21   A sample from the breast cancer data, where the class label representing the diagnosis is either benign or malignant.

Radius	Texture	Perimeter	Area	Label
17.99	10.38	122.80	1001.0	benign
20.57	17.77	132.90	1326.0	benign
19.69	21.25	130.00	1203.0	benign
7.76	24.54	47.92	181.0	malignant
10.86	21.48	68.51	360.5	malignant
11.13	22.44	71.49	378.4	malignant

Example 4.11. The data set described features from scans of breast cancer patients recording the mean radius, texture, perimeter, and area of breast tissue; a sample from the data is shown in Table 4.21. The last column in the table represents whether the diagnosis is labelled benign or malignant.

A scatter plot of the breast cancer data points is shown in Figure 4.35, where the first two principal components are plotted against each other. In this example, the first two components accounts for approximately 0.63 of the total explained variance, with the first principal component accounting for 0.44 of the variance and the second one for 0.19 of the variance.

PCA is one of the most used methods for dimensionality reduction. It is well understood and effective in capturing correlated features. In reducing the dimensionality

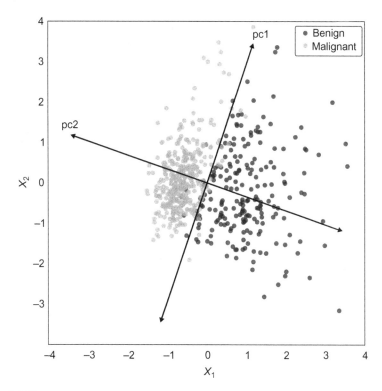

Figure 4.35 A scatter plot of the data points in the breast cancer data set associated with the two principal components. As in Figure 4.34 the x-axis is labelled by pc1, the first principal component, while the y-axis is labelled by pc2, the second principal component.

of a data set, PCA will potentially improve the computational performance of a machine learning task and reduce overfitting. As shown in Figure 4.34, PCA allows better visualisation of high-dimensional data. On the other hand, the principal components, which are linear combinations of existing features, may be hard to understand and consequently to interpret. There is also the issue that the data may be inherently nonlinear, when an extension of standard PCA would need to be used.

4.4.4 Topic Modelling

In topic modelling we will concentrate on clustering textual data and, in particular, we will assume the data set is a corpus consisting of a large number, m, of instances, called *documents* in this case, each consisting of words taken from a vocabulary of V *words*; that is, the feature values are words. To gain a better understanding of the corpus, we assume that there are k latent *topics*, $\mathbf{T} = \{t_1, t_2, \ldots, t_k\}$, which best describe a corpus $\mathbf{U}$ and are to be discovered. The topics are akin to clusters in k-means. There is, however, a twist, in that we will consider distributions rather than point estimates, and thus we concentrate on probabilistic topic modelling. So, in probabilistic topic modelling (or simply topic modelling), each document is a distribution over topics (also referred to as a mixture of topics), and each topic is a distribution of words.

To make this discussion more concrete, assume we have three news topics: *politics*, *technology*, and *sports*, that is, $k = 3$. The *politics* topic may be described by words such as "minister," "parliament," and "talks"; the *technology* topic by words such as "device," "app," and "hacker"; and the *sports* topic by words such as "football," "basketball," and "golf." Each word in a topic will have a probability attached to it, and the sum of these probabilities will be 1. In addition, each document will be a mixture of these three topics. It is important to note that a topic model does not know what the name of a topic may be; rather its function is to discover the distribution of words in the discovered topics. So, if *politics*, *technology*, and *sports* have strong presence in the corpus, a probabilistic topic model would uncover them and, when we inspect the words describing the topics, we would recognise them for what they are. Thus, a word will generally have a different probability in different topics—for example, the probability of the word "game" appearing in both the *sports* and *technology* topics.

Topic modelling is therefore about discovering latent topics in textual data, and the method for describing the topics is probabilistic. To be more specific, we will employ the *bag-of-words* assumption from information retrieval to model words in a document. This assumes that the order of words in a document is not important, and what we are interested in is the number of word occurrences or their proportion relative to the total number of words (including duplicates) in the document. A secondary assumption is that the order of the documents in the corpus does not matter. Although in our setting we have assumed that each instance, that is, document, **x**, has n features, we do not, in general, need to assume documents are of a fixed length. A simple way around this is to equate n with V, the vocabulary size, and for each i to record the ith feature values as the number of occurrences of word i in document **x**, which could be zero if the word does not occur in the document; this is consistent with the bag-of-words assumption.

We now introduce a topic model called *probabilistic latent semantic analysis* (PLSA), which formalises the probability of observing a word w in a document d. In particular, the joint probability $P(w, d)$ of w and d is given by the mixture over topics such as t, of the conditionally independent probabilities of t given d and words w given t:

$$P(w, d) = P(d) \sum_{t \in \mathbf{T}} P(t|d)P(w|t),$$

where $P(d)$ is the prior probability on document d (see Section 4.3.2 for the Bayesian definition of a prior); $P(d)$ may, for example, be proportional to the norm of d.

A probabilistic model showing the dependencies between random variables is called a *graphical model*, and the manner in which they are repeated is described using *plate notation*, as shown in Figure 4.36. In this case, the random variables d, t, and w are depicted as circles and the shading of d and w indicates that they are observable as opposed to t, which is a *latent*, that is, unobservable, variable. The rectangle surrounding $P(w|t)$, where the dependence of w on t is depicted as a link from the representative circle of t to that of w,

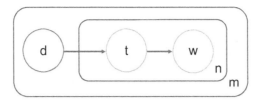

Figure 4.36   Graphical model plate notation for probabilistic latent semantic analysis.

implies that the surrounding subgraph is repeated $n = V$ times, once for each word in the vocabulary. Moreover, the second rectangle surrounding the full graphical model is repeated m times, once for each document in the corpus.

The graphical model for PLSA shown in Figure 4.36 induces a generative model for word-document co-occurrences as follows: (i) first, select a document d with probability $P(d)$; (ii) then pick a latent topic t with probability $P(t|d)$; and (iii) finally generate a word w with probability $P(w|t)$.

We will now demonstrate another way to understand PLSA, as a *matrix factorisation* problem, but first we will present a bit of terminology. We often prefer to work with the transpose $\mathbf{U}^T$, which is the n-by-m matrix obtained by flipping $\mathbf{U}$ over its diagonal, that is, by interchanging its rows and columns. Now, let $\mathbf{W}$ be an n-by-k matrix, whose individual values are indexed by w_{ij}, and $\mathbf{H}$ be a k-by-m matrix, whose individual values are indexed by h_{ij}.

The generative PLSA model can be seen to lead to the approximate factorisation of the data set $\mathbf{U}^T$ into two matrices: an n-by-k matrix $\mathbf{W}$ and an k-by-m matrix $\mathbf{H}$ such that

$$\mathbf{W} \times \mathbf{H} \approx \mathbf{U}^T,$$

where $\approx$ denotes approximately equal to and $\times$ is the multiplication symbol, which is usually omitted whenever no confusion arises. In more detail, suppose individual values of $\mathbf{W}$ are indexed by w_{ij}, those of $\mathbf{H}$ are indexed by h_{ij}, and those of $\mathbf{U}^T$ are indexed by $x_{ij} = x_{ji}^T$. In more detail, the factorisation of $\mathbf{U}^T$ is given by

$$\begin{bmatrix} w_{11} & w_{12} & \cdots & w_{1k} \\ w_{21} & w_{22} & \cdots & w_{2k} \\ \vdots & \vdots & \ddots & \vdots \\ w_{n1} & w_{n2} & \cdots & w_{nk} \end{bmatrix} \times \begin{bmatrix} h_{11} & h_{12} & \cdots & h_{1m} \\ h_{21} & h_{22} & \cdots & h_{2m} \\ \vdots & \vdots & \ddots & \vdots \\ h_{k1} & h_{k2} & \cdots & h_{km} \end{bmatrix} \approx \begin{bmatrix} x_{11} & x_{12} & \cdots & x_{1m} \\ x_{21} & x_{22} & \cdots & x_{2m} \\ \vdots & \vdots & \ddots & \vdots \\ x_{n1} & x_{k2} & \cdots & x_{nm} \end{bmatrix},$$

where

$$x_{ij} = w_{i1}h_{1j} + w_{i2}h_{2j} + \cdots w_{ik}h_{kj} = \sum_{r=1}^{k} w_{ir}h_{rj},$$

Table 4.22 A sample from the news-group data set showing the date of publication and headline text of ABC news articles.

Publish date	Headline text
20030219	aba decides against community broadcasting lic...
20030219	act fire witnesses must be aware of defamation
20030219	a g calls for infrastructure protection summit
20030219	air nz staff in aust strike for pay rise
20030219	air nz strike to affect australian travellers

for $i = 1, 2, \ldots, n$ and $j = 1, 2, \ldots, m$ describes the mechanics of the matrix multiplication.

In particular, with appropriate normalisation of the columns of $\mathbf{W}$ and $\mathbf{H}$, each topic is a distribution over words and each document is a distribution over topics. With this in place, we have $w_{ik} = P(w_i|t_k)$ and $h_{kj} = P(t_k|d_j)$. Since both w_{ik} and h_{kj} are non-negative, this type of factorisation is known as *non-negative matrix factorisation* (NMF). In addition, the factorisation of the data set can also be viewed as a dimensionality reduction exercise because we can generally expect the number of topics k to be much less than either the number of words n or the number of documents m. It can easily be seen that, given these assumptions, $nm \ll k(n + m)$, where $\ll$ reads "much less than."

Example 4.12. The ABC news data set contains a corpus of news articles covering 20 topics, including computer hardware, items for sale, and religion; see Table 4.22 for a sample from the data set. We apply NMF to the data set generating 20 topics and plot, in Figure 4.37, four of the 20 topics with their top-ten words ordered by weight. Topic 1 does not appear to be well defined and may represent general news stories. On the other hand, topic 2 is defined by words that are associated with war and conflict. Topic 3 appears to describe computer technology and software, while topic 4 describes news stories around space exploration.

In Figure 4.38 we show the topic coherence plot for the number of topics ranging from $k = 2$ to $k = 30$ for the NMF model, where k indicates the number of generated topics. The topic coherence on the y-axis is the average of the topic coherence scores for the k topics generated by the NMF model. The plot demonstrates that $k = 20$ topics are sufficient for describing the corpus due to the high coherence score for $k = 20$ in the plot.

Topic modelling is a popular technique for discovering clusters of words in textual data in the form of latent topics that can be used to summarise documents. The topics are interpretable, and the probabilistic model is well defined. On the other hand, it is hard to evaluate the quality of topics and, as in k-means, the number of topics k needs to be set in advance.

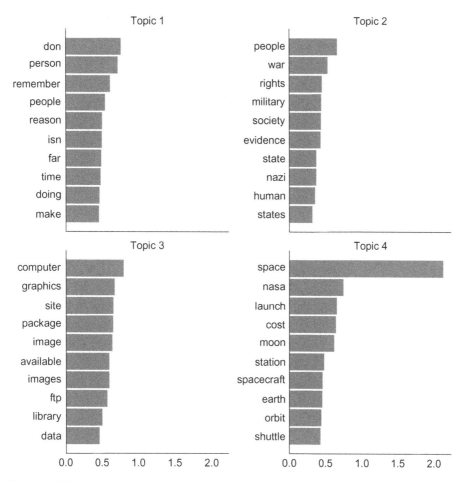

Figure 4.37 A plot of the four topics from the ABC news group data set with the top-ten words per topic in descending order ordered by weight.

A more elaborate model than PLSA that has a better mechanism to assign probabilities to previously unseen documents is *latent Dirichlet allocation* (LDA), which assigns a prior distribution to topics.

4.4.5 DBSCAN

Density-based clustering algorithms have been developed to detect arbitrary shapes in a space of n-dimensional points. Clusters are typically considered to be high-density regions in the space, separated by regions of low density that may be considered as noise. This type of clustering is especially suited for applications dealing with spatial data.

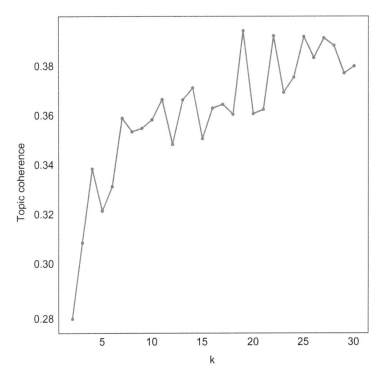

Figure 4.38   A plot of the average topic coherence scores for the NMF model, with the number of topics ranging from $k = 2$ to $k = 30$.

For clarity of exposition, let us assume that the points, which are the instances of the unlabelled data set **U**, are embedded in a two-dimensional Euclidean space, and so the Euclidean distance is the appropriate one to use in this case. The central idea of the DBSCAN (*Density-Based Spatial Clustering of Applications with Noise*) algorithm is that for each point in a cluster, its neighbourhood within a given radius must contain a minimum number of points, implying that the density of the neighbourhood is above a specified threshold. While k-means and hierarchical clustering are suitable for discovering spherical shapes, which are convex clusters, DBSCAN can detect nonconvex clusters such as ones having an S shape.

Prior to presenting the DBSCAN algorithm, we introduce some preliminary concepts, where *eps* and *minPts* are two specified parameters: *eps* is a distance threshold specifying a radius, while *minPts* is a frequency threshold specifying a minimum number of points. An *eps-neighbourhood* of a point **x**, denoted by $N_{eps}(\mathbf{x})$, is defined as the set of points in the data set **U** that are within a distance of *eps* from **x**. That is, a point **z** is in $N_{eps}(\mathbf{x})$ if $D_E(\mathbf{x}, \mathbf{z}) \leq eps$, where D_E is the Euclidean distance measure.

In DBSCAN a point is either *core* (in the interior of a cluster), *border* (on the border of a cluster), or *noise* (neither core nor border, i.e., on the exterior of a cluster), defined as follows.

Core points: These are points within the interior of a cluster. Specifically, $\mathbf{x}$ in $\mathbf{U}$ is a *core* point if there are at least $minPts$ within a distance eps from $\mathbf{x}$. That is, the number of points in $N_{eps}(\mathbf{x})$ is greater or equal to $minPts$.

Border points: These are points on the border of a cluster. Specifically, $\mathbf{z}$ in $\mathbf{U}$ is a *border* point if it is not a core point, but it is in the neighbourhood of at least one core point. That is, the number of points in $N_{eps}(\mathbf{z})$ is less than $minPts$, but for some core point $\mathbf{x}$ in $\mathbf{U}$, $\mathbf{z} \in N_{eps}(\mathbf{x})$.

Noise points: These are points on the exterior of a cluster. Specifically, $\mathbf{z}$ in $\mathbf{U}$ is a *noise* point if it is neither a core point nor a border point. That is, the number of points in $N_{eps}(\mathbf{z})$ is less than $minPts$, and there is no core point $\mathbf{x}$ in $\mathbf{U}$, such that $\mathbf{z} \in N_{eps}(\mathbf{x})$.

See Figure 4.39 for a visual depiction of the concepts of core, border, and noise points. Pseudocode for DBSCAN is given in Algorithm 4.10. In the algorithm, two points $\mathbf{x}$ and $\mathbf{z}$ are said to be *connected* if there is a sequence of points $(\mathbf{x}_1, \mathbf{x}_2, \ldots, \mathbf{x}_{k-1}, \mathbf{x}_k)$ such that $\mathbf{x} = \mathbf{x}_1$, $\mathbf{z} = \mathbf{x}_k$, and for $i = 1, 2, \ldots, k-1$, there is a *link* (as created in Algorithm 4.10) between $\mathbf{x_i}$ and $\mathbf{x}_{i+1}$. In the special case when $k = 2$, $\mathbf{x}$ and $\mathbf{z}$ are connected, since there is a link between them, and also when $k = 1$, where $\mathbf{x}$ and $\mathbf{z}$ are in fact the same point, the degenerate sequence of a single point is assumed to be connected. A *connected group* is a maximal collection of points such that each pair of points in the collection is connected to each other.

DBSCAN can handle clusters of arbitrary shapes and sizes. Moreover, it is generally resistant to noise or outliers, and the number of clusters does not need to be specified.

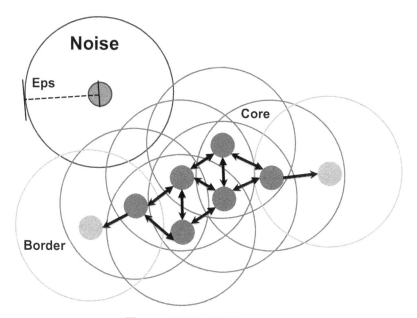

Figure 4.39   DBSCAN concepts.

Algorithm 4.10 DBSCAN

Input: $minPts$, eps, **U**,
  1: Construct two sets **C** and **B** containing, respectively, all the core and border points in **U**
  2: Create a *link* between all points **x** and **z** in **C** such that $\mathbf{z} \in N_{eps}(\mathbf{x})$
     % If there is a link from **x** to **z**, then there will also be a link from **z** to **x**
  3: For each border point $\mathbf{z} \in \mathbf{B}$, create a link to it from a random core point $\mathbf{x} \in \mathbf{C}$ such that $\mathbf{z} \in N_{eps}(\mathbf{x})$
     % The choice of point linking to it is random, since there may be more than one core point satisfying the condition $\mathbf{z} \in N_{eps}(\mathbf{x})$
  4: Create a cluster for each connected group of points, and label each point in the cluster with its label
  5: Let **S** become **U**   % Each point is now labelled by its cluster
  6: **return S** $= \{(\mathbf{x}_1, y_1), (\mathbf{x}_2, y_2), \dots, (\mathbf{x}_m, y_m)\}$

On the other hand, DBSCAN is sensitive to the value of eps, in particular when clusters are of varying densities. If eps is too small, then clusters that are sparse will be categorised as noise, whereas if eps is too large, then clusters that are denser will be merged into a larger cluster. Another problem with DBSCAN is that it operates on data that could be of high dimensionality, and distance measures on such data tend to be more complex.

Example 4.13. The swan data set is based on a study participating in the Arctic Animal Movement Archive (AAMA) analysing the flights of the Latvian Whooper Swans to different moulting sites in Russia throughout the year. The data set is composed of the latitudinal and longitudinal coordinates for four Whooper swans; see Table 4.23 for a sample from the data set.

DBSCAN was applied to the data set, resulting in a total of 22 clusters, with an overall silhouette coefficient score of 0.77, which suggests a good clustering. A plot of the clusters after removing noise points is shown in Figure 4.40.

Table 4.23 A sample from the Latvian Whooper Swan data set with the unique identifier for the swan and its geolocation at the specific time and date it was recorded at the moulting location.

Swan ID	Timestamp	Longitude	Latitude
9E10	2016-07-27 06:24	22.282067	57.062600
9E07	2016-07-27 06:50	22.282617	57.062683
9E05	2016-07-27 07:07	22.284017	57.062883
9E04	2016-07-27 07:22	22.283800	57.063150
9E06	2016-07-27 07:37	22.283950	57.062900

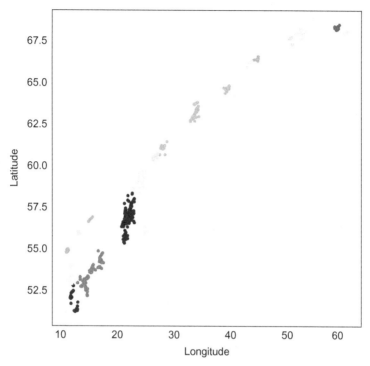

Figure 4.40 A plot of the clusters obtained from DBSCAN applied to the Whooper Swan data set, representing the moulting sites of the swans.

4.5 Semi-Supervised Methods

In many situations there is a sparsity of labelled data, and so a pure supervised algorithm may not give sufficiently good results. To motivate semi-supervised learning, let us consider a classification task with **S** containing a small amount of labelled data and **U** holding a much larger amount of unlabelled data. We start by training a model using the available labelled data, say, **S**, and then use this model to classify an unlabelled instance, say $\mathbf{z} = \langle z_1, z_2, \ldots, z_n \rangle$, for a pair $(\mathbf{z}, ?) \in \mathbf{U}$ as y, and as a result replace the pair $(\mathbf{z}, ?)$ by $(\mathbf{z}, y)$. As a next step, we remove the pair $(\mathbf{z}, y)$ from the unlabelled data set **U** resulting in **U'** and add it to the labelled data set **S** resulting in **S'**. This process is then repeated on the new labelled data set **S'** and unlabelled data set **U'**.

This form of semi-supervised learning is called *self-learning*. More specifically, in self-learning, (i) a new model is trained using **S'**, (ii) a pair $(\mathbf{z}', ?) \in \mathbf{U}'$ is classified as $(\mathbf{z}', y')$, (iii) the classified pair is removed from **U'**, and finally, (iv) the pair $(\mathbf{z}'y')$ is added to **S'**, and so on until all the unlabelled data in **U** is classified. (We have assumed without loss of generality that the test data is separate from **S**.) So, in essence, in addition to the original labelled data set **S**, a semi-supervised algorithm will have available to it supplementary data originating from **U**, whose labels were added through an intermediate supervised process.

Now, assume that the values from pairs such as $(\mathbf{z}, y)$ come from random variables **Z** and Y, respectively. A necessary condition for a semi-supervised algorithm to be a viable proposition is that we can use the probability $P(\mathbf{z})$ of the **Z**-value $\mathbf{z}$ from an unlabelled pair $(\mathbf{z}, ?)$ to gain useful information for estimating the conditional probability $P(y|\mathbf{z})$ for a predicted Y-value y. Otherwise, we could not vouch for the accuracy of the predictions of the semi-supervised machine learning algorithm.

The manner in which $P(\mathbf{z})$ and $P(y|\mathbf{z})$ may interact gives rise to semi-supervised assumptions. The most common one is the *smoothness assumption*, which states that if $\mathbf{z}$ and $\mathbf{z}'$ are close, then their respective labels, y and y', are likely to be the same. An immediate benefit arising from this assumption is that, by transitivity, if $\mathbf{z}_1$ is close to $\mathbf{z}_2$ and $\mathbf{z}_2$ is also close to $\mathbf{z}_3$, then one can expect their labels to be the same, even if $\mathbf{z}_1$ is not so close to $\mathbf{z}_3$. Another assumption that is often made is the *cluster assumption*, which states that instances belonging to the same cluster are likely to have the same label.

Another form of semi-supervised learning, apart from self-learning, is called *graph-based learning*, which is a form of *transductive learning* as opposed to *inductive learning*. In the traditional, inductive learning, we build a model from training data and then use the model to infer labels from test data. In transductive learning we observe all the data, both training and test, and use these to add labels to the unlabelled instances; when new data instances are encountered, we rerun the algorithm.

In graph-based learning, we construct a network (called a *graph* in this context) having nodes, denoting the data instances, and bidirectional links (called *edges* in this context, leading to a graph that is *undirected* as opposed to *directed* where the link has a direction), denoting similarity (the opposite of distance) between the two nodes they connect. The edges are labelled with a weight to indicate the similarity strength, and the nodes are labelled with either the class given by a training data pair or the class predicted by the graph-based learning algorithm that has been used, when the data comes as unlabelled. We may wish to further restrict the constructed graph to a *k-neighbourhood graph*, where a node in the network has at most k edges (i.e., its *degree* is at most k, with $k \geq 1$) to its *nearest neighbours*, that is, only keeping the (at most) k edges with the highest weights.

Now to instigate the semi-supervised algorithm on the k-neighbourhood graph, we mark the labelled nodes from the training data as the *seed* nodes. We then proceed to propagate the labels to neighbouring unlabelled nodes, starting from the seeds, thereby labelling neighbours when their similarity is high, without changing any of the seed labels. This process continues iteratively until the algorithm converges.

To give a bit more detail, assume that the weights are represented by an m-by-m square matrix, **W**; that is, we assume that the total number of instances in **S** and **U** is m and that w_{ij} in **W** gives the weight between nodes i and j in the k-neighbourhood graph. We may safely assume that $w_{ij} = 0$ when there is no edge between i and j in the graph. Note that **W** is symmetric, since $w_{ij} = w_{ji}$ for all weights w_{ij} in **W**; that is, **W** is equal to its transpose $\mathbf{W}^T$.

Now let $\mathbf{y} = \langle y_1, y_2, \ldots y_m \rangle$ be a vector containing the labels of the m instances, and assume for simplicity that the classifier we are trying to construct is binary; that is, for

$i = 1, 2, \ldots, m$, $y_i = 0$, or $y_i = 1$ when y_i is labelled as class 0 or 1, respectively, and $y_i = ?$ when y_i is unlabelled. The *energy function* for $\mathbf{y}$, denoted by $E(\mathbf{y})$, is given by

$$E(\mathbf{y}) = \sum_{i=1}^{m} \sum_{j=1}^{m} w_{ij} \left(y_i - y_j \right)^2.$$

Pairs such as y_i and y_j satisfying $y_i = y_j$, that is, sharing the same label, reinforce low-energy configurations, while those satisfying $y_i \neq y_i$ reinforce higher-level configurations. In this setup the semi-supervised algorithm can be viewed as an optimisation problem, whose goal is to assign labels to the unlabelled instances in $\mathbf{y}$ in such a way that the energy function is minimised.

We can simplify the optimisation problem through a simple iterative label propagation process as follows. Let $\mathbf{T}$ be an m-by-m matrix holding the propagation probabilities of labels from one instance to another, where $\mathbf{T}_{ij}$ is given by the normalisation

$$\mathbf{T}_{ij} = \frac{w_{ij}}{\sum_{h=1}^{m} w_{hj}}.$$

In addition, let $\mathbf{P}$ be an m-by-c matrix holding the class distributions; that is, its rows sum up to one for each instance in the data set, where c denotes the number of classes to be classified (in the binary case, we consider, $c = 2$). The value of p_{ij} in $\mathbf{P}$ is initialised in one of two ways: (i) when y_i was originally labelled by 0 or 1, then its value is either $(1, 0)$ or $(0, 1)$, respectively; this is referred to as *clamping*, or (ii) when y_i was originally unlabelled, then its value is set to $(p_i, 1 - p_i)$, for some p_i between 0 and 1. The pseudocode for the label propagation algorithm, LP, is given in Algorithm 4.11. The algorithm returns a class distribution, which would allow unlabelled instances to be labelled if the class probability was above some predetermined threshold.

Algorithm 4.11 LP

Input: T, y,
1: Initialise the class distribution $\mathbf{P}$
2: **repeat**
3: $\quad \mathbf{P} = \mathbf{T} \times \mathbf{P}$
4: $\quad$ Clamp the labelled data
5: **until P** converges
6: **return P**

Example 4.14. This example is based on a modified version of the breast cancer data set. We reuse the breast cancer data set, shown in Figure 4.35, where a patient diagnosed with malignant breast cancer is assigned a class label 1 and a patient diagnosed with benign breast cancer is assigned a class label 0. The semi-supervised model is trained using the label propagation method. The resulting confusion matrix is shown in Figure 4.41, and the precision, recall, and F1 for the semi-supervised model are shown in stylised form in Table 4.24.

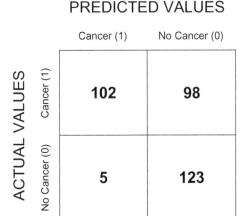

Figure 4.41   The confusion matrix for a semi-supervised model trained on the breast cancer data set.

Table 4.24   The precision, recall, and F1 score for a semi-supervised model trained to label data points as benign (labelled as class 0) or malignant (labelled as class 1).

Label	Precision	Recall	F1	Support
$Class_0$	0.56	0.96	0.70	128
$Class_1$	0.95	0.51	0.66	200
Total support:	328			
Micro-averaged F1:	0.68			
Macro-averaged F1:	0.68			

Semi-supervised learning is important when there is a sparsity of labelled data, and unsupervised methods are not deemed to be sufficient for the application in hand. We have introduced self-learning, an inductive method, and graph-based learning, a transductive method, as representative semi-supervised algorithms. For semi-supervised learning to perform well, some assumptions that were discussed need to be satisfied, although in practice, even when it is not easy to verify whether these conditions hold, the performance of the algorithms is generally encouraging.

In cases when labelled data is scarce, and manual labelling is costly, we may wish to resort to *weak supervision*, where heuristics are employed to automatically label data that can be used for training. The heuristics may come in the form of rules, which create potentially noisy labels, but these can still be useful as training data for a machine learning algorithm.

4.6   Chapter Summary

In this chapter we covered one of the central topics of the book, introducing the most-used machine learning methods and algorithms. In some sense, this is the tip of the iceberg because machine learning is a very fluid subject that is evolving as we speak. Despite this, we believe that we have covered the fundamentals that will provide you with a sound footing in the art and science of machine learning.

In supervised learning algorithms, we use labelled data to construct a model, whereas in unsupervised learning, we construct a model using unlabelled data. We also touched upon semi-supervised methods, when the amount of labelled data is sparse and supervised learning on its own is not adequate. For all methods, evaluation is crucial for assessment of the quality of the produced models. We introduced the important topic of neural networks and deep learning, but we are completely aware that many dedicated books already cover these topics in much greater depth than we have here.

5

Data Science Topics

In this chapter, we look at several topics that we believe are at the heart of data science and well worth knowing about. (That is not to say other topics are less important, simply that we had to make a choice.) We concentrate on three major topics:

(i) Search engines, with reference to how instances or items are ranked, or ordered in a list from the most relevant to the least relevant, and rated, that is, a numerical score is attached to them—the higher, the more relevant. (Although for search engines instances are generally ranked and rated according to relevance, in other contexts ranking can be done according to some other criteria, the main takeaway being that the higher the ranking and rating of an item, the "better" it is; an example of this is when the items are game players.)

(ii) Social networks, which hold a prominent place in our day-to-day lives, allow us to analyse patterns of interaction that emerge from the network structure. A social network is, of course, a network, its nodes representing the *actors* or *agents* in the network and the links representing relationships or connections between actors. (We will generally assume that in social networks the links are bidirectional and will often refer to them as edges to emphasise this.)

(iii) Sentiment analysis (SA), often referred to as opinion mining, and named entity recognition (NER) are both fundamental tasks in natural language processing pertaining to textual data. We introduce SA and NER and also throw in a short introduction to word embeddings, which operationalise the quotation by the well-known linguist Firth in the late 1950s: "You shall know a word by the company it keeps."

5.1 Searching, Ranking, and Rating

Searching is ubiquitous in data science and has been central to the internet revolution. There is, from a practical perspective, an infinite amount of information available, but we, the *users*, are interested in only a very small quantity, which is *relevant* to us at a given moment.

What is relevant and what is not is evasive and philosophical to some degree; we will take a pragmatic approach and presume that the user submits a *query* to the search engine and, from the system's perspective, the query encapsulates what is relevant to the user. The search engine is at liberty to use additional information that may help narrow it down the amount of information returned to the user, such as the past history of the user's searches; a user profile, which if available provides the search engine with information about the user's preferences; the overall popularity of specific information that may be presented to the user; and any other clues that are available. In general, the use of any heuristics, that is, rules of thumb, is fair play.

For discussion purposes we may assume that the search engine is dealing with textual data, though, of course, data comes in many guises such as image, video, and audio (see Chapter 3 for more on types of data). The field that provides the underlying formalisms for search engine technology is *information retrieval* (IR). Since the advent of the *World Wide Web* (WWW, also known as the web), the remit of IR has become much broader than its traditional role, and this is reflected in our coverage of search.

We will highlight the tasks of search engines in the context of the WWW, although search has applications on all data-rich major internet-based platforms such as e-commerce online shopping portals and social networks. We will assume that the unit of retrieval is a *web page* (or simply a page), each of which acts as an instance (or item) in the data set at hand, that is, the WWW. Also, as we are concentrating on text, web pages can be viewed as documents; the terminology is chosen to emphasise that we are searching within a network of documents. The WWW is thus a network, called the *web graph*, of pages (the nodes, collectively viewed as the corpus) and *hyperlinks* (or simply links) that connect pairs of pages in the network.

More formally, the *web graph*, denoted by **G**, is an abstract representation of the WWW, consisting of N nodes $\mathbf{W} = \{W_1, W_2, \ldots, W_N\}$ and a collection $\mathbf{L}$ of links, such as $W_i \to W_j$ in $\mathbf{L}$ that connects web pages W_i and W_j; W_i is called the *source* of the link, and W_j is called its *destination*. The links in the subcollection of $\mathbf{L}$, whose source is W_i, are called the *outlinks* from W_i, denoted by $OUT(W_i)$, and the links in the subcollection of $\mathbf{L}$, whose destination is W_i, are called the *inlinks* to W_i, denoted by $IN(W_i)$. We emphasise that the web graph is a directed network, since for two distinct web pages W_i and W_j, $W_i \to W_j$ being in $\mathbf{L}$ does not imply that $W_j \to W_i$ is also in $\mathbf{L}$. In addition, it is important to mention that the web graph is *sparse*, since on average the number of links in $OUT(W_i)$ is very small compared to N, the number of web pages in $\mathbf{W}$; this, generally, has a positive effect on the complexity of computations over the web graph.

In the big picture, information seeking is the process we go through when locating information within a repository such as the WWW. This process is quite broad in nature and includes browsing, say with the aid of a web browser and the tools it provides, navigating (often referred to as "surfing") by following links and using various cues to make sure we are on the right track and querying a search engine, which is what we concentrate on here.

The fundamental architecture of a search engine is shown Figure 5.1. It includes several components, which interact on a continuous basis with each other and the web, in order

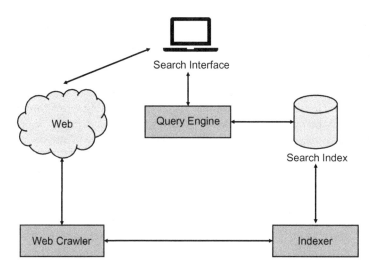

Figure 5.1   The architecture of a prototype search engine.

to provide users with an up-to-date search experience. The *query interface* is the point of interaction of the user with the system. It is very important in terms of the usability of a search engine and within the realms of human–computer interaction (known as HCI). The *query engine*, which is the algorithmic heart of a search engine, is what we will concentrate on from a modelling perspective, so that we can understand its inner workings. The *search index* is the data repository that holds all the information the search engine needs to match and retrieve web pages that satisfy users' search queries. It is worth mentioning that the search index makes use of inverted file indices that allow the search engine to retrieve all the web pages that contain a word in a user's query. This assumes, as is customary, that the query that is submitted to the search engine is simply a list of keywords, that is, a list of words that describe what the user is looking for. The *indexer* is responsible for indexing the web pages that are harvested by a *crawler* (also called a *spider*), which is a software program that runs continuously, following hyperlinks it finds in the web pages it has visited and sending their content to the indexer; the basic crawling algorithm is shown in Figure 5.2. Crawling and indexing are mammoth computing tasks given the size of the web, and therefore both these tasks are distributed as much as resources will allow. From an engineering perspective, running a global search engine is not an easy task, to say the least, and thus only few technology companies can compete in this space.

The objective of a search engine is to retrieve the most *relevant* pages given a user query and to present them to the user in a ranked list from the most relevant to the least relevant. There is no point in showing the user too many results because users will, on average, inspect a few of these; it seems that most users do not even click on results beyond the fifth ranked one. Moreover, there is a presentation position bias, which means that even if a user clicks on several results, the distribution of clicks over these results is not uniform; the click rate decreases very fast as the user moves down the ranking.

List of URLs to visit

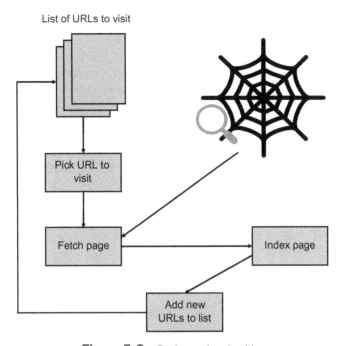

Figure 5.2   Basic crawler algorithm.

We will take a pragmatic approach to relevance and define it algorithmically according to the IR model we choose to base our search on; here we will follow the *vector space model*, which has proven to be very successful in practice. It is important, though, that once we choose our model, we have a means to evaluate it. We will opt to use precision and recall, which were defined in Subsection 4.2.1 in Chapter 4 as

$$precision = \frac{TP}{TP + FP}, \text{ and}$$
$$recall = \frac{TP}{TP + FN}$$

The TP search results are the ones that were retrieved by the search engine and are relevant, the $TP + FP$ results are the retrieved results, while the $TP + FN$ are the relevant ones. To unpack this a bit more, the retrieved results (i.e., the results presented to the user) contain both relevant results (the TPs) and ones that are not relevant (the FPs). Moreover, the relevant results contain both the retrieved and relevant results (the TPs) and ones that were not retrieved but are still relevant (the FNs).

We can further refine precision to the top-k search results, called *precision at k*, which only considers the k most highly ranked results when computing precision. In addition, we can also average the precision scores by summing the precision at k scores after each relevant result is retrieved, and then dividing by the number of relevant results considered to obtain an average precision value. If we further compute the average precision for several queries and then take the average of these, we obtain the *mean average precision* (MAP) score.

We also mention the *discounted cumulative gain* (DCG), which is a measure of the effectiveness of a search engine. The DCG accumulates the relevance of returned results based on their rank in the returned list of results for a given query and applies a discounting factor to each result so that the lower the rank, the heavier the discount. Relevance can be measured in a binary fashion, that is, 0 for not relevant and 1 for relevant, or can be graded into a more refined scale. Thus, the DCG at rank k sums the k discounted relevances, called gains in this context, for the results ranked from 1 to k.

DCG is based on two assumptions: (i) highly relevant documents are more useful than less relevant ones and (ii) the lower-ranked results are less useful because they are less likely to be viewed by the user. DGC can be normalised, giving the *normalised discounted cumulative gain* (NDCG), by dividing the DCG at rank k by the *ideal* DCG at rank k, obtained by ordering the results according to their grades (binary or otherwise), and then computing the resulting DCG.

5.1.1 The Vector Space Model

Here we will assume, as in topic models, that we are dealing with textual data and thus web pages are documents, each represented, as in Subsection 4.2.2 in Chapter 4, by a vector such as $\mathbf{x} = \langle x_1, x_2, \ldots, x_n \rangle$, having n features, one for each word (or term) in a vocabulary V. (Here, we use the terms "web page," "page," and "document" interchangeably.) In particular, the ith feature value x_i in $\mathbf{x}$ is the number of occurrences of word i in document $\mathbf{x}$, which is zero if the word is not in the document; this value is called *term frequency* (TF), denoted by $TF_i(\mathbf{x})$. This method of representing documents is based on the *bag-of-words* assumption, where the order of words in a document is not considered to be important; see Subsection 4.4.4 for some discussion on the bag-of-words assumption in the context of topic modelling.

We define *cosine similarity* for documents $\mathbf{x} = \langle x_1, x_2, \ldots, x_n \rangle$ and $\mathbf{z} = \langle z_1, z_2, \ldots, z_n \rangle$, denoted as $S_C(\mathbf{x}, \mathbf{z})$ as one minus the cosine distance as introduced at the end of Section 4.1 in Chapter 4; that is, we have

$$S_C(\mathbf{x}, \mathbf{z}) = \frac{\sum_{i=1}^{n} x_i z_i}{\sqrt{\sum_{i=1}^{n} x_i^2} \sqrt{\sum_{i=1}^{n} z_i^2}}.$$

Cosine similarity is already normalised by document length, which is a sensible way to avoid giving an unfair advantage to long documents over short documents. Normalising by document length is also a practical way to penalise high-frequency terms, which occur in long documents, and may cause bias, since, due to the importance of being visible on search engines, some websites inflate the number of occurrences of keywords in the hope that a higher TF will result in a higher ranking of their pages for queries containing these terms. Search engine manipulation practices such as keyword inflation are obviously frowned upon by commercial search engines.

The most common model for IR, although not the only one, is the vector space model, which represents both web pages (or documents) and queries as vectors having n

dimensions, noting that a query is simply also a list of words and so can be viewed as a document, albeit, in most cases, a very short one. Thus, given a document $\mathbf{d}$ and a query $\mathbf{q}$, the relevance (or more specifically, content relevance) of $\mathbf{d}$ to the query $\mathbf{q}$ is given by $S_C(\mathbf{d}, \mathbf{q})$.

We now refine the representation of word features in web pages from TF to TF-IDF, where IDF stands for *inverse document frequency*. As mentioned previously, inflating the number of keywords in documents causes problems, and moreover some keywords such as "the," "is," "at," "on," and others, called *stop words*, are very common and appear in almost all documents. In most cases stop words have little meaning in terms of relevance and thus are often ignored for efficiency purposes; there are exceptions to this, the most known sequence being "to be or not to be." IDF is a measure over the whole corpus, which is higher for low-frequency terms in the corpus and lower for high-frequency terms. The intuition behind this is that query keywords, which are rarer in the corpus, appear in fewer documents and thus limit the number of documents that are relevant given a user query. Thus, keywords with high IDF allow for better discrimination of relevant documents.

Given a word (or term), which is the ith feature of a document, its IDF is given by

$$IDF_i = \log\left(\frac{N}{\#(i, \mathbf{W})}\right),$$

where $\#(i, \mathbf{W})$ is the number of pages (documents) $\mathbf{x} \in \mathbf{W}$ such that $x_i > 0$, that is, the number of documents in the corpus (web graph) that contain the word of interest. The logarithm is used to dampen the effect of IDF, so doubling the size of the corpus only adds 1 to IDF values rather than doubling it, assuming the base of the logarithm is 2.

We can thus modify the x_i feature values in documents such as $\mathbf{x}$, from $TF_i(\mathbf{x})$ to $TF_i(\mathbf{x}) \times IDF_i$. We observe that for a document $\mathbf{x}$, when $\#(i, \mathbf{W}) = 0$, then $TF_i(\mathbf{x}) = 0$, and thus the TF-IDF score, $TF_i(\mathbf{x}) \times IDF_i$, is taken to be 0. This method of scoring documents is known as TF-IDF and is one of the pillars of the vector space model. Many other heuristics can be used to improve the quality of retrieval, such as stop word removal, stemming (reducing parts of words to expose their root form known as their stem, for example, by removing prefixes and suffixes of words), matching phrases in addition to single words, detecting synonyms, and weighting markup tags present in the document structure. However, within the vector space model, TF-IDF provides the essential foundation for content retrieval.

Example 5.1. To illustrate TF-IDF, we make use of a small corpus of BBC news articles on recent events including inflation brought about by rising energy costs and recent military conflicts; for a sample of the data, see Table 5.1. The data is composed of the text from each article, which is preprocessed into words (or tokens) and with stop words removed. The TF values of a sample of the documents are shown in Table 5.2, while the IDF values for the full ten documents are shown in Table 5.3 and the TF-IDF values are shown in Table 5.4.

So the vector space model is actually quite simple once we know how to represent documents as vectors, and we can measure the similarity of documents in vector space. Of the other IR models that have been formulated, we mention *statistical language models*,

Table 5.1 Sample data composed of five BBC news articles on recent events including inflation, politics, and world conflicts.

Document ID	Headline text
1	Bank of England warns the UK will fall into recession this year
2	China fires missiles near Taiwan after Pelosi visit
3	As it happened: Sunak and Truss clash over economy in TV grilling
4	Tory leadership: I took money out of deprived urban areas, says Sunak
5	Bank's recession warning matters to everyone

Table 5.2 Sample of the term frequency of words in the corpus of BBC news articles. Five news articles are identified by the document ID (docid), with words in the vocabulary of all documents in the columns, document IDs in rows (in column Docid), and the cells represent the term frequency of words given the document.

DocID	Inflation	Bank	Interest	Tax	Russia	China	US	Ukraine
1	3	5	4	0	1	0	0	1
2	0	0	0	0	0	4	3	0
3	0	2	0	0	0	0	0	0
4	0	1	0	0	0	0	0	0
5	3	6	3	1	1	0	1	1

Table 5.3 A sample of the inverse document frequency (IDF) of words in the corpus of BBC news articles.

Word	IDF
inflation	1.322
bank	0.514
interest	2.322
tax	3.322
Russia	0.737
China	2.322
US	0.737
Ukraine	0.514

Table 5.4 A sample of the term frequency–inverse document frequency (TF-IDF) of words in the corpus of BBC news articles. Five news articles are identified by the document ID (docid), with words in the vocabulary of all documents in the columns, document IDs in rows (in column Docid), and the cells represent the TF-IDF of words given the document.

DocID	Inflation	Bank	Interest	Tax	Russia	China	US	Ukraine
1	3.965	2.572	9.287	0.000	0.736	0.000	0.000	0.514
2	0.000	0.000	0.000	0.000	0.000	9.287	2.210	0.000
3	0.000	1.029	0.000	0.000	0.000	0.000	0.000	0.000
4	0.000	0.514	0.000	0.000	0.000	0.000	0.000	0.000
5	3.965	3.087	6.965	3.321	0.736	0.000	0.736	0.514

which are probability distributions over sequences of words, in contrast to the bag-of-words assumption of the vector space model. So the probability of a sequence of k words is $P(w_1, w_2, \ldots, w_k)$. Most of the possible sequences will not be observed in the data set, due to the sparsity of data sequences, which provides motivation for the assumption that the probability of a given word depends only on its $n - 1$ previous words, resulting in what is called an n-gram model.

Specifically, when $n = 1$, we have a *unigram* language model, and the words in the sequence are independent of each other; that is, we have

$$P(w_1, w_2, \ldots, w_k) = \prod_{i=1}^{k} P(w_i) = P(w_1)P(w_2) \cdots P(w_n),$$

where $\prod$ is the symbol denoting a product.

When $n = 2$, we have a *bigram* model, and words are dependent on their predecessory; that is, we have

$$P(w_1, w_2, \ldots, w_k) = P(w_1) \prod_{i=2}^{k} P(w_i | w_{i-1}),$$

which is a classical *Markov model*; in general, n-gram models result in $(n - 1)$-order Markov models. Given a data set, a language model will estimate the conditional probabilities by counting the appropriate number of sequences in the data set and applying some form of smoothing to deal with unseen sequences. How this estimation works is at the heart of language modelling; nevertheless, we will leave readers to follow that trail independently, as it is is not in the scope of this introductory text.

On the whole, unigram models seem to perform well in the context of IR; compare the naive Bayes classifier in Subsection 4.3.2 in Chapter 4. However, combining a unigram model with a bigram or both bigram and trigram models may be beneficial for retrieval. In a language model for IR, both documents such as **d** and queries such as **q** are modelled as sequences of words. This allows us to specify retrieval in terms of $P(\mathbf{q}|\mathbf{d})$, that is, the probability of $\mathbf{q}$ given the document language model for $\mathbf{d}$.

The sound statistical foundations of the language model approach can lead to a productive synergy with other statistical approaches used in data science; however, in comparison to the vector space model, this may lead to higher complexity both in terms of modelling and the computational methods used.

5.1.2   Ranking with PageRank

The vector space model, introduced in the previous subsection, uses content to rank web pages, but web pages also contain links as recorded in the web graph. A link added to a web page by the page's author can be viewed as a recommendation, endorsement, or vote of the destination web page of the link. This is a form of popularity ranking, "vox populi," which means voice of the people in Latin.

There are two simple ways to measure popularity: the first is to count the number of user visits to a web page, and the second is to count the number of inlinks to a web page. The number of user visits strongly favours commercial brands and temporary fads and is easy to manipulate because users can easily visit a popular web page multiple times and, taking this even further, users could even be hired to visit the web page to increase its popularity and therefore its ranking. The second method to measure popularity of a web page is to count the number of inlinks to that page. This would be similar to counting the number of citations to an academic paper, a metric commonly used in citation analysis. As with user visits, this method is volatile and can be manipulated (or using stronger language, spammed) by recruiting website owners to add links to the web page; however, one may argue that adding a link is harder than merely visiting a web page. In any case, the higher the benefits of being ranked higher, the bigger are the incentives for spammers to try and manipulate the ranking. Search engines are not oblivious to these practices and will respond with counter-measures to stop spammers; this is a classical data science problem.

PageRank is a more sophisticated method for measuring popularity. Instead of simply counting the number of inlinks, it takes into consideration the quality of recommendation of each inlink pointing to it. The quality of an inlink is thus determined by the quality of the source web page of the inlink, so a vote to a web page is more important if the web page that voted for it is itself more important. Note that this definition is recursive and, therefore, PageRank involves an iterative algorithm; it cannot be computed by merely inspecting a web page and its inlinks. We further note that PageRank is independent of any user query and thus may be precomputed by the search engine prior to answering specific queries.

PageRank can be explained precisely, via the *random surfer* model. Navigating the web, colloquially known as *surfing*, is the process users partake in when following web links (i.e., the outlinks on the web page being browsed) by clicking on one of them to move from one web page to another. Surfing often occurs in sessions, when a user has some, possibly vague, objective in mind to find information. The navigation session may lead to a website the user is looking for (or even "it" if the user is a "robot"), acquiring some information about a topic, or performing some activity such as downloading a file or completing a transaction mediated by an online shopping site.

The navigation session of our random surfer, which we call RS, is never-ending. In fact, RS clicks on links randomly as they appear on web pages landed on; that is, if there happen to be n links on the web page RS is currently browsing, then the probability of choosing any one of them to click on is proportional to $1/n$. However, RS eventually gets bored clicking on links and, when this happens, RS is "teleported" randomly to one of the N pages in the web graph, only to resume surfing the web from the web page RS actually lands on. The probability of teleportation is T, where $0 \leq T \leq 1$, and the probability of continuing surfing by following a link on the current page being browsed is $1 - T$; that is, teleportation is a Bernoulli random variable.

Two special boundary cases of T deserve attention. When T is 1, RS simply hops indefinitely from one of the N random web pages to another, visiting any one of these with equal probability. On the other hand, when T is 0, no teleportation ever occurs, and RS simply continues surfing by following one of the available links on the web page currently being browsed. However, what happens if the current web page being browsed has no links on it (i.e., it is *dangling*)? In this case, RS is stuck and will definitely get bored because there is no link to click on and teleportation becomes inevitable. We can imagine that a dangling web page has links to all other web pages, and one is chosen with probability proportional to $1/N$, avoiding infinite boredom. So, it is sensible for T to be strictly between 0 and 1, avoiding these undesirable circumstances. Another undesirable situation motivating nonzero teleportation is the *rank sink*. In this case, RS gets stuck in a loop, when at each step from the current web page being browsed, say W_i, there is only one link to choose from, which will inevitably lead RS back to W_i, and thus RS is stuck in an infinite loop.

PageRank is formalised as a vector $\mathbf{PR} = \langle PR_1, PR_2, \ldots, PR_N \rangle$ that induces a distribution of web pages such that the probability of a web page W_i is PR_i. The probability PR_i is defined as the proportion of times the random surfer, RS, will visit a web page during its never-ending surfing activities, normalised so that the sum of the PR_is is 1, and thus PR_i can be viewed as a probability. You may wonder if PR_i actually converges, since whether this happens may not seem obvious; indeed it does, but we will not prove this here. (To whet your appetite, the convergence follows from *Markov chain* theory, since teleportation, which solves the problems of dangling web pages and rank sinks, leads to a well-defined convergent Markov chain, modelling the stochastic activities of the random surfer on the web graph.)

Now, let $IN(W_i) = \{W_{1i}, W_{2i}, \ldots, W_{hi}\}$ be the h inlinks to a web page W_i and $\#OUT(W_{ji})$ be the number of outlinks from W_{ji}, for $h = 1, 2, \ldots, h$. Then, PR_i is defined by the equation

$$PR_i = \frac{T}{N} + (1 - T) \left(\frac{PR_{1i}}{\#OUT(W_{1i})} + \frac{PR_{2i}}{\#OUT(W_{2i})} + \cdots + \frac{PR_{hi}}{\#OUT(W_{hi})} \right).$$

Pseudocode for the random surfer model is given in Algorithm 5.1. In the algorithm, the vector $\mathbf{PRC}$ of N PageRank counts holds the number of visits PRC_i of the random surfer to the web page $W_i \in \mathbf{W}$, for $i = 1, 2, \ldots, N$, at any stage during the computation of the PageRank vector; the final result is independent of the initial values assigned to $\mathbf{PRC}$.

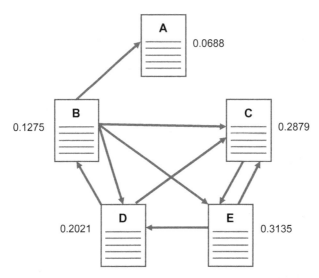

Figure 5.3 A small web graph with five web pages, used to illustrate PageRank; the actual
PageRank values are shown beside the web pages.

Example 5.2. In Figure 5.3 we show a simple web graph with five web pages. The
random surfer starting at page B has four choices, so with probability of $1/4$, the surfer will
choose one of them, say C. Page C has only one outlink to E, so the surfer must move to
that page. From E there are two outlinks, one back to C and the other to D. Thus, the
random surfer continues on the mission ad infinitum. But, what does the surfer do when
reaching page A? This page, which does not have any outlink, is *dangling*, and so the user is
teleported from this page to a random one; we assume that $T = 0.15$ in this case.

As a real-world example, we use data released in 2002 as a part of Google's
programming contest. The web graph contains over 916,000 web pages with 5.1 million
links. For the purpose of illustration, we use a small sample of 1,299 web pages, that is, its
nodes, with the 2,773 links between them, that is, its edges; ten of the web pages from the
small sample of this web graph are shown in tabular form in Table 5.5.

In light of this, what would be a "good" default setting for the teleportation
probability? By "good," we mean two things. First, the number of iterations of the
repeat-until loop in Algorithm 5.1 prior to convergence is reasonable in the sense that the
computation time needed to determine the PageRank is feasible. Second, we wish T to be
relatively close to 0 because the further it is away from 0, the more random PageRank
becomes. A good empirical compromise is to set T to be 0.15.

We now take a brief detour to look at *bibliometrics*, involving the study of the structure
and process of scholarly communication, encompassing the study of citation analysis.
We assume that a researcher has n publications, where $n \geq 0$, which are represented by a
citation vector of positive integers,

$$\mathbf{c} = \langle c_1, c_2, \ldots, c_n \rangle,$$

Table 5.5 Ten web pages from the Google 2002 web graph sample, in descending order of inlinks. The first column gives the node ID of the web page, the second column gives the number of its inlinks, and the final column give its PageRank, with T set to 0.15.

Node	#Inlinks	PageRank
71	134	0.00161
211	136	0.00070
718	193	0.00052
827	137	0.00047
1049	79	0.00047
280	258	0.00045
943	276	0.00040
1285	77	0.00036
1068	71	0.00036
1167	71	0.00036

Algorithm 5.1 The random surfer model

Input: W, T

1: Let **PRC** $= \langle 1, 1, \ldots, 1 \rangle$ % Initial assignment of the PageRank counts
2: Let $Count = N$ be the initial number of visited web pages
3: Start the navigation at a random web page W_i out of the N web pages
4: Set $Current = W_i$
5: **repeat**
6:      Toss a biased coin, with success probability $1 - T$ and failure T
7:      **if** Success % Navigate **then**
8:          Choose a random page, $W_i \in OUT(Current)$ to navigate to
9:      **else** Failure % Teleport
10:          Choose a random page $W_i \in \mathbf{W}$ to teleport to
11:      **end if**
12:      $Count = Count + 1$
13:      $PRC_i = PRC_i + 1$ % Increment the value of PRC_i
14:      $Current = W_i$ % The current web page being visited becomes W_i
15: **until PRC**$/Count$ converges % i.e., does not change by much
16: **return PR** = **PRC**$/Count$ % **PR** is the normalisation of **PRC**

---

where c_i is the number of citations to publication i, sorted in descending order, that is, $c_i \geq c_j$ for $1 \leq i < j \leq n$.

The simplest citation indices are (i) the number of publications, n, which is regarded as a measure of quantity, and (ii) the total number of citations, $\sum_{i=1}^{n} c_i$, which is regarded as a measure of quality. An ingenious index combining quality and quantity is the h-index, which is defined as the maximum number h of the researcher's publications such that each has at least h citations; that is, for a citation vector, $\mathbf{c}$, the h-index is the largest h for which $c_h \geq h$.

Example 5.3. To illustrate the h-index, we have to count citations of every publication for an author. We can then create a citation vector by ordering the publications according to the counts of citations in descending order. We present the h-index for two researchers, Albert Einstein (with citation statistics: min=1, mean=434, max=22,202, h-index=165) and an anonymous theoretical physicist (with citation statistics: min=1, mean=166, max=3,004, h-index=63); min, mean, and max denote the minimum number, mean number, and maximum number of citations per paper, respectively. In Table 5.6, we show the top-ten cited papers contained in Albert Einstein's citation vector, where his top-cited publication, which received a total of 22,202 citations, appears as rank 1. Figure 5.4 shows a plot of the top-200 cited papers of Albert Einstein and the anonymous theoretical physicist; these plots are called *citation curves*. We note that their h-indices induce a square under the citation curve, as highlighted in the figure.

A variant of the h-index for ranking web pages, called the hw-index, is defined for web pages. To make this more concrete, the citation vector $\mathbf{c}(W)$ of a web page W having n inlinks, $W_1, W_2, \ldots, W_n$, such that each W_i, for $i = 1, 2, \ldots, n$, has at least one inlink, is defined as

$$\mathbf{c}(W) = \langle c(W)_1, c(W)_2, \ldots, c(W)_n \rangle,$$

where $c(W)_i$ is the number of inlinks to W_i.

Table 5.6   A sample including the top-ten cited publications contained in Albert Einstein's citation vector.

Publication ID	#Citations
1	22,202
2	18,073
3	16,596
4	7,034
5	6,792
6	6,687
7	6,656
8	6,614
9	6,164
10	5,966

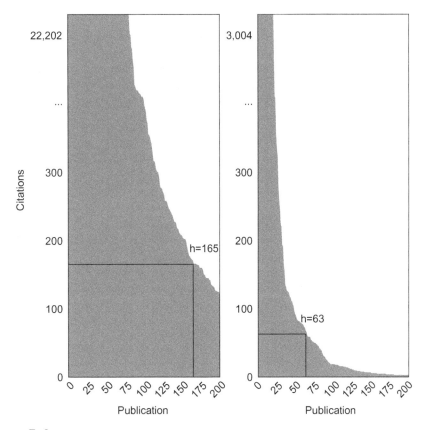

Figure 5.4 The citation curve of the top-200 cited publications contained in Albert Einstein's citation vector, whose *h*-index is 165 (left plot) and, correspondingly, the citation curve of the top-200 cited publications contained in the citation vector of an anonymous theoretical physicist whose *h*-index is 63 (right plot). The index of publications is shown along the x-axis and the number of citations per publication is shown on the y-axis.

Now, in analogy to the h-index, the hw-index is thus defined as the maximum number hw of the web page's inlinks such that each has at least hw web pages linking to it; that is, for a citation vector, $\mathbf{c}(W)$ of a web page, W, the hw-index is the largest hw for which $c(W)_{hw} \geq hw$.

5.1.3 Rating with the Elo System

The Elo rating system was formulated by Arpad Elo in 1960 for calculating the relative skill of chess players and is based on the theory of pairwise comparisons, where judgement is made regarding the preference between two entities. It does, however, have applications in competitive domains other than chess. For instance, it can be applied to other board games such as Go, to online competition involving multiplayer games, and also to sports such as tennis and football. It is hard to know objectively how well the Elo system measures true skill; however, it has served chess players for quite a few decades now and is accepted by the community both offline and online as an estimate of players' strength.

To formalise the Elo rating system, assume two players A and B, with *ratings* having values R_A and R_B, respectively, reflecting the players' strengths. The probability that a player of strength R_A beats a player of strength R_B, denoted by p_{AB}, is given by

$$p_{AB} = logistic\left(C\left(R_A - R_B\right)\right) = \frac{1}{1 + \exp\left(-C\left(R_A - R_B\right)\right)},$$

where C is a positive scaling factor; see Section 2.5 in Chapter 2 for a brief discussion on the logistic function. We note that as the difference of strengths, $R_A - R_B$, between players A and B decreases, p_{AB} tends to 0, as it increases it tends to 1, and when $R_A = R_B$, $p_{AB} = 0.5$. Moreover, $p_{AB} + p_{BA} = 1$, that is, the probability that A beats B plus the probability that B beats A is 1, as one would expect.

The score of the game for player A against player B is denoted by S_{AB}, where S_{AB} is 1 if A wins, 0 if A loses, and 0.5 if the game is a draw. Its expected value is assumed to be equal to p_{AB}, that is,

$$E(S_{AB}) = logistic\left(C\left(R_A - R_B\right)\right),$$

where we have

$$C = \frac{\log(10)}{400} = 0.00576.$$

The magical number 400 is the point at which the difference $R_A - R_B = 400$ implies that $E(S_{AB})$ is approximately $0.9091 = 10/11$; that is, player A is ten times more likely to win against player B than otherwise. So, for example, if $R_A - R_B = 100$, then $E(S_{AB})$ is approximately 0.64, and if $R_A - R_B = 200$, then $E(S_{AB})$ is approximately 0.76.

After playing a game against player B, player A's rating is adjusted according to

$$\text{new } R_A = \text{old } R_A + K(S_{AB} - E(S_{AB})),$$

where K, known as the K-factor, is the maximum number of points by which a rating can be changed as a result of a single game. In particular, a high K-factor gives more weight to recent results, while a low K-factor increases the relative influence of results from earlier games. In the Elo system, the K-factor is typically between 10 and 30.

The term $S_{AB} - E(S_{AB})$ reflects the disparity between the score that was observed and the score that was expected. When it is positive, player A achieved more than the rating R_A predicted, so A's rating is increased to reflect this, whereas if it is negative, A achieved less than predicted and the rating is decreased accordingly.

So, for the preceding example, for $K = 20$, if $R_A = 2000$ and $R_B = 1900$, and A wins against B, A's rating R_A will go up by 7.2 points, but if A loses, its rating will go down by

Table 5.7   The top-ten Elo ratings of chess players as of June 2022.

Rank	Name	Nationality	Elo score
1	Magnus Carlsen	Norway	2,864
2	Ding Liren	China	2,806
3	Alireza Firouzja	France	2,793
4	Fabiano Caruana	United States	2,783
5	Levon Aronian	United States	2,775
6	Wesley So	United States	2,775
7	Ian Nepomniachtchi	Russia	2,766
8	Richard Rapport	Hungary	2,764
9	Anish Giri	Netherlands	2,761
10	Maxime Vachier-Lagrave	France	2,760

12.8 points. Player B's rating R_B is updated similarly. We note that, after updating both A's and B's ratings, the sum of their ratings remains unchanged. The preceding method can be straightforwardly extended to the case of the number of games of a player competing in a tournament, or to a number of games played over a given period of time.

Example 5.4. The Elo rating of the top-ten ranking chess masters as of June 2022 is shown in Table 5.7. The Elo score of each player will go up or down depending on how well they perform in tournaments against other rated players. We note that a novice chess player typically has a rating of 1,200 or below, while a chess masters rating is typically 2,200 or above. The ratings of the top-ten players are far above 2,500, which is the threshold for grandmaster status. Moreover, players achieving a rating of 2,700 or above are considered to be super grandmasters; the rating list as of June 2022 contained 38 super grandmasters. The top-100 players, as of June 2022, all had an Elo rating of 2,650 or above.

5.1.4   Recommender Systems and Collaborative Filtering

Considering online shopping as one of the major applications of e-commerce, the question online vendors ask themselves is, What products should be recommended to users? Products are not limited to books, movies, music, or computer equipment because other types of artifacts can be recommended, such as images, news items, or social media.

Recommendations can be made on the basis of *content* (CB) or *collaborative filtering* (CF). CB recommendation is about finding the best-matched items for a user based on the similarity between the user profile and the description of items. A user's profile is represented as an n_1 feature vector storing the user's details and preferences (e.g., the user may prefer nonfiction books, classical music, and documentary movies), and an item's description is represented as an n_2 feature vector storing the product details (e.g., that the book is in the fiction category or the movie is in the action category). To discover the extent to which a product matches a user, the vector-space model can be employed to compute the cosine similarity between the relevant n' features in the product description and the user profile, resulting in a score indicating how close the match is between the user and product. This score can be scaled (see Section 3.7 in Chapter 3) according to the rating system used, resulting in a *pseudo-rating* of the user for the product under consideration.

In the rest of this section, we will concentrate on CF recommendations, which are recommendations based on "word of mouth," that is, people recommending (or not recommending) products to other people according to their personal experiences.

The data set input to a recommender system is an unlabelled data set $\mathbf{U}$, comprising m instances, where the instance $\mathbf{u} = \langle u_1, u_2, \ldots, u_n \rangle$ in $\mathbf{U}$ is a vector of n feature values. Each of the m instances, such as $\mathbf{u}$, represents a *user*, and each of the n features for a user represents an *item* from a collection I of n possible items. In particular, the jth feature value u_j of $\mathbf{u}$ is the rating assigned to this item by the user represented by $\mathbf{u}$, which is normally a number between 1 and 10 (this is the standard 5-star rating system, allowing for half stars, leading to a 10-point rating system); the rating is recorded as 0 when the user did not assign a rating to the jth item.

We can also refer to the data set $\mathbf{U}$ as an m-by-n matrix, called the *rating matrix*, where each of the m row vectors, say $\mathbf{u}_i$, is the ith instance in $\mathbf{U}$ representing user i, and each of the n columns vectors, say $\mathbf{c}_j$, is the vector containing the jth feature values.

Correlation (see Section 2.4 in Chapter 2) is often used as a similarity measure in collaborative filtering. Thus, we define *correlation similarity* for users $\mathbf{x} = \langle x_1, x_2, \ldots, x_n \rangle$ and $\mathbf{z} = \langle z_1, z_2, \ldots, z_n \rangle$, denoted as $S_R(\mathbf{x}, \mathbf{z})$ as 1 minus the correlation distance, as introduced at the end of Section 4.1 in Chapter 4; that is, we have

$$S_R(\mathbf{x}, \mathbf{z}) = \frac{\sum_{i=1}^n (x_i - \bar{\mathbf{x}})(z_i - \bar{\mathbf{z}})}{\sqrt{\sum_{i=1}^n (x_i - \bar{\mathbf{x}})^2} \sqrt{\sum_{i=1}^n (z_i - \bar{\mathbf{z}})^2}}.$$

The two main approaches to collaborative filtering are *user-based* CF and *item-based* CF. We make use of the following notation:

(i) r_{aj} is the rating prediction for the active user $\mathbf{u}_a$, for the jth item.

(ii) k is a parameter denoting the number of nearest neighbour users (see Subsection 4.3.1) of the active user $\mathbf{u}_a$, with respect to a similarity measure such as cosine or correlation, used for the purpose of prediction.

(iii) $S(\mathbf{u}_a, \mathbf{u}_i)$ is the similarity between users $\mathbf{u}_a$ and $\mathbf{u}_i$; this is the same as the similarity measure used to determine the nearest neighbours.

(iv) For user $\mathbf{u}_i = \langle u_{i1}, u_{i2}, \ldots, u_{in} \rangle$, u_{ij} is the rating $\mathbf{u}_i$ assigned to item j and $\bar{\mathbf{u}}_i$ is the average rating of items for that user, noting that when computing the average rating we include only rated items, that is, those for which $u_{ij} > 0$.

The user-based CF prediction is now given as

$$r_{aj} = \bar{\mathbf{u}}_a + \frac{\sum_{i=1}^{k} (u_{ij} - \bar{\mathbf{u}}_i)\, S(\mathbf{u}_a, \mathbf{u}_i)}{\sum_{i=1}^{k} |S(\mathbf{u}_a, \mathbf{u}_i)|},$$

recalling that $|v|$ is the absolute value of v.

We augment the notation for item-based CF as follows:

(i) For the active user $\mathbf{u}_a = \langle u_{a1}, u_{a2}, \ldots, u_{an} \rangle$, u_{aj} is the rating $\mathbf{u}_a$ assigned to item j.

(ii) The ratings given to item j are represented by the transpose $\mathbf{c}_j^T$ of the column vector $\mathbf{c}_j$ of the rating matrix $\mathbf{U}$.

The item-based CF approach prediction is now given as

$$r_{ai} = \frac{\sum_{j \text{ rated by } a} S(\mathbf{c}_i^T, \mathbf{c}_j^T)\, u_{aj}}{\sum_{j \text{ rated by } a} |S(\mathbf{c}_i^T, \mathbf{c}_j^T)|}.$$

Example 5.5. We first demonstrate item-based CF on a movie data set constructed by *MovieLens*, consisting of 9,742 movies. The data set is represented in a *item-user matrix*, where each row in the data set represents an item (in this case a movie), while each column represents a user (or alternatively, a viewer); note the item-user matrix is the transpose of the rating matrix. The number in each cell is a rating between 1 and 10 given by the viewer, or an empty cell when the viewer did not rate that item (corresponding to a 0 rating). In practice, recommender systems often use a star system, where there are five stars or equivalently ten half stars, which is identical to the 10-point rating system. A sample of the item-user matrix for five users and movies is shown in Table 5.8. Viewers only watch and rate a small subset of the full movies available, and so the full matrix of movies and user scores is very sparse. Thus, there are very few scores for each movie, which may have an impact on the results of recommendation systems. The mean movie rating is derived from only those viewers who rated the movie and does not take into account movies that have no ratings. The top-five movies watched by V_a are shown in Table 5.9.

Table 5.8 A sample of movies and viewer ratings per movie, with the *mean movie rating* in the final column and the *mean user rating* in the final row.

Movie title	V_1	V_2	V_3	V_4	V_5	Mean movie rating
Sudden Death		6			10	8.00
Sabrina	8	8			8	8.00
Toy Story			6	8	4	6.00
Jumanji	6		2	6		4.66
Tom and Huck	10		8	8	6	8.00
Mean user rating	8.00	7.00	5.33	7.33	7.00	9.32

Table 5.9   The top-five movies watched by viewer V_a, including the title and rating.

Title	Score
Adventures of Robin Hood, The (1938)	10
Alice in Wonderland (1951)	10
20 Dates (1998)	8
Abyss, The (1989)	8
13th Warrior, The (1999)	8

Table 5.10   The top-five recommended movies for V_a based on the history of movies watched by the viewer, employing KNN with $k = 3$.

Title	Predicted rating
101 Dalmatians (1996) - predicted rating	10
Austin Powers: The Spy Who Shagged Me (1999)	10
Best in Show (2000)	10
Brady Bunch Movie, The (1995)	10
Close Encounters of the Third Kind (1977)	10

For recommendation purposes, we apply the k-nearest neighbour (KNN) algorithm with $k = 3$. The list of recommended movies, based on the ratings given to movies watched by viewer V_a, include a mix of Disney, comedy, and sci-fi movie recommendations, which are considered to be similar to movies they scored highly in the past; see Table 5.10 for the top-five recommendations.

We now demonstrate user-based CF of viewers' ratings on a subset of the MovieLens data set. The data set contains 597 unique users and their rating of over 9,000 movies; as before, the ratings are integers between 1 and 10. Based on viewers' (or users') rating of movies, we can recommend to them movies that they may enjoy based on the viewing habits of other viewers. The matrix, shown in Table 5.11, presents a small sample of 11 random users from the *user-user correlation matrix* displaying the correlation similarity between several viewers of the platform, with the correlation values ranging from -1 to 1 (see Section 2.4 in Chapter 2). Based on this matrix, we can recommend new movies to a viewer, say V_a, by employing user-based CF, as described earlier. Table 5.12 shows the top-five recommended movies for V_a, based on the user-user correlation matrix. We note that in this example the average scores of the movies recommended to viewer V_a are low.

Another method for collaborative filtering is similar to the way topic modelling is formalised in Subsection 4.4.4 in Chapter 4 as a non-negative matrix factorisation (NMF) problem.

Table 5.11 A small sample of 11 random users V_{r1} to V_{r11} from the user-user correlation matrix, based on their movie rating profile. The matrix showing how similar their movie ratings are to other users is in the range of -1 to 1.

Viewers	V_{r6}	V_{r7}	V_{r8}	V_{r9}	V_{r10}	V_{r11}
V_{r1}	1.00	-0.58	0.00	-1.00	0.00	0.00
V_{r2}	0.00	0.00	0.00	0.00	0.00	0.00
V_{r3}	0.36	-0.23	0.56	0.16	-0.15	0.90
V_{r4}	-0.77	0.00	0.23	0.13	0.06	-0.24
V_{r5}	0.95	-0.29	-0.03	-0.12	-0.17	0.06

Table 5.12 Top-five recommended movies for viewer V_a, based on the movie ratings of V_a and the user-user correlation matrix of similar users who have rated similar movies.

Title	Mean score
Harry Potter and the Chamber of Secrets (2002)	3.76
Eternal Sunshine of the Spotless Mind (2004)	3.76
Ocean's Eleven (2001)	1.76
Bourne Identity, The (2002)	1.76
Inception (2010)	1.36

In this case, the m documents are the m users, and the n words are the n items (i.e., the vocabulary V is the item set I). In addition, the k latent topics become k latent factors.

As a result of NMF, the transpose $\mathbf{U}^T$, of the rating matrix, is factorised into two matrices: an n-by-k matrix $\mathbf{W}$ and an k-by-m matrix $\mathbf{H}$ such that

$$\mathbf{W} \times \mathbf{H} \approx \mathbf{U}^T,$$

and thus the product $\mathbf{W} \times \mathbf{H}$ will contain the desired predictions.

Two notable problems in collaborative filtering are the *sparsity* and *first-rater* problems. The sparsity problem arises from the fact that most of the values in the rating matrix $\mathbf{U}$ are actually 0s, since any user will only be able to rate very few items of the many available ones. Although the sparsity problem has a positive effect on the complexity of computations over $\mathbf{U}$, it raises the question whether reliable predictions can be made when either a user has not rated many items or an item has not been rated by many users. The first-rater problem arises when a new item is added to the item set, but it has not been rated by any users. In this case, collaborative filtering will not be able to recommend this new item at all.

One resolution to these problems is to deploy a hybrid context-based and collaborative filtering approach to recommender systems. The idea is simply to replace a rating of 0, when a user did not rate an item, by the corresponding pseudo-rating by the user for the item, as described earlier, and then carry on with the user-based or item-based approaches as before. We are assuming that each user and item have a profile, so that the pseudo-rating can be computed on demand when needed. We may further wish to weight the predictions according to the number of items the user has rated, as we expect the predictions to be more accurate as this number grows.

Another form of weighting to improve the quality of predictions is to take into account temporal aspects, giving higher weight to more recent ratings. This is based on the fact that user tastes may change in time, and the more recent rating will better reflect users' current preferences.

There is another dimension we briefly touch upon, that is, the role played by product advertisements, which can also be viewed as a form of recommendation called *paid* recommendations. We distinguish between *paid* recommendations and *algorithmic* (or *organic*) recommendations as described previously, which we assume are purely data-driven and not paid for. (There is a fine line here, which we do not wish to go into, of whether the rating data or the actual code implementing the preceding algorithms are free from bias created by some indirect form of advertising.) We point out that the same distinction, between organic and paid, also applies to search engine results because these can be viewed as a form of recommendation. Without going into detail, paid advertising normally goes to the highest bidder, and may be targeted, for example, to the user's browsing history. Paid advertising is normally clearly marked as such to distinguish it from organic recommendations because this is mandated by consumer agencies.

5.2 Social Networks

Social networks fall with the realm of *network science*, whose broad aim is to provide an understanding of networks as a mechanism to understand the relationships between the actors in a network; see Section 3.6 in Chapter 3, where social network data was introduced.

We cover the basic concepts in Section 5.2.1, and in Section 5.2.2 we introduce some centrality measures, allowing us to ascertain the importance of actors in the network from several different perspectives. The 80-20 rule, which states, for example, that 80% of friendship relationships in a social network originate from 20% of the actors, is covered in Section 5.2.3. It may not be precisely 80-20 as stated, but it indicates that the distribution of friendship is approximately skewed in that manner. (In practice, rather than 80-20, it may be 90-10 or some other skewed proportions.) More precisely, the 80-20 rule is typical in power law (or Pareto) distributed relationships, in contrast to the normal (or Gaussian) distributed ones. In Section 5.2.4, we briefly cover another broad topic, that of modelling the spread of infectious diseases, when, according to the model, individuals are deemed to come in contact with each other at random. These types of models, when actors meet randomly rather than with their friends as determined by the structure of the network, are a simplification but, maybe surprisingly, lead to meaningful results providing many useful insights.

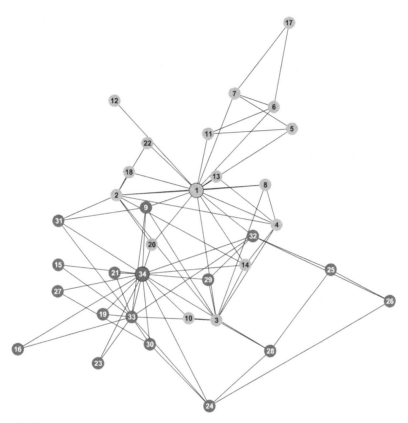

Figure 5.5 A visualisation of the Karate Club social network, with blue nodes representing followers of the administrator (node 1) and orange nodes representing followers of the instructor (node 34).

Example 5.6. To introduce social networks, we consider the Karate Club social network data set, captured by Wayne Zachary over a period of three years from 1970 to 1972. The network is based on 34 individuals who were members of a karate club. The data set records the edges (representing ties) between pairs of members (the nodes, representing actors) in the network, who interacted socially outside of the club. Figure 5.5 illustrates the conflict that arose between followers of the administrator (blue nodes) and followers of the instructor (orange nodes). This conflict resulted in the division of the club, where half of the members moved on to create a new club with the previous instructor (orange nodes), and the other group of members either found a new club or gave up karate completely (blue nodes).

5.2.1 The Basics of Social Networks

A social network in its basic form is a graph G having a node set, N, containing m nodes, representing the *actors* in the networks, and a set of edges, E, which are bidirectional links between nodes in N, representing a form of *tie* or interaction between the actors; see the definition of an *undirected graph* in Section 4.5 in Chapter 4 where graph-based learning was introduced. A common type of social network is one where the actors are people and the edges denote a relationship such as friendship between two actors. (When there is no ambiguity, we will refer to a social network, which is an undirected graph, simply as a network.)

Nodes n_1 and n_2 that form an edge, that is, a pair (n_1, n_2) in E, are said to be *adjacent* and are also referred to as being *neighbours* of each other. The number of neighbours of a node is called its *degree*. We note that since the graph is undirected, (n_1, n_2) and (n_2, n_1) denote the same edge, while in a directed graph, these would represent distinct arcs. We also assume for simplicity that the nodes n_1 and n_2 in an edge (n_1, n_2) are distinct; that is, there are no loops and thus $n_1 \neq n_2$. For a node set N of m nodes, the *adjacency matrix* of G is an m-by-m square matrix A such that $A_{ij} = 1$ if there is an edge $(n_i, n_j) \in E$ and $A_{ij} = 0$, otherwise. Because the graph is undirected, the resulting matrix is *symmetric*. The no loops assumption implies that the diagonal of the adjacency matrix A contains only 0s.

We repeat the definition, from Subsection 4.4.5, of a *connected component* in a graph due to its importance in a social network. Two nodes $n_h, n_j \in N$ are said to be *connected* if there is a sequence of nodes $(n_1, n_2, \ldots, n_{k-1}, n_k)$ in N such that $n_h = n_1, n_j = n_k$, and for $i = 1, 2, \ldots, k - 1$, there is an edge $(n_i, n_{i+1}) \in E$; note that in the special case when $k = 2$, n_h and n_j are connected since $(n_h, n_j) \in E$, and also when $k = 1$, and n_h and n_j are in fact the same point, and the degenerate sequence of a single point is assumed to be connected. The sequence of nodes $(n_1, n_2, \ldots, n_{k-1}, n_k)$, whose nodes can be assumed to be distinct, is called a *path* from n_1 to n_k, and its *length*, denoted by $len(n_1, n_k)$, is $k - 1$, that is, the number of edges in the path. The *distance* between any two nodes is the length of a shortest path between these two nodes, that is, a path between these nodes containing the minimal number of edges.

A *connected component* is a maximal collection of nodes such that each pair of nodes in the collection is connected to each other. In other words, there is a path between every pair of nodes in the component. If the collection of nodes includes all the nodes in N, that is, there is only a single connected component, then the graph is said to be *connected*. We will assume by default that a social network is connected since, in the case that it is not connected, we may consider its connected components as separate *sub*-social networks. In this context an edge is a *bridge* if its removal causes the network to separate into two connected components.

A social network is *weighted* when each edge, say (n_i, n_j) in E, has a *weight* w (i.e., a value w) attached to it representing the strength of the tie between nodes n_i and n_j; in a weighted network, edges become triples (n_i, n_j, w).

Consider an actor's neighbours to be its friends, and for an actor n_i, let $f(n_i)$ be the number of friends of n_i, that is, the number of neighbours it has. The *friendship paradox* states that if X generates a randomly chosen actor and Y generates a randomly chosen actor from a randomly chosen edge in the network, that is, from a friendship relationship, then

$$E(f(Y)) \geq E(f(X)).$$

This is often stated informally as "on average your friends have more friends than you do." Now, the average number of your friends is just the average degree, since X is a random variable over nodes. However, the average number of friends takes into account the friendship relationships, since Y is a random variable over all nodes in edges. Now, if all actors have the same number of friends, then we get equality in the preceding equation; however, in real social networks, we expect some actors to have quite a few more friends than others and, therefore, Y is more likely to choose one of them when the random selection is over edges.

In 1967, Milgram, a renowned American social psychologist, carried out a seminal experiment in social network analysis. Milgram's so-called *small-world* experiment tested the hypothesis that within a social network, short paths, or chains as he called them, exist between any two actors in the network. It is a relatively common occurrence that two people who meet each other at a party discover that they have an unlikely mutual acquaintance, and then say "isn't it a small world."

The small-world problem can be rephrased in terms of the social network structure as follows, where edges between actors denote the relationship of being acquainted with each other. Suppose you choose two random actors in the network, then the small-world problem is to find the shortest path of acquaintances between these two actors, which is termed the *number of degrees of separation* in the network. The small-world property holds, if this number is small, or more precisely the expected value of the shortest path between any two nodes in the network is of the order of $\log(m)$, that is, logarithmic in the number of nodes m in the network.

Milgram's 1967 experiment involved measuring the length of chain of acquaintances it took to deliver a parcel originating from a random "starter" person to a "target" person in an unknown city distant from that of the starter. When receiving the parcel, each person in the chain was given some information about the target and was asked to mail the parcel to someone they knew on a first-name basis, whom they believed would be more likely either to know the target or to know someone who would know the target. The information they received about the target was meant to help them choose who to send the parcel to, without revealing any information regarding the location of the target. The average chain length of the 30% completed chains, when the parcels actually reached the target, was found to be six; hence the famous hypothesis that any two people are connected by "six degrees of separation." The relatively low completion rate casts some doubt on any firm conclusions that can be deduced from Milgram's study; however, it seems that people are generally comfortable with this hypothesis. As further evidence, the number of degrees of separation in the largest existing social network was found to be close to five.

Although we may know that short acquaintance paths exist, a question that arises is, How does one find the shortest path to the target? Moreover, if we only use a local search strategy, where we can pass the message on to only one of our neighbours, will we be able to find the target efficiently? A reasonable local strategy is that at each step we choose the nearest neighbour believed to be closest in distance to the target; this type of strategy results in what is known as a *greedy* algorithm. Here we assume that the network distance, in terms of the length of the shortest path, corresponds to geographic distance in some well-defined manner, when navigating in a physical rather than virtual network. To make

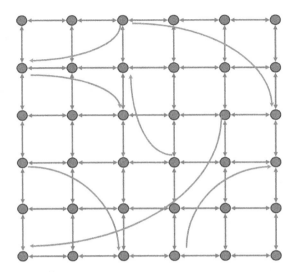

Figure 5.6   A two-dimensional grid with random shortcuts.

this more concrete, we may model the network in terms of a two-dimensional grid, where each node has exactly four neighbours and where the distance d between any two nodes in the grid is the Manhattan distance between them. To shorten the length of paths, random edges, called *shortcuts*, are added to the grid, where the probability of adding a shortcut between any two nodes decreases with the distance between them, as shown in Figure 5.6. In particular, for the two-dimensional grid, the probability of adding a shortcut is proportional to $1/d^2$, where d is the Manhattan distance between the nodes. The greedy algorithm is, in fact, efficient, only in this case, when the exponent of d is 2. The intuitive reason for this is that if the exponent is greater than 2, there will not be enough shortcuts and, conversely, if the exponent is less than 2, there will be too many of them.

The *clustering coefficient* of an actor n_i is the ratio of the number of edges all of n_i's neighbours including itself, to the maximum possible number of edges between all the neighbours of n_i including n_i, obtaining a number between 0 and 1. (For an actor having $k-1$ neighbours, the maximum number of edges between them is $k(k-1)/2$.) Why is the clustering coefficient important, and how does it relate to small-world networks? Well, a world network is defined as one that satisfies the small-world property and whose clustering coefficient is much higher than that of a random network, where each edge in the network is present with a fixed probability. The importance of the clustering coefficient is grounded in empirical evidence, which suggests that in real networks, such as social networks, the clustering coefficient tends to be much higher than in random networks.

5.2.2 Centrality Measures

Centrality addresses the issue of how important or influential an actor is in a social network. The simplest centrality measure is *degree centrality*, which is the number of neighbours of a node. This is quite intuitive but only gives a localised view of how central an actor is in the network. In *closeness centrality* we measure how close, on average, nodes in the network are to each other. So, an actor is more central if its average distance to other actors in the network is smaller. This is related to the facility location problem, which is the problem of where to locate a facility such as a hospital or supermarket that maximises its accessibility in terms of transportation. The control of flow of information in a social network is captured by *betweenness centrality*, which records, for a given actor, the quotient of the number of all shortest paths between actors that passes through the given actor and the totality of shortest paths between any two actors excluding the given one.

Two additional centrality measures are presented, *eigenvector centrality* and the *geometric potential gain* (or simply the potential gain), that take into account the influence of nodes beyond the neighbouring nodes. Eigenvector centrality, also known as *prestige*, can be viewed as a generalisation of PageRank (introduced in Subsection 5.1.2), where the importance of nodes is determined by the importance of its neighbours and so on for the neighbours and neighbours of neighbours, which leads to an iterative definition of centrality, whose computation involves the whole network. The potential gain makes the further assumption that the importance of a node decays in a geometric fashion as a function of the node's distance from the source node (and, yes, there is also a variant of the potential gain in which the importance decays in an exponential fashion).

To define centrality, we let A be the adjacency matrix of the social network G, and construct an m feature vector, $\mathbf{c} = \langle c_1, c_2, \ldots, c_m \rangle$, whose ith feature represents the centrality score of node $n_i \in N$.

We now present the formal definitions of the above-mentioned centrality measures, where n_i is a node in N. The *degree centrality*, c_i, of a node, $n_i \in N$, is simply its number of neighbours, that is, its degree. The *closeness centrality* c_i of the node n_i is given by

$$c_i = \frac{m - 1}{\sum_{n_j \in N} len(n_i, n_j)},$$

where the denominator divided by $m - 1$ is the distance of n_i to other nodes in the network. We note that $m - 1$ in the numerator is often replaced with m (the number of nodes in the network), since for large networks the difference will be very small.

Let $short(n_h, n_j)$ be the number of shortest paths in G from node $n_h \in N$ to node $n_j \in N$, and $short(n_h, n_j, n_i)$ be the number of shortest paths in G from n_h to n_j that pass though n_i. The *betweenness centrality* c_i of the node, n_i, is given by

$$c_i = \sum_{\substack{n_h \neq n_i \neq n_j \\ n_h, n_j \in N}} \frac{short(n_h, n_j, n_i)}{short(n_h, n_j)}.$$

In eigenvector centrality the importance of a node (in this case its centrality) is determined by the importance of its neighbouring nodes rather than just by the number of neighbours, as in degree centrality. So, as in PageRank, which is a variant of eigenvector centrality, a node may have fewer neighbours but higher importance, depending on the importance of its neighbours. More formally, the *eigenvector centrality* c_i of the node $n_i \in N$ is given by

$$c_i = \frac{1}{\lambda} \sum_{j=1}^{n} A_{ij} c_j,$$

for some constant λ, which in matrix notation reduces to

$$A\mathbf{c} = \lambda \mathbf{c},$$

where $\lambda = \rho(G)$, called the *spectral radius* of the graph G, is seen to be the largest absolute value of its eigenvalues, and the vector of centrality scores, $\mathbf{c}$, is seen to be its corresponding eigenvector; eigenvalues and eigenvectors were introduced in Subsection 4.4.3 in Chapter 4 in the context of PCA.

Let α, where $0 < \alpha < 1$ is a constant, called the *discount factor*, which determines the level of decay in moving to neighbouring nodes, and let $\mathbf{u}$ be the all-ones m feature vector $\mathbf{u} = \langle 1, 1, \ldots, 1 \rangle$. The *geometric potential gain* of G with respect to α, denoted by $GPG(G, \alpha)$, is given by

$$\mathbf{c} = GPG(G, \alpha) = A \left(I + \alpha A + (\alpha A)^2 + \cdots \right) \mathbf{u} = A \left(I - \alpha A \right)^{-1} \mathbf{u},$$

where I is the identity matrix and M^{-1} denotes the inverse of a matrix M, which in this case arises due to a geometric series of matrices.

Moreover, the spectral radius of the graph induced by the matrix $A \left(I - \alpha A \right)^{-1}$ is given by

$$\frac{\rho(G)}{1 - \alpha \rho(G)},$$

where, as in the case of eigenvector centrality, $\mathbf{c}$ is the eigenvector corresponding to $\rho(G)$. So, for the geometric potential gain to converge, we should constrain α as follows,

$$\alpha < \frac{1}{\rho(G)}.$$

Example 5.7. In Table 5.13 we show the centrality measure scores of the top-three node scores in the Karate Club social network shown in Figure 5.5, noting that the centrality scores have been normalised to add up to 1. It can be verified that the spectral radius of this social network is 6.7257, and for the computation of the potential gain, we set $\alpha = 0.5/\rho(G)$, which gives $\alpha = 0.0743$.

We have introduced several centrality measures that attempt to assess how important or influential an actor is within a network. An important question to ask is, What characteristics should a centrality measure possess? A sound approach in this respect is the *axiomatic* method, which suggests axioms, each of which comprises a set of properties to be

Table 5.13 Normalised centrality measures for the Karate Club data set, with the top-three scores for each measure, where ID is the node identifier of a member of the Karate Club and score is the centrality measure.

Degree		Closeness		Betweenness		Eigenvector		Potential gain	
ID	**Score**	**ID**	**Score**	**ID**	**Score**	**ID**	**Score**	**ID**	**Score**
33	0.1090	0	0.0392	0	0.2925	33	0.0750	33	0.0866
0	0.1026	2	0.0386	33	0.2032	0	0.0714	0	0.0833
32	0.0769	33	0.0379	32	0.0971	2	0.0637	32	0.0666

satisfied by a centrality measure. Several sensible axioms have been proposed such as (i) a requirement that the larger the centrality of the neighbours of an actor, the larger the centrality of that actor, and (ii) if a bridge (see Subsection 5.2.1) (n_1, n_2) is removed from the network, and the component containing n_1 has a larger node set than the component containing n_2, then n_1 is more central than n_2.

5.2.3 Power Laws and the 80–20 Rule

The tails of the common bell-shaped normal distribution decay at a very fast, exponential rate. For example, the height and weight of people are normally distributed as they do not vary that much from the average. So, for example, you will not find anyone twice as tall as the average grown man. On the other hand, if we consider the distribution of wealth in the population, it is by no means normal; rather, it is distributed as a power law. This means that the tail of the distribution decays only polynomially fast, which is by far slower than the exponential decay of the normal distribution. The power law is a skewed distribution, as opposed to the symmetric normal distribution, so we distinguish between the head of the distribution (the left side of the distribution when plotted) and its tail (the right side of the distribution when plotted). The 80–20 rule of thumb emanates from the power law distribution, although the precise proportions vary according to the application at hand. Power law distributions are abundant in nature. So there are a few very large earthquakes but many small ones; there are a few heavily populated cities but most are lightly populated; and there are few very large firms but most are rather small in size. In natural language texts, there are a few very frequent words but most are relatively rare; and in bibliometrics there are a few very highly cited authors but most receive only a few citations. In the web graph, few web pages have very many inlinks but most have only a few; also few websites are very large but most have only a few pages in them; in addition a few websites receive a very high number of daily visitors, that is, clicks, but most will have only a few, if any, visitors on a daily basis. In a social network the degree distribution is generally found to be a power law, where only a few actors have many friends, but most actors actually have only a few friends.

The probability density function (PDF) f_X of a *power law* distribution (also known as a *Pareto distribution*; see Section 2.1 in Chapter 2) takes on the form

$$f_X(x) = Cx^{-(\alpha+1)},$$

for a positive exponent α and some positive constant C acting as a normalisation constant (since the integral of f_X over all values x of X must be equal to 1), with the constraint that the data value x satisfies $x > 0$, recalling that $x^{-\alpha} = 1/x^\alpha$ (see Section 2.1 for the definition of probability distribution).

Now, let x_{min} be the positive lower bound of values x of X. Then, since the exponent α satisfies $\alpha > 0$, we can compute C to obtain

$$f_X(x) = \alpha \, (x_{min})^\alpha \; x^{-(\alpha+1)}.$$

The survival function, $S_X(x)$, of the Pareto distribution is thus

$$S_X(x) = (x_{min})^\alpha \; x^{-\alpha}.$$

The median of the power law distribution can be seen to be $x_{min}2^{1/\alpha}$, by setting $S_X(x) = 0.5$ and solving for x. Moreover, its mean, μ, is given by

$$\mu = \begin{cases} \infty & \text{if } \alpha \leq 1 \\ \dfrac{\alpha \, x_{min}}{\alpha - 1} & \text{if } \alpha > 1, \end{cases}$$

and its variance, σ^2, is given by

$$\sigma^2 = \begin{cases} \infty & \text{if } \alpha \leq 2 \\ \dfrac{\alpha x_{min}^2}{(\alpha - 1)^2 (\alpha - 2)} & \text{if } \alpha > 2. \end{cases}$$

Compared to the normal and exponential distributions, the power law distribution decays more slowly, and its tail events, although unlikely, are much more likely than the tail events of the exponential distribution. Combined with the fact that for power law distributions, its variance may be infinite (when $\alpha \leq 2$) and even its mean (when $\alpha \leq 1$), this leads to a fundamental difference compared to the normal and exponential distributions whose mean and variance are finite. Thus (when the variance is infinite), the power law distribution is metaphorically known as being *fat-tailed*, *long-tailed*, or *heavy-tailed* rather than being *light-tailed* or *thin-tailed*, as are the normal and exponential distributions. (Strictly speaking, there is a technical difference between fat-tailed distributions, which are properly included in the class of long-tailed distributions, which in turn are properly included in the class of heavy-tailed distributions; here we will not distinguish between them.)

The power law distribution, which was originally used by Vilfredo Pareto to describe the distribution of wealth in society, is a well-known example of a heavy-tailed distribution (with the exponent α typically being around 1.5), as is the distribution of word frequencies in natural language texts (with the exponent α typically being around 1.0), originally investigated by George Kingsley Zipf. The distribution of word frequencies is an example of a *rank-order distribution*. To obtain the distribution in this case, we rank words from 1 to the number of words, say n, where the word at rank 1 is the most frequent, the word at rank 2 the second most frequent, and so on until the nth word, which is the least frequent. We can then plot the frequency, appropriately normalised, against rank, resulting in the desired rank-order distribution. Heavy tails are also referred to as *long* or *fat tails* (as mentioned above); for example, in book sales the long tail is mentioned when explaining the phenomenon in e-commerce, where the total volume of sales of all the items in the tail is comparable to that of the most popular items.

Now consider the *degree distribution* of a network, which is the distribution of the degree centrality of the network. The minimum degree centrality is 1, since we have assumed the network is connected, and thus $x_{min} = 1$ in this case. The survival function of the degree distribution gives us the probability $P(X > i)$ in the network, that is, the probability that a node has degree centrality greater than i, where $i \geq 1$. Now an interesting point to note is that degree centrality is discrete, while the Pareto distribution, as we have defined it, is a continuous distribution. However, it is common practice to approximate discrete distributions with continuous ones, since they are mathematically easier to deal with.

It turns out that the degree distribution of many real-world networks is empirically fitted to a power law distribution. For example, in the web graph, which is a directed network, the in-degree distribution, that is, the distribution of inlinks, is a power law with exponent around $\alpha = 1.1$, while the out-degree distribution, that is, the distribution of outlinks, is a power law with exponent around $\alpha = 1.7$. As another example, consider the Twitter social media network, where users interact by posting short messages. Users can "follow" other users leading to a directed network, but if we restrict the network to the case when the follow relationship is reciprocated, the resulting network, called the mutual graph, is undirected, as in a social network where an edge typically denotes friendship. The degree distribution of the mutual graph is empirically a power law distribution with an exponent around $\alpha = 0.4$. Not all degree distributions of social networks are power laws, so, for example, that of the massive social network Facebook is not a strict power law. In fact, it is not so surprising given that Facebook has an artificial limit on the number of friends anyone can have in the network. In such situations, when there is evidence that the degree of actors decays exponentially beyond a certain value, it may be possible that adding an exponential cutoff to a power law would provide a better fit to the data than a strict power law.

It is also worth mentioning that power law distributions are also known to be *scale-free*, referring to the fact that their distributions look the same at all scales. For example, assuming that the degree distribution is a power law, if we observe actors in a social network having between 10 and 100 friends, they would be distributed in the same way as actors having between 100 and 1,000 friends. In practice, this means that if a distribution obeys a power law, then detecting the power law at a given range of values allows prediction of its values outside the range. This characteristic, of having the same properties at all scales, is also known as *self-similarity* or that of possessing *fractal* behaviour.

The most direct method to determine whether, say, the degree distribution of a network is a power law is to plot the data set on a logarithmic scale, giving rise to a *log-log plot*. If the data set comes from a power law distribution, then the plot will reveal a straight line (or a good approximation thereof), which can be fitted with linear regression (see Section 2.5 in Chapter 2). The reason we expect a straight line when the distribution is a power law is that taking logarithms on both sides of the PDF of a power law results in the linear equation

$$\log(y) = \log(C) - (\alpha + 1)\log(x),$$

where $y = f_X(x)$ for a data value x.

Log-log plots can be problematic, since in some cases the head of the distribution (the left part of the plot) does not appear to follow a power law distribution, and, in addition, there may be quite a bit of noise in the tail of the distribution (the right part of the plot), making it difficult to position the slope α of the regression line. The noise in the tail is, essentially, owing to the fact that for a finite sample the number of observations that are likely to fall in the range of, say 1 to 100, is much larger than the number that are likely to fall in the larger range, say 1,000 to 10,000, despite the fact that on the logarithmic scale these two intervals have the same size.

One way to get around noise in the tail of the distribution is to use a technique called *logarithmic binning*. The data set is collected into bins, in such a way that the bin sizes increase exponentially. So, taking the base of the logarithm to be 2, the first bin covers the range with the single value 1, the second bin the range 2–3, the third bin the range 4–7, and so on. The bins are then normalised by dividing the number of data points in each bin by the width of the bin. Once the data is preprocessed in this manner, we proceed to plot it on a log–log scale, so that the widths of the bins appear to be even, and then carry out linear regression as before. Another way to deal with the problem of noise is to take a log-log plot of the survival function (or complementary CDF) rather than the PDF, which can be viewed as a smoothing operator.

Example 5.8. We consider a data set containing the degree distribution of inlinks for the web graph from a web crawl in 1999 of over 200 million nodes and 1.5 billion links, performed by researchers from AltaVista, Compaq, and IBM. The inlinks degree distribution for the 1999 crawl is shown on the left-hand side of Figure 5.7, while the log-log plot (see Section 3.7 in Chapter 3) of the data set, after the application of logarithmic binning, is shown on the right-hand side of the figure. The exponent of the power law distribution fitted with linear regression to the log-log data results in $\alpha = 1.105$, while the exponent fitted to logarithmically binned data results in $\alpha = 0.492$. On the other hand, the maximum likelihood estimate of the exponent of the resulting power law distribution (see below) for the inlinks degree distribution is $\alpha = 0.500$, with the lower bound of the scale parameter of X set to $x_{min} = 1.0$.

A different method of estimating α, given a data set $x_1, x_2, \ldots, x_n$, where for $i = 1, 2, \ldots, n$, $x_i \geq x_{min}$, is the *maximum likelihood* method, recalling that $x_{min} > 0$. This method involves maximising a log likelihood function given some unknown parameters; in this case, the likelihood function is the PDF of the power law distribution

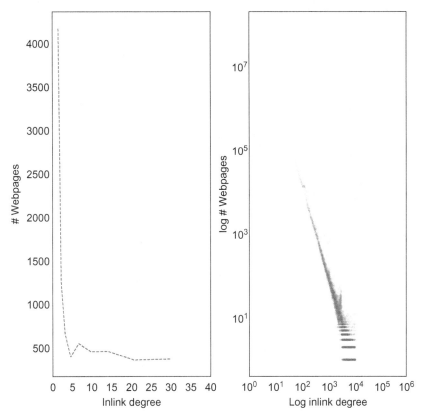

Figure 5.7   The inlinks degree distribution plot (left) and the log-log plot (right) of the 1999
crawl data set.

and there is a single unknown parameter α (we will assume that x_{min} is estimated
separately). In this case, the maximum likelihood estimator for α is given by

$$\alpha = n \left[\sum_{i=1}^{n} \log \left(\frac{x_i}{x_{min}} \right) \right]^{-1},$$

where we have used the same notation, α, for both the true value of the exponent and its
estimate as derived from the data set. For this method to work, we need to estimate x_{min}
from the data, prior to estimating α. We could simply take x_{min} to be the smallest
observed value in the data set. However, power law behaviour may actually occur only
above some of the values in the data set, which could be ignored by setting x_{min} to be
above these values but below the others.

As we have done with α, we use the same notation for both the true x_{min} and its
estimate. For a specified value x_{min}, we can measure the distance between two cumulative

distributions by the *Kolmogorov-Smirnov* (KS) statistic, which is the maximum distance between the two. More precisely, the KS statistic in this context is given by

$$D = \max_{x \geq x_{min}} |F_n(x) - F_X(x)|,$$

where F_n is the empirical distribution function (EDF, see Section 2.1 in Chapter 2) for the data set whose smallest value is greather than or equal to x_{min}, F_X is the CDF of the power law distribution fitted by the maximum likelihood estimator to this data set, and $|y|$ is the absolute value of y. So the estimate of x_{min} is the one that minimises the value of D.

The 80-20 rule in the context of degree centrality states that 80% of the edges that contribute to degree centrality come from 20% of the actors. In terms of the distribution of income or wealth, the 80-20 rule would say that 80% of the wealth or income lies with 20% of the population. The 80-20 rule is a rule of thumb, indicating a skewed relationship rather than a precise statement.

To find the exponent α that satisfies the 80-20 rule, we first need to solve $S_X(x) = 0.8$ to get an expression for x, and then solve $f_X(x) = 0.2$ to get a second expression for x. We then equate both expressions, as given by

$$\left(\frac{0.8}{(x_{min})^{\alpha}}\right)^{-\frac{1}{\alpha}} = \left(\frac{0.2}{\alpha\,(x_{min})^{\alpha}}\right)^{-\frac{1}{\alpha+1}},$$

and solve this equation for α. We can replace 0.8 and 0.2 in the preceding equation by any fractions as long as they add to 1, and obtain α, for example, for the 90-10 rule. We note that as we increase the first percentage (80%) and decrease the second one (20%), α decreases, and vice versa.

Example 5.9. A Pareto chart is a bar chart with the bars sorted in descending order that also depicts a line plot that shows the corresponding cumulative distribution. In particular, the Pareto chart shows the largest bars that contain, say, 95% of the cumulative distribution. In Figure 5.8 we show the Pareto chart for the 1999 web crawl data set with a horizontal broken line at the 95% value of the cumulative distribution of inlinks.

An interesting question to ask is, What is the mechanism by which a power law distribution arises in a social network or, say, in the web graph? One answer, which is quite compelling, can be illustrated using the degree distribution of a social network as an example. The social network evolves at discrete time steps through two mechanisms. The first is the continuous *growth* of the network by adding to it new actors, and the second is forming new friendships through a mechanism called *preferential attachment*. To begin with, the network is initialised with m_0 actors, and the friendships between them are chosen randomly with the constraint that each actor has at least one friend. At each step a new actor is added to the network in such a way that this actor will form k ($k \leq m_0$) new friendships with other actors in the network. Each of these new friendships is formed through preferential attachment, which means the actor with whom the friendship is formed is chosen in proportion to the number of friends that this actor already has. Thus, an actor having twice as many friends than a second actor is twice as likely to receive the new friend than the second actor.

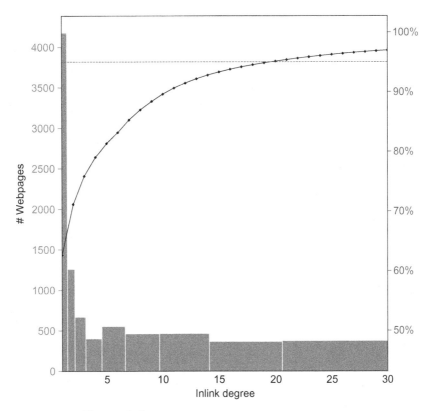

Figure 5.8   A Pareto chart for the 1999 crawl data set.

In reality it is rare that pure preferential attachment actually occurs, since some friendships may form due to random chance; however, as long as there is preferential attachment, the resulting distribution is a power law. Moreover, in the extreme case when the choice of friend is purely random, then the distribution will be exponential rather than a power law. The mechanism of preferential attachment is not new, and has been known under different names. Some of these are the "rich get richer" phenomenon in economics; the "Matthew effect"in sociology, according to the Gospel of Matthew; and "cumulative advantage" in bibliometrics.

An interesting byproduct of preferential attachment is the correlation between the length of time an actor has been present in the network and its degree; this phenomenon is known in economics as the *first-mover advantage*. The longer an actor has been in the network, the more friends it is likely to have. This is not strictly the case in practice, as at times new actors join the network and become "popular" very quickly, where we are using the degree of an actor as a proxy for popularity; for example, this may happen when a celebrity joins the network. Modelling the evolution of a network is well studied, and many extensions have been proposed. Still the basic model gives a good idea of how a power law distribution may emerge in a network.

As we have seen in this section, the power law, or Pareto, distribution is a frequent visitor in real-word data sets such as social network data, whose degree distribution is typically heavy-tailed. As opposed to the normal distribution, power laws are skewed and scale-free. This implies that in a social network, it is possible for an actor to have many more friends than one would expect under the normal distribution. As an example of the 80-20 rule, it has been observed that in online social networks 80% of the content is generated by roughly 20% of the actors.

5.2.4 SIS and SIR Models for the Spread of Disease

Modelling the spread of infectious diseases is at the heart of mathematical epidemiology and of major interest to data scientists, since data analytics is key to decision makers who need to react to disease outbreaks and form policy when intervention is needed. We will concentrate on *compartmental models*, which simplifies the modelling process by partitioning the population into groups, where each individual in a compartment is treated in the same way and individuals can move between compartments according to the progression of the diseases. The basic compartments used in an epidemic model are (i) *susceptible* (S), the number of individuals in the population that have not yet been infected but are at risk of infection; (ii) *infected* (I), the number of individuals in the population that have been infected with the disease; and (iii) *removed* (R), the number of individuals in the population that have either recovered from the disease, are immune for some other reason, or may have died; here we will refer to R as *recovered*.

At any time, t, the number of individuals in the three compartments are $S(t)$, $I(t)$, and $R(t)$ and, if we assume the size of the population is a constant, N, independent of t, then

$$S(t) + I(t) + R(t) = N,$$

although in reality $N = N(t)$, since deaths will reduce the population size and births will increase it. Whenever t is understood from context, we will assume $S = S(t)$, $I = I(t)$, and $R = R(t)$.

An epidemic model determines how individuals flow from one compartment to another, and this is commonly formalised by differential equations; we will present a deterministic rather than stochastic model, since it is simpler to analyse yet capture the essential components necessary in an epidemic model. Some parameters that we may obtain from an epidemic model are

1) The *transmission rate*, β, which is the average number of contacts per individual per unit of time.

2) The *recovery rate*, γ, which is the reciprocal of the average duration D over which an infected individual is infectious, that is, $\gamma = 1/D$.

3) The *basic reproductive number*, $\mathcal{R}_0$, which is the expected number of new infections from a single infected individual in a population where all the individuals are susceptible, that is, $\mathcal{R}_0 = \beta/\gamma$.

4) The *force of infection*, $\beta I/N$, which is the transition rate proportion from the susceptible compartment to the infected compartment.

5) The *final epidemic size*, which is the final numbers of S and R when I eventually becomes zero.

6) The *duration of the epidemic*, which is the time it takes for I to become zero.

7) *Herd immunity*, which is an indirect form of protection from infection, when a large enough proportion of the population has already been infected or vaccinated.

We now briefly present the two simple yet powerful models: the *susceptible-infected-susceptible (SIS)* model and the *susceptible-infected-recovered (SIR)* models. In the SIS model, the flow is from susceptible to infected and then back to susceptible, illustrated as $S \rightarrow I \rightarrow S$; the transfer diagram for the SIS model is shown in Figure 5.9. This model captures the situation when there is no lasting immunity once an infected individual has recovered; an example of this is the common cold. The dynamics of the SIS model are captured by the following system of differential equations:

$$\frac{dS}{dt} = -\frac{\beta SI}{N} + \gamma I$$

$$\frac{dI}{dt} = \frac{\beta SI}{N} - \gamma I,$$

where β is the transmission rate and γ is the recovery rate.

Setting $S = N - I$ in the second equation for the SIS model, we can rewrite it as

$$\frac{dI}{dt} = (\beta - \gamma) I - \frac{\beta I^2}{N},$$

We can now further rewrite the second equation as

$$\frac{dI}{dt} = rI \left(1 - \frac{I}{K} \right),$$

where $r = \beta - \gamma$ and $K = rN/\beta$, whose solution is a logistic function (see Section 2.5 in Chapter 2). Recalling that $\mathcal{R}_0 = \beta/\gamma$, it can now be shown that when $\mathcal{R}_0 \leq 1$, then as t

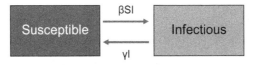

Figure 5.9   Transfer diagram for the SIS compartmental model.

gets larger, $I = I(t)$ tends to 0, that is, the epidemic dies out, and when $\mathcal{R}_0 > 1$, as t gets larger, I tends to

$$\left(1 - \frac{\gamma}{\beta}\right) N,$$

that is, the number of infected individuals is a fixed fraction of the population size, N. In the SIS model, we have $N = S + I$, so $S = N - I$.

In the SIR model, the flow is from susceptible to infected and then from infected to recovered, illustrated as $S \to I \to R$; the transfer diagram for the SIR model is shown in Figure 5.10. This model captures the situation when an infected individual becomes immune over a lasting period once that individual has recovered; an example of this is measles. The dynamics of the SIR model are captured by the following system of differential equations:

$$\frac{dS}{dt} = -\frac{\beta SI}{N}$$

$$\frac{dI}{dt} = \frac{\beta SI}{N} - \gamma I$$

$$\frac{dR}{dt} = \gamma I,$$

where β is the transmission rate and γ is the recovery rate.

We proceed with an analysis of some salient properties of the SIR model. Starting with the susceptible group S, we divide the first equation for the SIR model by the third equation to obtain

$$\frac{dS}{dR} = -\frac{\mathcal{R}_0 S}{N},$$

whose solution can be seen to be

$$S = S(0) \exp\left(-\frac{\mathcal{R}_0 R}{N}\right) \geq S(0) \exp\left(-\mathcal{R}_0\right) > 0,$$

where $S = S(t) = S(0) > 0$ at time $t = 0$. Thus, the final size of the epidemic, which is the limit of $S(t)$ as t tends to infinity, must be greater than 0.

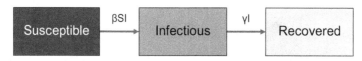

Figure 5.10   Transfer diagram for the SIR compartmental model.

Continuing with the infected group I, the second equation of the SIR model can be rewritten in terms of $\mathcal{R}_0$ as

$$\frac{dI}{dt} = \left(\frac{\mathcal{R}_0 S}{N} - 1\right)\gamma I,$$

where the solution can be seen to be

$$I = I(0)\exp\left(\left(\frac{\mathcal{R}_0 S}{N} - 1\right)\gamma\right),$$

where $I = I(t) = I(0) > 0$ at time $t = 0$. Thus, if

$$S = S(t) > \frac{N}{\mathcal{R}_0},$$

then the number of infected individuals will grow at the next time step, while, if

$$S < \frac{N}{\mathcal{R}_0},$$

then the number of infected individuals will decrease at the next time step; the right-hand side of the preceding two equations is called the *threshold value*. Finally, the maximum value of I is attained when S is equal to the threshold value, since at that point the derivative of I with respect to t is equal to 0.

However, while the limit of $S(t)$ as t tends to infinity is greater than 0, the corresponding limit of $I(t)$ as t tends to infinity is 0; that is, the epidemic eventually dies out. To see this, we first note that by the first equation for the SIR model, the number $S(t)$ is monotonically decreasing with t, but, as we have shown previously, it is always greater than 0. In addition, the limit of the derivative of $S = S(t)$ with respect to t is 0 and, since it cannot fall below 0, this is written as

$$\lim_{t\to\infty}\frac{dS}{dt} = \frac{\beta S(\infty)I(\infty)}{N} = 0,$$

where $S(\infty)$ and $I(\infty)$ denote the values of $S(t)$ and $I(t)$ at infinity. So, since $S(\infty) > 0$, the only option remaining is that $I(\infty) = 0$.

Now, dividing the second equation for the SIR model by the first equation, we get

$$\frac{dI}{dS} = -1 + \frac{\gamma N}{\beta S},$$

where the solution can be seen to be

$$I + S - \frac{\gamma N}{\beta}\log(S) = C,$$

for some constant of integration C. From this we can derive

$$I(0) + S(0) - \frac{\gamma N}{\beta} \log\left(S(0)\right) = S(\infty) - \frac{\gamma N}{\beta} \log\left(S(\infty)\right),$$

noting that $I(\infty) = 0$ and, with some straightforward manipulation, we obtain a solution for $\mathcal{R}_0$, given by

$$\frac{\beta}{\gamma N} = \frac{\mathcal{R}_0}{N} = \frac{\log\left(S(0)\right) - \log\left(S(\infty)\right)}{I(0) + S(0) - S(\infty)}.$$

Now, the severity of the epidemic is given by

$$R(\infty) = \frac{N}{\mathcal{R}_0}\left(\log\left(S(0)\right) - \log\left(S(\infty)\right)\right),$$

where $R(\infty) = S(0) - S(\infty)$ is the number of recovered individuals at the end of the epidemic, noting that at the beginning of the epidemic $I(0)$ is approximately 0.

Example 5.10. In Figure 5.11 we demonstrate the SIS model based on a 365-day period, recorded on a daily basis, with a population size of $N = 58,500$. Its model parameters include an initial group $I(0) = 2$ of infected individuals, a transmission rate per day of $\beta = 0.259$, and a recovery rate per day of $\gamma = 0.045$. Thus, in this case, $\mathcal{R}_0 = 0.259/0.045 = 5.756$. Table 5.14 shows the progression of the disease for the SIS model over the first 100 days.

In Figure 5.12 we demonstrate the SIR model based on a 365-day period, recorded on a daily basis, with a population size of $N = 58,500$. Its model parameters include an initial group $I(0) = 2$ of infected individuals, a transmission rate per day of $\beta = 0.2$, and a recovery rate per day of $\gamma = 0.1$. Thus, in this case, $\mathcal{R}_0 = 0.2/0.1 = 2.0$. Table 5.15 shows the progression of the disease for the SIR model over the first 100 days.

There are various extensions of the SIS and SIR models. In particular, it is common to add an *exposed* compartment between S and I, when individuals undergo an incubation period when they are infected but not yet infectious.

Moreover, these models can be extended to operate over social networks, which complicate the models but make them more realistic. Imposing a social network structure on the spread of a disease results in more realistic models than the basic SIS and SIR models. In this case, there is a constraint that an individual may only come in contact with its neighbours within the network, which is more true to life than random encounters as in the basic models. For example, contact tracing, which is the activity of determining who may have come in contact with an infected individual, can be viewed as the construction of a restricted social network in which only targeted individuals are considered as neighbours. Making use of a social network to monitor the spread of a disease also allows us to detect *superspreaders*, which are individuals who are more likely to infect others compared to a randomly encountered individual. Superspreaders may indeed satisfy the 80-20 rule (see Section 5.2.3) where 20% of the infected individuals are responsible for 80% of the transmissions of the disease.

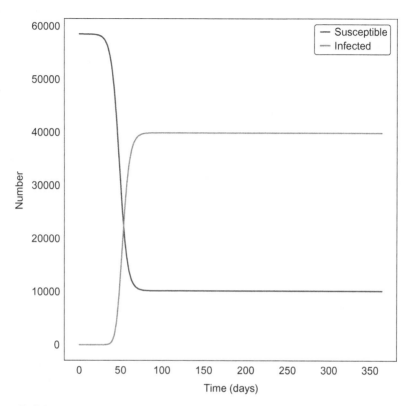

Figure 5.11   A plot showing the dynamics of the SIS model, where the x-axis is time in days and the y-axis is the number of individuals in a compartment; blue=susceptible and red=infected.

Table 5.14   A sample of the SIS model output showing the number of susceptible $S(t)$ and the number of infected individuals $I(t)$, both at time t.

Time	Susceptible	Infected
0	58,498	2
20	58,384	116
40	51,381	7,119
60	13,780	44,720
80	10,230	48,270
100	10,176	48,324

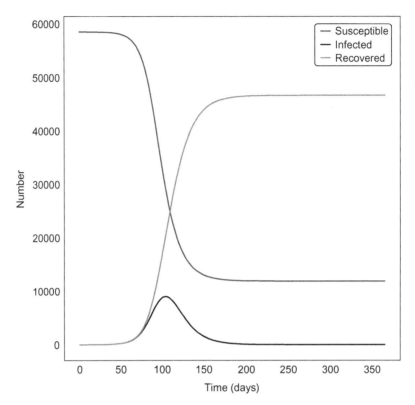

Figure 5.12 A plot showing the dynamics of the SIR model, where the x-axis is time in days and the y-axis is the number of individuals in a compartment; blue=susceptible, red=infected, and green=recovered.

Table 5.15 A sample of the SIR model output showing the number of susceptible $S(t)$, the number of infected $I(t)$, and the number of recovered individuals $R(t)$, all at time t.

Time	Susceptible	Infected	Recovered
0	58,498	2	0
20	58,477	12	11
40	58,323	89	88
60	57,216	636	648
80	50,610	3,653	4,237
100	32,351	8,823	17,326

5.3   Three Natural Language Processing Topics

We briefly introduce three topics from *natural language processing* (NLP). The first two, sentiment analysis (SA) and named entity recognition (NER), are specialised *text classification* tasks, while the third topic, word embeddings, are *distributional representations* of words in NLP texts.

SA detects the polarity in a fragment of text, the polarity being sentiment, opinion, emotion, or mood; here we will concentrate on sentiment. There are many examples from e-commerce and social media, where sentiment from customer reviews and reader comments often has a strong effect on other people's decisions to buy products or on their attitudes toward social media posts. NER, on the other hand, is concerned with labelling of text with semantic tags corresponding to predefined classes, which enhance the understanding of natural language text. Named entities (NEs) are objects from these predefined classes, such as Person, Location, Organisation, and Company. An example of the application of NER is that of labelling news content, which is rich in named entity objects. Another example where NER can help is in the area of semantic search, where search engines make use of meaning, in this case named entities in user queries, to improve the quality of retrieval.

Word embeddings are distributional representations of text in the statistical sense, that have application in boosting the performance of NLP tasks that make use of word similarity. This reduces to computing vector similarity, since the embeddings are operationalised by mapping words to vector representations. Word embeddings are grounded on the hypothesis that linguistics terms with similar distributions have similar meaning. A well-known quote from the English linguist Firth in 1957 is "you shall know a word by the company it keeps," which implies that, in natural language texts, the meaning of a word is correlated with its context.

5.3.1   Sentiment Analysis

We will briefly review detection of sentiment polarity, which examines textual content using NLP and classification methods. A coarse classification will only distinguish between positive (+1), neutral (0), and negative (−1) sentiment. However, it is possible to have a finer grain classification, commonly based on the star rating on a scale of 1 to 5 or the finer 1 to 10 range (adding half stars), or even a continuous range of sentiment values if this is needed.

Assuming that our aim is to derive the sentiment from a document, which could be a user review or a news article, this could be done at the document level, or at a finer granularity, that is, at the sentence level, or at the level of a specific feature, also referred to as an *aspect*. Examples of aspect-based sentiment are "the battery life of the tablet was too short" and the "the weight of the tablet was very reasonable." Aspect-based sentiment analysis involves an additional step, involving the extraction of the aspects (or features) from the text, and segmenting the text in order to delineate the context words, surrounding the feature, that are relevant to the feature and from which sentiment can be detected.

Sentiment is a subjective statement rather than an objective, purely factual one, which does not contain explicit sentiment. So for example, "the movie was very good" is a subjective statement, while the "the movie was filmed in London" is an objective statement, which does not contain an explicit sentiment. In our brief overview, we will assume that sentences that are objective statements have been filtered out and are thus ignored, although this is not to say that these are always neutral. Another type of sentiment is exemplified by a *comparative* statement such as "this book is better than that book" rather than a typical sentiment such as "this book is great." A comparative statement involves a relation between two objects, say books or laptops, examples of which are "better," "cheaper," "faster," or "equal." In this case, sentiment analysis first detects whether a sentence is comparative or not, and only after positive discovery is the comparative relationship extracted.

An important ingredient of SA is the sentiment dictionary or *lexicon*, which is a list of sentiment words that are annotated with their polarity; a lexicon may also include sentiment phrases that contain more than a single word, although we generally ignore these for simplicity of the exposition. The lexicon may be created manually, or starting from a small seed set may be augmented with additional words via an automated method. Such a method may make use of an externally available dictionary from which synonyms and antonyms can be added to an existing lexicon. This is especially useful if we have available a distance measure between words. So, assuming such a distance measure, D, the sentiment of a word (which is often an adjective), w, called its *sentiment orientation* and denoted by $SO(w)$, can be measured by its relative distance from two seed words, w_1 and w_2, acting as reference words, where w_1 is known to be positive and w_2 is known to be negative. Sentiment orientation is defined more formally as

$$SO(w) = \frac{D(w, w_1) - D(w, w_2)}{D(w_1, w_2)},$$

where, if $SO(w) > 0$, then the w is considered to be a positive sentiment word and, if $SO(w) < 0$, then it is considered to be negative; otherwise, it is considered to be neutral. The strength of the sentiment is given by the absolute value of $SO(w)$ and can be used to determine whether to add the word w to the lexicon, provided it is greater than a preset threshold. A distance measure between words can be constructed with graph-based learning in a semi-supervised fashion, as described in Section 4.5 in Chapter 4. As an alternative to this method, or to augment it, we could also make use of a word embedding, as introduced in Subsection 5.3.3, which induces a vector similarity measure between words.

To simplify matters we will concentrate on document sentiment classification, rather than on sentence or aspect-based classification. Aspect-based SA concentrates on a single entity, for example, a tablet or a book, while a sentence may express sentiment on more than a single entity and, moreover, be completely neutral. Due to its typically shorter length, sentence-based classification is normally harder than document-based classification;

however, to ensure that the SA task is meaningful, we will assume that the document expresses sentiment on a single entity and that there is a single sentiment holder; that is, the sentiment is expressed by a single person. We will also ignore the time at which the sentiment was expressed, although in some cases time may be relevant, when sentiment changes according to time.

As a baseline method for SA, we can use a sentiment lexicon in combination with a rule-based classifier. In particular, we can deploy several rules to form a lexicon-based SA classifier. First, a simple rule is to sum the values of all the detected sentiment words and return the sign of the score; a more nuanced approach would use a preset threshold above and below zero to decide whether the sentiment is positive, negative, or neutral. We can refine this by adding a rule for intensifiers, which are words, such as "very" and "really," that modify sentiment polarity by a certain value; when the sentiment is positive, its value will be increased and, when it is negative, it will be decreased. We can also add a rule to take into account negation words, implying the oppositive sentiment, in which case the sentiment polarity will be multiplied by -1; so, for example, the sentiment value of "not bad" is modified to that of "good." However, a lexicon-based SA classifier is somewhat limited, since natural language is generally ambiguous and difficult to deal with, so the rule set is bound to be incomplete. An example of potential difficulties is sarcasm detection, as in "the tablet has all the features you would want, a shame they do not work."

Turning to a machine-learning-based SA algorithm, we will make a further simplification by viewing the problem as a binary classification one, where we only have two classes positive and negative, ignoring the neutral case. It is still worth mentioning that as we have seen in Chapter 4, a machine learning algorithm can output a probability that can readily be translated into, for example, a star rating scale. In this manner, SA is reduced to a text classification problem, and we can readily employ the vector space model described in Subsection 5.1.1. Still, sentiment classification is different from other text classification problems due to the importance of sentiment words in the classification process.

Finally, a hybrid sentiment classification approach makes use of both a lexicon rule-based approach and a machine learning algorithmic approach. Essentially, the idea is to incorporate the features output from the lexicon-based approach, such as its overall score and the detection of individual sentiment words combined with the rules that modify its sentiment polarity, into the feature set of the machine learning algorithm. Apart from enhancing the training of the machine learning, it also enhances the testing, since it allows the detection of sentiment words that were not present in the training data.

Example 5.11. We apply sentiment analysis to a movie review data set, containing reviews collated from three different sources including IMDB, Amazon, and Yelp, where each collection of reviews is composed of 500 positive and 500 negative sentences, labelled as 0 or 1, respectively. We apply sentiment analysis to a sample of 1,000 reviews using naive Bayes classifier as the machine learning algorithm; the model was trained without a lexicon. The test set is labelled by the classifer with sentiment values ranging from -1 to 1, where -1 is negative, 0 is neutral, and 1 is positive sentiment. A sample of the sentiment output from the classifier is shown in Table 5.16.

Table 5.16 A sample of sentences from the data set with the learned sentiment in the first column and the text representing the sentence in the second column.

Score	Text
−0.55	Not sure who was more lost—the flat characters or the audience.
−0.42	A very, very, very slow-moving, aimless movie about a distressed, drifting young man.
−0.25	The rest of the movie lacks art, charm, meaning.... If it's about emptiness, it works I guess, because it's empty.
0.00	Very little music or anything to speak of.
0.00	A bit predictable.
0.49	And those baby owls were adorable.
0.59	Loved the casting of Jimmy Buffet as the science teacher.
0.70	Saw the movie today and thought it was a good effort, good messages for kids.

5.3.2 Named Entity Recognition

Named entity recognition is concerned with detecting and labelling textual fragments with tags corresponding to entities belonging to predefined classes such as Person, Location, Organisation, Company, or even Time expressions or Monetary values. In particular, named entities are linguistically proper nouns; for instance, "Dan Silver" is a person, "London" is a location (or more specifically a City), "New Zealand" is a location (or more specifically a Country), "Arm" is a company, "24 hours" is a time expression, and "£30" is a monetary value. The implementation of NER is broken down into two phases. The first is to identify the entities in text fragments, referred to as *named entity detection*, and the second is to tag the text with the appropriate labels, referred to as *named entity classification*.

We will concentrate on NE classification, as it will often include NE segmentation as a subtask in its computation. We do, however, mention that NE detection typically involves several rules, such as deploying initial capitalisation for detecting named entities; using *gazetteers*, which are dictionaries containing lists of named entities for given classes such as lists of cities and countries; and applying other rules that can help with the detection of named entities from specific classes. In addition, NE detection may also involve parts-of-speech (POS) tagging, which is a standard component of NLP packages, that can recognise proper nouns, which are likely to be named entities.

To address the problem of NE classification, we introduce *conditional random fields* (CRFs), which is a probabilistic graphical model that is especially suited to NER but does have other applications. One of the notable ingredients of CRFs is that its output is also a sequence, providing class labels for all the words in the input sequence.

Now, let $\mathbf{x} = \langle x_1, x_2, \ldots, x_n \rangle$ be a vector of n features, called the input or *text* sequence, and let $\mathbf{y} = \langle y_1, y_2, \ldots, y_n \rangle$ be another vector of n features, called the output or *label* sequence. The features in $\mathbf{x}$ are typically words corresponding to those in a document containing n words, and the features in $\mathbf{y}$ are the labels corresponding to the named entity classes of the words. Named entities may be phrases containing more than a single word, as in "Dan Silver" or "New Zealand," so a tag may be prefixed by B–, denoting the beginning of a named entity or by I–, denoting the inside of a named entity. When the word is not recognised as a named entity, it is tagged as belonging to the Other class. So, for example, the input and output sequences may be

$$\mathbf{x} = \langle \text{Dan}, \text{Silver}, \text{lives}, \text{in}, \text{London} \rangle, \text{ and}$$
$$\mathbf{y} = \langle \text{B–Person}, \text{I–Person}, \text{Other}, \text{Other}, \text{B–Location} \rangle.$$

To classify the input text sequence $\mathbf{x}$, a CRF computes the conditional probability, $P(\mathbf{y}|\mathbf{x})$, with the output label sequence $\mathbf{y}$ holding the results of the classification. Here we concentrate on the special case of *linear-chain* CRFs, where each output label y_t may have some dependence on the previous label y_{t-1}, forming a simple chain of labels; y_0 is a "dummy" label denoting the start of the output sequence.

In addition, we make use of m real-valued *feature functions*,

$$f_k \left(y_{t-1}, y_t, \mathbf{x} \right),$$

where $k = 1, 2, \ldots, m$ and $t \in \{1, 2, \ldots, n\}$. Feature functions are an important component of CRFs, allowing the formulation of general rules over the whole input sequence and the output sequence at positions $t - 1$ and t as part of determining the conditional probability $P(\mathbf{y}|\mathbf{x})$. For example, feature functions allow us to combine information from gazetteers within CRFs. This can be implemented through binary feature functions that return 1 if the word x_t is found in, say, the Location gazetteer and y_t is a Location label (either $B–Location$ or $I–Location$), and returns 0 otherwise. Such a feature function can also make use of y_{t-1}, for example, when the named entity is a multiple word phrase.

Thus, recalling that $\prod$ is the symbol denoting a product, the linear-chain CRF computing $P(\mathbf{y}|\mathbf{x})$ is given by

$$P(\mathbf{y}|\mathbf{x}) = \frac{1}{Z(\mathbf{x})} \prod_{t=1}^{n} \exp \left(\sum_{k=1}^{m} \lambda_k f_k \left(y_{t-1}, y_t, \mathbf{x} \right) \right),$$

where $Z(\mathbf{x})$ is a normalisation function, which is dependent on the input $\mathbf{x}$, and the λ_k are weight parameters, one for each feature function, that are estimated from the input data set. We also note that CRFs can be viewed as a generalisation of logistic regression (see Section 2.5 in Chapter 2).

A *knowledge graph* is a kind of semantic network comprising *subject*, *predicate*, *object* triples. A triple takes the form $s \xrightarrow{p} o$, where s is a subject, o is an object, both labelling nodes in the network, and p is a predicate, which is a binary relation, labelling the directed link from s to o. In the context of named entities, we are particularly interested in the case when the subject is a proper noun (although it may also be just a noun). The predicate connects the subject and object, and grammatically is the action that the subject is completing. The predicate can be viewed as the property that the subject is characterised by and the object is the value of this property, which may be a proper noun or just a noun but not exclusively (e.g., sentiment is often expressed by adjectives).

Examples of knowledge graph triples are

$$\text{Dan Silver} \xrightarrow{isa} \text{Person},$$
$$\text{London} \xrightarrow{isa} \text{City, and}$$
$$\text{Dan Silver} \xrightarrow{lives\ in} \text{London},$$

where *isa* is a built-in relationship used to model hierarchical relationships.

Example 5.12. We make use of a data set, known as the CoNLL-2002 (Conference on Computational Natural Language Learning) named entity data set, which consists of text documents covering news topics with labels (also known as tags in this context) for each word, encoding whether the word is a type of named entity. Words tagged with O (denoting the Other class) are not considered to be named entities. The data set provides four types of named entities: (i) Per (denoting the Person class), (ii) Org (denoting the organisation class), (iii) Loc (denoting the location class), and (iv) Misc (denoting miscellaneous names), which are those that have been identified as named entities but are not part of the labelling schema. A sample of sentences from the test data set, together with their annotations, is shown in Table 5.17; the model was trained and tested on the CoNLL-2002 data set, with a 67-33 split.

Table 5.17   A sample of sentences from the CONLL-2002 data set, annotated with their named entities.

Text
Peter Blackburn BRUSSELS 1996-08-22 The European Commission said on Thursday it disagreed with German advice to consumers to shun British lamb until scientists determine whether mad cow disease can be transmitted to sheep.
B-Per I-Per I-Loc O O B-Org I-Org O O O O O O I-Misc O O O O O I-Misc O O O O O O O O O O O O
BRASILIA 1996-08-26 Japanese Prime Minister Ryutaro Hashimoto left Brasilia on Monday for Lima, the penultimate stop on a 10-day Latin American tour , a Brazilian Foreign Ministry spokeswoman said.
I-Loc O I-Misc O O B-Per I-Per O I-Loc O O O I-Loc O O O O O O O B-Misc I-Misc O O O I-Misc B-Org I-Org O O
Tsang said three sets of meetings with Chinese authorities on Hong Kong's 1997-98 budget which will span the transition period had gone smoothly.
I-Per O O O O O O I-Misc O O I-Loc I-Loc O O O O O O O O O O O O O
Atlanta Braves first baseman Fred McGriff owns the second-longest streak at 295 games.
B-Org I-Org O O B-Per I-Per O O O O O O O

Knowledge graphs are very useful for representing semantic information in, for example, the web graph and social networks, and are often introduced in the context of the *semantic web*. They allow search engines to make use of semantic concepts during the search process; for example, the query "Cinema in North London" can use the Location named entity "North London" to find relevant addresses of cinemas. In this way, the named entity information present in the knowledge graph enables the search engine to provide a more precise answer with a better understanding of the query, through information present in the knowledge graph.

Thus, on the one hand, existing knowledge graph data can provide valuable data for training a CRF to label named entities in textual data. On the other hand, the output named entity labelling from a CRF can augment a knowledge graph with additional machine-learnt information.

5.3.3 Word Embeddings

Word embeddings are distributional representations of textual data in the statistical sense that have application in improving the performance of many NLP tasks such as SA and NER. Word embeddings are constructed by mapping words to vector representations, which can be compared to each other using a vector similarity operation such as cosine similarity. Methods for constructing word embeddings are based on the hypothesis that words in similar contexts have similar meaning.

As an example, consider the sentence, assumed to be present in the input textual data, given by

"The *quick brown* $\boxed{\textbf{fox}}$ *jumps over* the lazy dog,"

which is often used to illustrate how word embeddings are created, and is by the way a pangram (i.e., it contains all the letters in the alphabet). We concentrate on the framed bold word "fox" as being the *focus* word (also known as the *target* word), for which an embedding is being created. We consider a window size of five, with a maximum of two *context* words in italics, on the left- and right-hand sides of the focus word. In this case, the immediate left context is the italicised word "brown," and the immediate right context is the italicised word "jumps"; the further left context is the italicised word "quick," and the further right context is the italicised word "over." We have used smaller font sizes for context that is further away from the focus word in order to emphasise that words that are further away from the focus word will have reduced weight when constructing the word embedding. This is due to the fact that, generally, context words that are more distant from the focus word are less related to it. So, on the basis of this small window centred at "fox," we may conjecture that "fox" and "dog" will have distributed vector representations that are quite similar.

The focus word **fox** in the preceding sentence induces the four focus/context word pairs

(**fox**, *quick*), (**fox**, *brown*), (**fox**, *jumps*), (**fox**, *over*), which provide input to the word embeddings construction algorithm, noting that a weight can also be added to each pair according to the distance of the context word from the focus word.

Creating word embeddings is, in principle, an unsupervised task because all that is needed as input to the training method is a textual corpus. The construction algorithm then slides over the text, starting from the first word; picks up the left- and right-hand context surrounding the current word being analysed; and feeds the pairs into the algorithm in the appropriate format demanded by the implementation. In particular, it uses the context words to adjust the embedding, so that two focus words with similar contexts become more similar, and then moves on to the next word. This process may be repeated several times on the input text. As in the vector space model (see Section 5.1.1), we make use of the bag-of-words assumption, so that the order of words (i.e., whether it comes from a left- or right-hand context) is not considered to be important; moreover, the words are assumed to come from a vocabulary of size V. Once a word embedding is pretrained, it can be used within an NLP task to improve its performance.

We will now introduce a particular implementation of an algorithm for creating word embeddings, known as *word2vec*, which offers two different training models: the *skip-gram* and the *continuous bag-of-words* (CBOW) models. We will introduce word2vec as a form of logistic regression (see Section 2.5 in Chapter 2) and then indicate how it could be implemented using a simple feedforward neural network with a single hidden layer (see Subsection 4.3.5 in Chapter 4).

Suppose we have an input textual data set and consider a focus word, w, and its context words, $c_1, c_2, \ldots, c_{k-1}, c_k$, for a window of size $k + 1$. In addition, let $\mathbf{w}$ and $\mathbf{c}_i$, $i = 1, 2, \ldots, k$, be the distributional vector representations of w and the c_i's, respectively. The number of dimensions of the vector representations is taken to be N, where it is typically but not exclusively around 300.

To introduce the skip-gram model, we consider a binary random variable Y taking on the value 1 when a pair (w, c_i) is such that c_i is the context of the focus word w within the input data set, and 0 otherwise, when the pair does not come from the input data set. Its probability can be modelled via a sigmoid function, as

$$P(Y = 1 | w, c_i) = \frac{1}{1 + \exp\left(-\mathbf{w} \cdot \mathbf{c}_i\right)},$$

implying that $P(Y = 0 | w, c_i) = 1 - P(Y = 1 | w, c_i)$, where $\mathbf{w} \cdot \mathbf{c}_i$ is the dot product between $\mathbf{w}$ and $\mathbf{c}_i$ (see Subsection 4.3.3 for the definition of the dot product).

Thus the skip-gram model is a dynamic form of logistic regression, where both the word and context vectors are being learnt. The skip-gram neural network architecture is shown in Figure 5.13. The input to the network is a *one-hot encoding* vector $\mathbf{x} = \langle x_1, x_2, \ldots, x_V \rangle$, having V dimensions, one for each word in the vocabulary. To encode the jth word, we have $x_j = 1$ and, for all $i \neq j$, we have $x_i = 0$.

So, the input to the network is a one-hot vector, of size V, representing the current focus word presented to the network, and these are presented one at a time in order of appearance, according to the current focus/context word pair, as described previously. The output of the network is also a one-hot vector representing one of the context words surrounding the current focus word, in such a way that all context words will appear as an

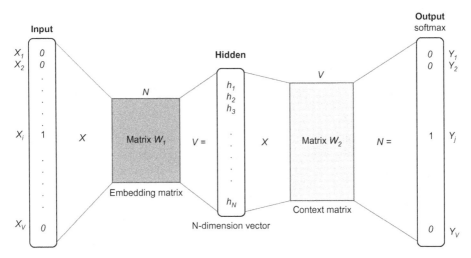

Figure 5.13   The skip-gram word2vec neural network architecture.

output for the given input focus word depending on the window size. The hidden layer $\mathbf{h}$ is a distributional vector representation, of size N, so

$$\mathbf{h} = W_1^T \mathbf{x},$$

recalling that W_1^T is the transpose of W_1, where W_1 is a V-by-N weight matrix holding the weights of the network connecting the input to the hidden layer; we note that the activation function between the input and the hidden layer is the identity function. In addition, W_2 is an N-by-V weight matrix, holding the weights in the network connecting the hidden layer to the outputs, so

$$\mathbf{y} = W_2^T \mathbf{h}$$

is a vector of size V, such that $\mathbf{y} = \langle y_1, y_2, \ldots, y_V \rangle$ and y_i replaces $\mathbf{w} \cdot \mathbf{c}_i$ in the sigmoid activation function given by $P(Y = 1 | w, c_i)$, that computes the output probability of the network for each context c_i.

To present the CBOW model, we introduce a variant Z of the preceding random variable Y, taking on the value 1 when the pairs (w, c_i) are such that c_i is the context of the focus word w, for $i = 1, 2, \ldots, k$, within the input data set, and 0 otherwise, when at least one of these pairs is not part of the context of w within the input data set. Its probability can be modelled via a sigmoid function as

$$P\left(Z = 1 | w, c_1, c_2, \ldots, c_k\right) = \frac{1}{1 + \exp\left(-\left(\mathbf{w} \cdot \mathbf{c}_1 + \mathbf{w} \cdot \mathbf{c}_2 + \cdots + \mathbf{w} \cdot \mathbf{c}_k\right)\right)},$$

implying that $P(Z = 0 | w, c_1, c_2, \ldots, c_k) = 1 - P(Z = 1 | w, c_1, c_2, \ldots, c_k)$.

Now, assuming that, given w, the pairs (w, c_i) and (w, c_j) are independent of each other, when $i \neq j$, we have

$$P\left(Z = 1 | w, c_1, c_2, \ldots, c_k\right) = \prod_{i=1}^{k} P(Y = 1 | w, c_i) = \prod_{i=1}^{k} \frac{1}{1 + \exp\left(-\mathbf{w} \cdot \mathbf{c}_i\right)},$$

where $\prod$ stands for product.

Thus, as with the skip-gram model, the CBOW model is a dynamic form of logistic regression, where both the word and context vectors are being learnt. The CBOW neural network architecture is shown in Figure 5.14. The input to the network are one-hot vectors, each of size V, representing the context words in the input for the present focus word. The algorithm slides over the focus words in order of appearance one at a time before presenting them to the network, according to the current focus/context word pair, as described earlier, where the number of context words depends on the window size. The output of the network is a one-hot vector representing the focus word pertaining to the context words input to the network. The hidden layer $\mathbf{h}$ is a distributional vector representation, of size N, where

$$\mathbf{h} = \frac{1}{k} W_1^T \sum_{i=1}^{k} \mathbf{x}_i,$$

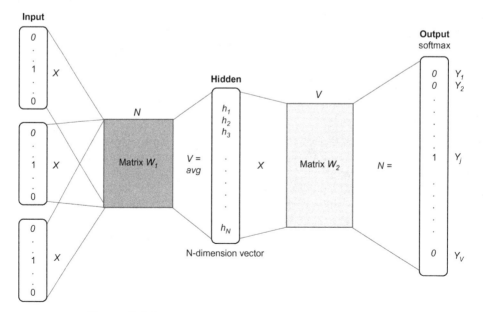

Figure 5.14   The CBOW word2vec neural network architecture.

recalling that W_1^T is the transpose of W_1, where W_1 is a V-by-N weight matrix holding the weights of the network connecting the input to the hidden layer and $\mathbf{x}_i = \langle x_{i1},$ $x_{i2}, \ldots, x_{iV}\rangle$, that is, $\mathbf{x}_i$ is the ith one-hot input vector; we note that, as with the skip-gram model, the activation function between the input and the hidden layer is the identity function. In addition, W_2 is an N-by-V weight matrix, holding the weights in the network connecting the hidden layer to the output, so

$$\mathbf{y} = W_2^T \mathbf{h}$$

is a vector of size V, as for the skip-gram model, such that $\mathbf{y} = \langle y_1, y_2, \ldots, y_V\rangle$ and y_i replaces $\mathbf{w} \cdot \mathbf{c}_i$, for $i = 1, 2, \ldots, k$, in the sigmoid activation function given by $P(Z = 1|w, c_1, c_2, \ldots, c_k)$, that computes the output probability of the network for the focus word w.

We note, just in case it was not clear, that the matrices W_1 and W_2 are the input and output embedding matrices that hold the word embeddings generated by word2vec. For the skip-gram model W_1 is the embedding matrix of words when viewed as focus words, while W_2 is the embedding matrix of words when viewed as context words. On the other hand, for the CBOW model, the reverse is true; that is, W_1 is the embedding matrix when words are viewed as context words, while W_2 is the embedding matrix when words are viewed as focus words.

A common heuristic to speed up the computation of word2vec is *negative sampling*, which we briefly describe. As each iteration of the neural network needs to update $V \times N$ weights for both the input and output embedding matrices, it makes sense to modify the update step so that only a few weights are actually being updated.

Now, suppose we are training a skip-gram model with the pair (**fox**, *quick*); that is, the input is the one-hot vector representing the word **fox**, and the output should be the one-hot representation of the context word *quick*. So, the pair (**fox**, *quick*) is a positive (i.e., true) example presented to the network and, in this case, all pairs of the form (**fox**, ?), where "?" is a placeholder for all context words apart from *quick*, can be viewed as negative examples (i.e., false). In negative sampling, we choose a small number of random words, say 5, and pair them up with **fox** to provide negative examples. Two negative random examples could be (**fox**, *red*) and (**fox**, *and*); note that the context word *and* is very frequent in all texts and therefore unlikely to be a useful discriminator for word embeddings. Thus, only $6 \times N$ weights, between the hidden and output layers, 1 for the positive example and 5 for the negative examples, will need to be updated. Regarding the weights between the input and the hidden layers, only $1 \times N$ weights will have to be updated, since the input is a one-hot vector having a 1 in only a single position.

Example 5.13. Here we explore word embeddings generated by the CBOW word2vec model from a corpus containing 100 billion words from a large snapshot of the Google News data set. Table 5.18 shows ten words related to "king" together with their cosine similarity scores. A visualisation of this small sample of word embeddings in two-dimensional vector space, where the algorithm that created the visualisation strives to maintain the cosine similarity between the embeddings, is shown in Figure 5.15.

Table 5.18 Ten words similar to "king," with their cosine similarity scores.

Word	Similarity
Kings	0.7138
Queen	0.6510
Monarch	0.6413
Crown prince	0.6204
Prince	0.6159
Sultan	0.5864
Ruler	0.5797
Princes	0.5646
Prince Paras	0.5432
Throne	0.5422

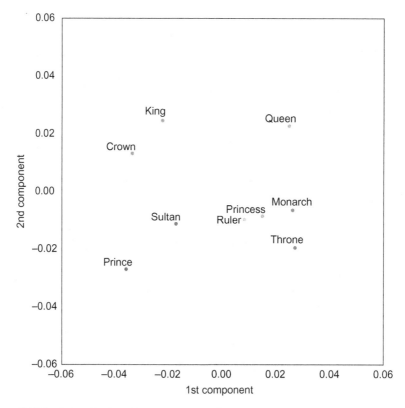

Figure 5.15 A visualisation of a small sample of word embeddings in two-dimensional vector space, which strives to maintain the cosine similarity between the embeddings.

Word embeddings can potentially be used in many NLP tasks to improve their performance. The word2vec algorithm, which comes in two flavours, the skip-gram and the CBOW models, can efficiently construct word embeddings over large corpora, that can be used in pretrained form within these NLP tasks. Many variants of these basic models exist, for example, to create embeddings for phrases, sentences, paragraphs, and even documents.

It is worth mentioning that word embedding can be viewed as an application of statistical language models (see Subsection 5.1.1). As such, contextualised word embeddings can extend traditional embeddings to capture the meanings of words in different contexts. For example, the focus word *bank* will have different meanings in "Dan withdrew money from the *bank*" and "Dan went for a walk along the river *bank*," and thus different contextualised representations.

5.4 Chapter Summary

In this chapter we have concentrated on several topics: search engines, social networks, and, from natural language processing, sentiment analysis, named entity recognition, and word embeddings. We have not covered other important topics such as image processing and speech recognition, but we had to make a choice.

In many cases, as a data scientist, you will be working on applications that will make use of tools we introduced in earlier chapters yet involve concepts and techniques from a wide variety of topics such as the ones we introduced here. Understanding these in some depth will always be a bonus in arriving at the best possible solution you can come up with as a seasoned data scientist.

Selected Additional Topics

Our objective in this book was to cover all the basic concepts of data science, reminding readers that our interpretation of machine learning is the algorithmic part of data science. In this respect, quite a few topics are not covered in the book, due to our desire to cover the least needed to know about the field and the fact that it is a fast-moving area. However, we would like to provide a short sampling of some additional topics we have selected; we still urge readers to carry out their own research and discover new and exciting developments in data science and machine learning. The presentation here will nonetheless be high-level, jumping from topic to topic, and we stress that, apart from delving deeper into these topics, the material in the preceding chapters should help in fleshing out some of the missing background details.

We start by mulling over the relationship between *artificial intelligence* (AI) and machine learning. AI is the theory and development of computer systems that are able to perform tasks that normally require human intelligence. AI systems may be adept in discovering new information, making inferences, and demonstrating reasoning capability.

It is customary to distinguish between three types of AI in increasing order of expressive power. *Narrow AI* (also known as weak AI) refers to AI systems that are designed to perform a specific task within well-defined boundaries. Examples of narrow AI are recommender and facial recognition systems. *General AI* (also known as strong or broad AI) is often referred to as artificial general intelligence (AGI), and refers to AI systems that perform as well as humans on a wide range of cognitive and intellectual tasks. General AI would be able to perform on tasks that it has not been explicitly trained on, but is still theoretical at this stage. The most powerful type of AI is *super AI* (also known as artificial superintelligence, or ASI), which refers to AI systems surpassing human intelligence in all respects. Whether ASI is possible or not is still a fierce topic of debate, notwithstanding the ethical issues that it raises.

6.1 Neuro-Symbolic AI

Machine learning (see Section 4.1) is a subset of AI focussing on AI methods that are able to learn and adapt. AI also includes symbolic computation, such as expert systems that are not considered to be part of machine learning, whereas machine learning builds statistical models of data that may be used for classification and prediction tasks to aid decision making. Although in this book we have not touched upon symbolic computation and its ability, in knowledge representation, to express information about the world, it is worth briefly mentioning *neuro-symbolic* AI, where neural networks and symbolic reasoning components are tightly integrated via neuro-symbolic rules. The neuro-symbolic rules employ symbolic logical rules to capture high-level reasoning, while the NN component is employed to discover patterns that are present in the data. Neuro-symbolic AI is adept in combining existing knowledge with data-driven discovery of patterns and relationships.

6.2   Conversational AI

Another important practical subarea of AI is that of *conversational AI*, also known as chatbot (or AI assistant) technology, whose objective is to allow computers to converse with humans through our most natural interface—human language. Machine learning plays an important role in conversational AI, building on techniques in natural language processing (NLP), information retrieval (IR), and question-answering (Q&A). In addition, speech recognition is also a key component of conversational AI as a prerequisite to utilising NLP. In particular, deep learning is often used to increase the accuracy of each component in a machine learning conversational AI pipeline, especially when the training data set is very large.

For example, named entity recognition (NER; see Section 5.3 in Chapter 5) is used in conversational AI to extract names of entities such as people, places, organisations, and products, to enhance the natural language understanding of the conversation and take an appropriate action. The use of NER gives rise to a technique called *transfer learning*, which allows the system to respond correctly in different contexts and domains. In particular, we may train a NN on a task in one domain and would like to use the trained model on another domain without fully retraining the existing model. This capability is particulary important when the application spans over several tasks and domains, as is often the case in conversational AI. One of the methods often used in transfer learning is known as *fine-tuning* when the parameters of an existing, pretrained model are adjusted by training with a smaller data set than the original one, starting from the existing model parameters.

6.3   Generative Neural Networks

Generative models (defined in Subsection 4.3.5 in Chapter 4) allow for the generation of original content in, for example, machine learning outputs. This has led to a significant subarea of machine learning called *generative deep learning*. We mention two prominent generative NN methods: *variational autoencoders* (VAEs) and *generative adversarial networks* (GANs).

VAEs are NNs that, apart from the input and output layers, consist of three components—an *encoder*, a *decoder*, and a *latent space*—in between the encoder and decoder. A VAE can be viewed as a probabilistic model that learns to encode the input data into a probabilistic latent space and then decode it back to generate novel content. One common application of VAEs is image reconstruction.

GANs are a type of deep NN composed of two NNs: the *generator* and *discriminator*. These networks work together to generate new data samples that resemble a training set of real data on the basis of a two-player game. The generator takes a sample as input and generates fake (i.e., not real) data samples that try to model the distribution of the training data. The discriminator's task is to compare both real and fake data samples and determine which is the fake sample. The main goal of a GAN is to generate high-quality, diverse, and realistic data samples that can be used for various applications such as image and video generation (known as *deep fakes*), text and speech synthesis, and data augmentation, which generates additional training data.

6.4 Trustworthy AI

The word "trustworthy" means "able to be relied upon as honest, responsible and truthful," which leads us to the concept of *trustworthy AI* (TAI), or more specifically *trustworthy machine learning*; here, we will not distinguish between the two and use the term "TAI" as the underlying concept. The motivation for TAI is the demand for demonstrating confidence in AI technology to be able to make responsible decisions when using it. In this sense, TAI can be viewed as a framework for managing the risk of potential negative impacts that may occur when employing AI systems.

The principles of TAI can be broken down into three broad themes:

(1) *Technical* characteristics such as reliability, robustness, generalisability, resilience, and security;

(2) *Socio-technical* characteristics such as interpretability, explainability, bias freeness, and privacy; and

(3) *Social* characteristics such as transparency, accountability, and fairness.

It is evident that TAI must also address the social issues, which are of concern to society as a whole. These include ethical issues, which are of prime importance, although we will not elaborate on these any further here. The socio-technical characteristics span the technical and social, emphasising that TAI introduces a third dimension, in addition to the algorithms and models, which includes the interaction of humans with the technology. As an example, explainability, that is, the ability to provide a clear explanation of why a machine learning system arrives at its outputs, is a key feature for promoting trustworthiness. Explainability also promotes fairness by increasing the transparency of the model, helping humans understand the decisions made by an AI system. It also addresses the "black-box" syndrome when a model is too complex to understand; this is especially prevalent in deep learning models, which typically have large numbers of parameters and features and may thus be hard to interpret.

The predicted output value of traditional machine learning methods is a point estimate, which does not indicate the uncertainty of the output. Because there is always some uncertainty that may be attached to the output of a machine learning algorithm, it is natural to quantify this uncertainty by using a probability distribution to model the degree of uncertainty. Quantifying the uncertainty of machine learning outputs can be viewed as an additional characteristic of TAI, since it increases transparency and enhances our confidence in its results. Uncertainty quantification can be added to NNs, leading to *Bayesian neural networks* (BNNs), where the parameters of the NN represent random variables coming from a distribution rather than simple variables mapping to fixed values. This extension of NNs enables BNNs to quantify the uncertainty of each of their outputs as a distribution.

6.5 Large Language Models

Foundation models (often called *large language models*, or LLMs) are very large pretrained generative deep NN models, trained at the outset on a vast corpus of unlabelled data. Their predictive capabilities include not only text (as in traditional language models; see Section 5.1.1 in Chapter 5) but also image, video, speech, and other possible modalities. To get a feel of the scope of an LLM, the number of parameters of its models is typically on the order of trillions or even more.

An LLM can be interrogated directly through a conversational AI interface (that is a chatbot) and can also be adapted to provide a solution to a downstream task through transfer learning. A downstream task is a specific task requiring a solution, such as a classification task, and the transfer learning mechanism used to implement such a task is fine-tuning, mentioned earlier. LLMs are a disruptive technology that will most likely affect user interaction with search engines and potentially revolutionise automated question-answering platforms. Wide use of LLMs have given rise to *prompt engineering*, which is the process of crafting and refining the instructions given to an LLM (known as prompts) so as to achieve the most desired output.

We give a few examples where LLMs provide serious challenges with regard to whether they are trustworthy, when tested against the TAI characteristics. In one example, where privacy is potentially violated, personal data is used in training an LLM. In this scenario, the personal data is extracted from the LLM and then used in an internet search; this is known as an inversion attack. In another example, the output of an LLM is interpreted by the user as a form of advice, which potentially may be misleading. Yet another example is the potential infringement of copyright when an LLM does not cite the source of its answer. Furthermore, bias may exist in the data on which the LLM was trained and remain present in its answers, also violating the principle of fairness.

6.6 Epilogue

It is time for us to be speculative. Data science has become an important field in its own right, just as machine learning has become an important subfield of AI and an integral part of data science. As time goes by, we can expect data science to be embedded in a multitude of both hardware and software systems to such a degree that we will be comfortable with their outputs having a statistical component.

Although we believe we have given you the minimum you need to know, technology is advancing at a fast pace, which makes it hard to predict what might bring a step change in the future. What we can say to a large degree of certainty is that data science and machine learning are here to stay. We hope that you have enjoyed the journey we have taken you through, as we have enjoyed writing this book.

7

Further Reading

We thank all the authors and contributors to the field of data science and machine learning. This book is based on their invaluable contributions to the field. Due to the increasing volume of publications in the areas we have covered, it would not be feasible to mention all of the publications and research on the subjects that we have covered. Instead, we provide a summary of some additional resources that readers might consider when exploring the topics we have introduced in greater depth, or simply out of pure curiosity.

7.1 Basic Statistics

Witte, R. S., and Witte, J. S. *Statistics*. Hoboken, NJ: John Wiley & Sons, 2021. [15]
   This book provides an introduction to basic concepts and approaches in descriptive and inferential statistical analysis, providing a wealth of additional information on the approaches mentioned in this book.

Wasserman, L. *All of Statistics: A Concise Course in Statistical Inference*. Germany: Springer, 2004. [14]
   This book covers a wide range of topics in statistics and probability, including more advanced topics in statistical inference, models, and methods.

7.2 Data Science

Barabási, A. -L., and Pósfai, M. *Network Science*. Cambridge, UK: Cambridge University Press, 2016. [1]
   This extensive textbook covers the science of networks applied in a wide variety of areas such as physics, computer science, economics, and social networks.

Hastie, T., Tibshirani, R., and Friedman, J. *The Elements of Statistical Learning: Data Mining, Inference, and Prediction*. New York, NY: Science+Business Media, 2009. [5]
   This comprehensive reference book covers machine learning within a statistical framework, emphasising the methods and their conceptual underpinnings.

Levene, M. *An Introduction to Search Engines and Web Navigation*. Hoboken, NJ: John Wiley & Sons, 2010. [7]

 This book provides a detailed overview at the introductory level of the technologies and approaches underlying the tools that assist us in finding information on the web. In particular, how search engine technology and the activity of navigating the web work are explained in detail.

Manning, C. D., Raghavan, P., and Schütze, H. *Introduction to Information Retrieval*. Cambridge, MA: MIT Press, 2008. [9]

 This book introduces the main approaches in information retrieval from a computer science perspective. Apart from introducing the foundations, it covers more advanced topics, including the use of machine learning in information retrieval.

Provost, F., and Fawcett, T. *Data Science for Business: What You Need to Know About Data Mining and Data-Analytic Thinking*. Sebastopol, CA: O'Reilly, 2013. [11]

 This book introduces many of the fundamental concepts of data science, using a data-analytic approach to identifying the appropriate data and choosing the appropriate methods to be used when thinking about the problems. It then applies data science techniques with examples from business.

Witten, I. H., Frank, E., Hall, M. A., and Pal, C. J. *Data Mining: Practical Machine Learning Tools and Techniques*. San Francisco, CA: Morgan-Kaufmann, 2016. [16]

 This highly accessible book is a practical machine learning book covering the tools and techniques. It introduces many of the core machine learning concepts, along with guidance on ways to apply these concepts and techniques to real-world data.

7.3 Machine Learning

Bishop, C. M. *Pattern Recognition and Machine Learning*. New York, NY: Springer Science+Business Media, 2006. [2]

 This book is a comprehensive introduction to Bayesian approaches applied to pattern recognition and machine learning.

Jurafsky, D., and Martin, J. H. *Speech and Language Processing: An Introduction to Natural Language Processing, Computational Linguistics, and Speech Recognition*. Upper Saddle River, NJ: Pearson Prentice Hall, 2009. [6]

 This book covers many important topics in statistical natural language processing, speech recognition, and computational linguistics.

Gonzalez, R. C., and Woods, R. E. *Digital Image Processing*. New York, NY: Pearson Education, 2018. [3]

 This book covers the basic techniques applied to image processing, as well as more recent topics in deep learning and deep neural networks.

Liu, B. *Sentiment Analysis: Mining Opinions, Sentiments, and Emotions*. Cambridge, UK: Cambridge University Press, 2015. [8]

The book introduces sentiment analysis and opinion mining techniques applied to text data.

Murphy, K. P. *Probabilistic Machine Learning: An Introduction*. Cambridge, MA: MIT Press, 2022. [10]
  This book is a comprehensive and detailed introduction to machine learning, covering the theoretical aspects of probabilistic modelling and Bayesian decision making. It also includes the topics of deep neural networks and other, non-neural approaches.

7.4   Deep Learning

Goodfellow, I., Bengio, Y., and Courville, A. *Deep Learning*. Cambridge, MA: MIT Press, 2017. [4]
  This well-received book provides an introduction to neural networks and deep learning, covering a broad range of topics that you will come across in deep learning both in industry and academia.

Roberts, D. A., Yaida, S., and Hanin, B. *The Principles of Deep Learning Theory*. Cambridge, UK: Cambridge University Press, 2022. [12]
  This book provides a theoretical approach to understanding the mechanics underlying deep neural network architectures and optimisers.

Russell, S., and Norvig, P. *Artificial Intelligence: A Modern Approach*. Pearson Education, Hoboken, NJ, 2021. [13]
  This comprehensive and in-depth book introduces the theory and practice of a very wide range of topics in artificial intelligence.

7.5   Research Papers

ArXiv
  This is a valuable open-access scholarly archive, where you will find many recent research papers on machine learning, data science, and other fields. The research articles are published in the archive as preprints and can be freely downloaded.

7.6   Python

All the data sets and the Python Jupyter notebooks used in this book are available on the companion website.

Bibliography

[1] A.-L. Barabási and M. Pósfai. *Network Science*. Cambridge University Press, Cambridge, UK, 2016.

[2] C. M. Bishop. *Pattern Recognition and Machine Learning*. Information Science and Statistics. Springer Science+Business Media, New York, NY, 2006.

[3] R. C. Gonzalez and R. E. Woods. *Digital Image Processing*. Pearson Education, New York, NY, fourth edition, 2018.

[4] I. Goodfellow, Y. Bengio, and A. Courville. *Deep Learning*. Adaptive Computation and Machine Learning series. MIT Press, Cambridge, MA, 2017.

[5] T. Hastie, R. Tibshirani, and J. Friedman. *The Elements of Statistical Learning: Data Mining, Inference, and Prediction*. Springer Series in Statistics. Springer Science+Business Media, New York, NY, second edition, 2009.

[6] D. Jurafsky and J. H. Martin. *Speech and Language Processing: An Introduction to Natural Language Processing, Computational Linguistics, and Speech Recognition*. Pearson Prentice Hall, Upper Saddle River, NJ, second edition, 2009.

[7] M. Levene. *An Introduction to Search Engines and Web Navigation*. John Wiley & Sons, Hoboken, NJ, second edition, 2010.

[8] B. Liu. *Sentiment Analysis: Mining Opinions, Sentiments, and Emotions*. Cambridge University Press, Cambridge, UK, 2015.

[9] C. D. Manning, P. Raghavan, and H. Schütze. *Introduction to Information Retrieval*. MIT Press, Cambridge, MA, 2008.

[10] K. P. Murphy. *Probabilistic Machine Learning: An Introduction*. Adaptive Computation and Machine Learning. MIT Press, Cambridge, MA, 2022.

[11] F. Provost and T. Fawcett. *Data Science for Business: What You Need to Know About Data Mining and Data-Analytic Thinking*. O'Reilly, Sebastopol, CA, 2013.

[12] D. A. Roberts, S. Yaida, and B. Hanin. *The Principles of Deep Learning Theory*. Cambridge University Press, Cambridge, UK, 2022.

[13] S. Russell and P. Norvig. *Artificial Intelligence: A Modern Approach*. Pearson Series in Artificial Intelligence. Pearson Education, Hoboken, NJ, fourth edition, 2021.

[14] L. Wasserman. *All of Statistics: A Concise Course in Statistical Inference*. Springer Texts in Statistics. Springer, Germany, 2004.

[15] R. S. Witte and J. S. Witte. *Statistics*. John Wiley & Sons, Hoboken, NJ, eleventh edition, 2021.

[16] I. H. Witten, E. Frank, M. A. Hall, and C. J. Pal. *Data Mining: Practical Machine Learning Tools and Techniques*. Morgan-Kaufmann, San Francisco, CA, fourth edition, 2016.

Index

Note: The italic letter *f* following page numbers refers to figures.

E

S